the slow cooking bible

the slow cooking bible

with more than 300 recipes

bay books

contents

This book celebrates the joy of flavours which can only be crafted from taking things slowly. Slow cooking allows the ingredients to coalesce, weaving a culinary magic which transcends the palate and feeds the heart and soul. These recipes span seasons, cuisines and cooking styles. Typically made by slowly simmering ingredients in stock or other liquid, such dishes make possible a world of unconstrained delicious possibilities. Don't be daunted by lengthy cooking times—curries, casseroles, soups and stews need little supervision after their initial preparation. Apart from an occasional quick stir or skim, they can be left to gently bubble away, undisturbed. Little more than a large casserole dish, wok or pot is required to create these dishes of lingering pleasure. If you are one of those lucky people who own a slow cooker, there is a chapter devoted to recipes designed for this appliance.

basics

Take it slowly

In our busy lives, there is a delicious pleasure in allowing food to cook slowly. As the aromas of the simmering food fill the house, you have the satisfaction of knowing that dinner is taken care of and you can get on with your other tasks. There are several main styles of cooking that suit slow cooking and this guide to the fundamentals will help you feel confident with them all.

CASSEROLES, STEWS AND CURRIES

The most important aspect of a casserole, stew or curry is the process of long, slow cooking which results in a tender, flavoursome dish. Whether this is achieved in an oven or on top of a stove doesn't matter. For this book we have defined casseroles as dishes that are cooked in the oven and stews as those that are cooked on the stove, but many people use the terms interchangeably.

One of the main benefits of this type of slow cooking is that it is generally better to use the more economical cuts of meat, which helps with the budget. As well as this, it is usually cooked and served in the same dish, which means less washing-up.

Most casseroles, stews and curries will improve in flavour if cooked in advance and refrigerated overnight or even for a couple of days. The same dish can be used for cooking, refrigerating, reheating and serving. When ready to use, remove from the refrigerator and skim off any fat that has formed on top. This will make for a much healthier meal.

Brown the meat in batches over a fairly high heat.

Cooking techniques

When cooking, there are just a few key techniques. For a successful result, it is important to seal in the juices of pieces of meat, fish or poultry by first browning them briefly over a fairly high heat. Do this in batches, turning frequently and setting aside each batch until it is all done. If the pan is too crowded, the meat will stew and become tough. Brown all sides, turning often to prevent sticking and burning. The idea is to seal in the juices and give a coating, not to cook the food.

Sometimes the meat is tossed in seasoned flour before browning. This helps to add flavour as well as thicken the liquid in the cooking process.

When browning pieces of meat, fish, chicken or vegetables, oil is usually a better medium than butter, because butter burns at a comparatively low temperature. However, some dishes use a mixture of both—the oil prevents butter from burning and butter adds a nutty flavour.

If you are cooking in advance and then reheating, the food should be brought to the boil and then simmered slowly for approximately 20 minutes. Alternatively, if you prefer, you can reheat it in the microwave on a medium–high setting. Any leftover casserole portions can be used as pie fillings, although if they are quite wet, they may need thickening with a little blended cornflour (cornstarch) and water over medium heat. For an extra dimension, casseroles can be varied by topping them with pastry, scone dough, mashed potato or pumpkin.

Read on to find some more helpful hints to use when cooking the recipes in this book.

Meats

For slow-cooked dishes, the cheaper cuts of meat are generally the best choice, not only for economy, but for increased flavour.

For beef dishes, cuts such as blade, chuck, round or topside steak are ideal. They generally have more flavour than expensive cuts like fillet or rump. The same applies to cuts of veal such as veal shanks, which have an excellent flavour and texture when cooked.

As for lamb, cuts which we don't often make use of produce very tasty meals. For example, neck chops and lamb shanks lend themselves to this type of cookery and are very easy on the budget.

Pork fillets and other cuts of pork which are suitable for casseroling have recently been made much more accessible to the home cook. They are reasonably priced, quite lean and absolutely full of flavour.

Unlike the expensive cuts, which are usually cooked quickly, the cheaper cuts of meat are best when slowly simmered in liquid in a casserole dish. This process tenderises the meat and produces a delicious meal. The fibres of cheaper cuts, while initially becoming tough, break down while cooking and become succulent. You can tell when the meat is cooked because the pieces will easily break up with a fork.

Poultry and game

Chicken, turkey, rabbit and duck are all suitable for stewing and casseroling. They become very tender and add variety to the dinner table. Even when larger old birds are used they are transformed into a tasty, tender meal. Make sure the food is simmered gently, not boiled, otherwise the meat will toughen.

Whole chicken, chicken pieces, thighs, drumsticks and wings are readily available from chicken shops and some butchers. They can all be used for slow cooking. Rabbit is available from some butchers. You will find duck and turkey in some chicken shops and shops that specialise in game. In the freezer section of supermarkets you will find turkey in pieces (like turkey breast roll), which are convenient to use.

Seafood

Seafood is high in protein and offers a wide variety of flavours and textures with the use of different types of fish, crustaceans and molluscs. Seafood is easy to prepare and does not take quite as long to cook as meat and poultry.

The secret of a moist fish casserole or stew is to ensure it is not overcooked and the cooking temperature is low. Otherwise, it will become tough and dry. For slow-cooked dishes, the sauce is often prepared first and fish added later.

Vegetables

Vegetables are highly nutritious and make an economical meal. Some vegetable dishes are more suitable for serving on the side with a main course or as a first course. Slow-cooking vegetables like potatoes, parsnips, turnips, or sweet potatoes are an ideal addition to meat and poultry casseroles. Not only do they add flavour but will help thicken the sauce, thus eliminating the need for any flour or thickening agent. The faster cooking vegetables such as snow peas, broccoli or

Vegetables can be used on their own or in combination.

11

mushrooms are usually added towards the end of cooking time to prevent them becoming too soft.

Legumes and pulses are high in protein and fibre and add variety to your cooking. Some need overnight soaking to make them soft and cut down cooking time. If you are in a hurry, place the pulses in a saucepan, cover well with hot water and bring to the boil. Simmer for a couple of minutes, skimming froth from the top. Remove from the heat and allow to soak for approximately 1 hour. After draining, they will be ready for use.

Cutting vegetables and herbs

When slicing vegetables, try to keep the pieces uniform in size. Some recipes are best with chunky vegetables, some with finely sliced ones which will merge into the sauce.

There's a trick to chopping fresh herbs. Use a large sharp knife and place one hand on the handle, the other hand on the top of the blade. Hold the top of the blade in one place, chop with the other hand in a swiveling motion to finely cut herbs. It's a very quick and efficient method.

Tinned tomatoes will often remain whole even after prolonged cooking. You can strain them and place the tomatoes on a board for chopping, but it is messy and inefficient. A simpler way is to roughly chop the tomatoes with a pair of kitchen scissors, while they are still in the tin.

Cutting meat

While cheaper cuts of meat are often well marbled with fat, any large pieces of fat and sinew should be removed. Neither of these will break down in the cooking process and it's a most unpleasant sensation to find a piece of fat or gristle. You will need a sharp knife to trim fat and sinew from meat.

Cut the meat into even-sized cubes. The size of the cubes depends on the type of meat and on the dish but somewhere between 2 and 3 centimetres (¾ and 1¼ inches) is the most usual. If the cubes are too small, the meat will fall apart into shreds during cooking and the dish will not look appetising.

Coating meat

If you coat the meat cubes in flour seasoned with salt, pepper and often herbs and cook them on all sides in oil or butter, a crusty brown coating will form on the meat, giving it an attractive appearance and a delicious taste.

Coating with flour will also help to thicken the casserole—usually once flour has been used to coat meat you don't need any other thickener.

There are two ways of coating meat in flour. Whichever method you use, try to avoid doing it too far ahead of the cooking time, or the flour will be absorbed by the moisture in the meat. It will no longer be a coating and in fact will change the whole texture of the dish. If for some reason the flour is absorbed by the meat, re-coat the meat just before use and shake off any excess.

The first method is to place plain flour on a sheet of greaseproof paper and mix in a little pepper and salt. Using your hands or tongs, turn the meat cubes in the flour, coating on all sides. Shake off the excess flour.

Trim off any fat, then cut into even-sized cubes.

Coat the meat in flour by tossing in a plastic bag.

The second method is to put flour and seasonings into a plastic bag, add meat cubes—not too many at a time—and shake until thoroughly coated. Remove from the bag. Shake off the excess flour.

Casserole dishes

When choosing a casserole dish, buy one that can be taken straight from the freezer to the oven or microwave. A tight-fitting lid is essential to ensure that moisture is retained. The size of the dish is important. If it's too small, the liquid might overflow. If it's too large, the food will dry out because the liquid will reduce too quickly. The food should come approximately three-quarters of the way up the dish for the best result.

If the dish becomes stained during cooking it is best to allow it to cool and then soak it overnight in cold water. This will make most stains easy to remove.

When to boil and when to simmer

As a general rule in casserole making, the ingredients are browned, liquid is added, the food is brought to the boil, the heat is reduced and then it is covered and simmered slowly until tender.

A dish is boiling when large bubbles appear in quick succession on the surface. Never boil a casserole for prolonged periods, otherwise the meat will become tough and stringy and any vegetables will break up and look unattractive.

Simmering is when tiny bubbles appear—at a slower pace—on the surface of the food. If there is too much liquid, uncover and simmer until liquid has reduced.

Slow cooking and the freezer

One of the best things about casseroles, stews and curries is that they store well in the freezer for up to 3 months, so they are great to cook ahead of time and keep until needed.

There are a few guidelines to make sure food is frozen and reheated safely. One of the key points is that food should be frozen as soon as it has cooled to prevent bacteria forming. Skim any fat from the surface of the cooled casserole before freezing for a healthier option.

Freezer bags or plastic bags are the easiest to use to freeze casseroles because of the irregular shapes of food. An ideal method is to place the bag inside a cake tin or other rigid container of suitable size and shape. Spoon the casserole into the bag, tie loosely and put the tin or container in the freezer. When the food is hard but not completely frozen, remove the bag from the container, squeeze out as much air as possible and seal securely with a twist tie or adhesive tape. Label and date before returning to the freezer until required. The date is necessary so you remember how long it has been frozen.

Of course, if you have cooked a large quantity, you may not wish to freeze the whole lot together. In this case, freeze in smaller bags in the portions required for future use.

It is best to thaw casseroles completely before reheating but if you are in a hurry it is possible to reheat straight from the freezer. Remove from the bag or container and heat either slowly in a saucepan on top of the stove or in a casserole dish in the oven. To avoid cracking the dish, place in a cold oven and heat to 220°C (425°F/Gas 7). Heat for about 30 minutes depending on the amount of food. If you are cooking dumplings or a pastry top, do not add these until the casserole is warm.

Brown meat in batches.

Add liquid and bring to the boil.

SOUPS

The ultimate in comfort food, soups are as good for the soul as they are for the body. They can vary from light, broth-based soups to thick, hearty chowders and spicy laksas.

Many soups are substantial enough to eat as a meal in themselves. Other soups are best served as a starter or for a light lunch.

As with other slow-cooked dishes, you will get the best result if you use a good-quality stock. If time doesn't permit you to make your own, there are a range of good commercially available stocks. See pages 16–17 for more information about stocks and for recipes for home-made stocks.

Asian soups

Many Asian soups use a spice paste to provide the underlying flavour. The spices are fried in a little oil, then liquid and other ingredients are added to make the soup. Woks are good for cooking Asian soups. When using a wok to cook soups, pay attention to the fluid levels because liquid can evaporate too quickly and will need to be replenished. It is also important to cover a wok with a lid (if the recipe specifies) otherwise the evaporation created by the wok's large surface area will concentrate the flavours and result in a very strong-tasting, thick soup.

Because woks have such excellent heat conductivity, it is important to cook long-simmered soups on as low a heat as possible, and to follow any instructions for using a lid. Additional water or stock may need to be added if the liquid evaporates too rapidly. When choosing a wok for soups, it is a good idea to pick a non-stick or stainless steel one for any soups that include a lot of tamarind or lime juice, as the acidity level of these ingredients can strip the seasoning layer off carbon steel woks.

The essence of flavourings

When flavouring soups, stews or casseroles with herbs, it's important to be able to remove the herbs when the dish is ready to serve. A piece of very wilted parsley or a well cooked bay leaf is not a pleasant surprise to the taste buds (and is difficult to remove with any grace). The suggestions below will all add flavour to a dish and are easy to remove.

Herb and celery bundles Tie a bunch of fresh herbs and a small piece of celery together with a piece of string. See page 16 for a picture of a herb bundle.

Clove-studded onion Peel an onion and press a few cloves into it.

Bouquet garni Place a mixture of fresh herbs such as parsley, lemon thyme and a bay leaf on a square of muslin (cheesecloth), then tie into a bundle with string.

SLOW COOKERS

From hearty soups such as seafood chowder and pea and ham soup to creamy chicken curry, country beef stew and lamb shanks in red wine, the hardest thing about using your slow cooker will be deciding what to make in it.

Trends come and go, and when it comes to kitchen gadgetry, we've possibly seen them all. From omelette makers, ice-cream machines and bread makers to plug-in tagines and electric tin openers, it seems there's been an electrical appliance invented for every culinary situation imaginable. Yet how many of us have succumbed to the latest, greatest gizmo, only to discover that it takes up too much space in our cupboards or is annoyingly hard to clean? Having said that, there are some machines and appliances we'd rather not live without. Food processors, blenders and electric beaters have removed a great deal of tedious elbow grease from much of our cooking and we'd be hard pressed to cook successfully without them. Slow cookers are another indispensable kitchen device that no busy household should be without. They've been around since the 1960s and have always had their devotees, but more and more cooks are wising up to the time- and budget-saving capabilities of the slow cooker.

Slow cookers transform many foods (particularly those tougher, tastier cuts of meat) from their raw state to melting tenderness, with not much more exertion than flicking a switch. They can be plugged in anywhere, they use less electricity than your oven, and there is only one bowl to wash up afterwards. You don't need to stir or hover over a meal simmering in a slow cooker and it's almost impossible to burn anything; there's such latitude in cooking times that an hour or two more isn't going to make much difference. In a slow cooker, meals practically cook themselves and they taste incredible—every last drop of the food's natural flavour is captured inside the cooker.

Slow cookers are also called 'Crock Pots'; Crock Pot is a brand name that was conjured up in America in 1971. Essentially, a slow cooker is an electrical appliance, comprising a round, oval or oblong cooking vessel made of glazed ceramic or porcelain. This is surrounded by a metal housing, which contains a thermostatically controlled element. The lid, which is often transparent, makes it easy to check the progress of what's cooking inside. The recipes in this book were developed using a 4.5 litre (157 fl oz/18 cup) slow cooker but they come in a variety of sizes, with the largest having a capacity of around 7 litres (245 fl oz/28 cups). Note that slow cookers work best when they are at least half, and preferably three-quarters, full (the operating manual that comes with your model will advise you on this).

Most models of slow cookers have a number of temperature settings and typically these are 'low', 'medium' and 'high'. The 'low' setting cooks foods at around 80°C (175°F) while 'high' cooks foods at around 90°C (195°F). 'Medium' is a combination of these two temperatures; when set to medium the slow cooker cooks for around an hour at 'high', then automatically clicks to 'low' and continues cooking at that temperature. As a general rule, cooking on 'low' doubles the cooking time from a 'high' setting and you can tweak the cooking times of recipes to longer or shorter. Recipe cooking times vary from 3 to 12 hours.

At its simplest, to use your slow cooker all you need to do is prepare and chop your ingredients, add liquid (water, wine or stock) and turn it on, leaving the contents to murmur away until cooked to lush tenderness. Time-strapped cooks can put ingredients in the slow cooker before work and return home at night to a dinner ready-to-go; or, meals can be cooked overnight. The cooking environment in a slow cooker is very moist, making it perfect for tough cuts of meat such as beef blade, lamb or veal shanks, or pork belly. Such cuts contain a great quantity of connective tissues and these can only be broken down with long, slow cooking. When preparing meat, it is important that you trim fatty meat well, as the fat tends to settle on top of the juices.

The slow cooker requires less liquid than normal stovetop or oven cookery, as there is no chance for the liquid to evaporate. In fact, many foods, including some meats, release moisture of their own during cooking (up to one cup per average recipe), so bear this in mind when you think a recipe doesn't have enough liquid in it, or when adapting recipes for the slow cooker (when adapting standard recipes for the slow cooker cut the liquid by 50 per cent). Resist the urge to lift the lid during cooking, particularly at the beginning, as the slow cooker takes a while to heat up, and always cook with the lid on unless the recipe instructs otherwise—perhaps when thickening a sauce. If you need to remove the lid to stir or to check the food is cooked, replace the lid as quickly as possible so the slow cooker doesn't lose too much heat.

It is difficult to overcook tougher meats but it is possible (the meat will turn raggedy and fall apart into thin shreds) so you still need to use the suggested cooking times for each recipe. Keep in mind, however, that cooking times may vary, depending on the brand and size of slow cooker you are using. And, because cooking times are fairly approximate, we have rounded our cooking times to the nearest 15 minutes.

While most recipes use the slow cooker as a true one-pot solution, where everything goes in together at the start, other recipes use the cooker as the primary mode of cooking but use other steps along the way. If you like, you can brown meats

Trim off any fat before adding meat to a slow cooker.

14

such as pork, beef or lamb on the stovetop first, before adding them to the cooker. Meat gains extra flavour when browned, as the outside surfaces caramelise over high temperatures (about 100°C/210°F) and this cannot be achieved in a slow cooker. Some recipes include this extra step but for any meat recipe, you can choose to brown first if you like.

Hard vegetables such as root vegetables can take a very long time to cook, so cut them into smallish pieces and push them to the base of the cooker or around the side, where the heat is slightly greater.

Green vegetables can lose some nutrients if cooked for prolonged periods, so blanch them first (if required) and add them at the end of cooking to heat through. Seafood and dairy products should also be added near the end of cooking.

Food safety

In the past there have been concerns about food safety issues with slow cookers, namely whether harmful bacteria that are present in foods, particularly in meats, are killed at such low temperatures. However, bacteria are killed off at around 68°C

(155°F), so users of slow cookers need not be concerned about bacteria. One rule here though is to never place meats that are still frozen, or even partially frozen, in a slow cooker as this scenario can cause food-poisoning bacteria to flourish; ALWAYS have meats thawed fully before cooking.

Another rule is to never use the ceramic insert after it has been frozen or refrigerated as the sudden change in temperature could cause it to crack.

A final caveat is that you cannot cook dried red kidney beans from their raw state in the slow cooker because the temperature is not high enough to destroy the natural toxins found in these beans. Dried red kidney beans, and other dried beans, need to be boiled for 10 minutes to destroy these toxins. Tinned beans, however, are safe for immediate use. To prepare dried beans, soak the beans in water for at least 5 hours, or overnight if time permits. Discard the water, then rapidly boil the beans in fresh water for 10 minutes to destroy the toxins.

NOTE: Make sure you read the manufacturer's instructions for the safe use of your slow cooker.

STOCKS

Home-made stock will give your dishes a richer, more flavoursome base and, although the cooking time is long, the preparation couldn't be easier. Browning meat bones beforehand adds flavour and colour.

A well-prepared stock is the foundation of most casseroles, soups and stews. Beef, veal and chicken are excellent to use and, fortunately, the cheaper cuts of meat like chuck steak have the most flavour.

The butcher will chop any bones into suitably sized pieces. These should first be browned in a little oil in the oven. Place browned bones in a large deep pan. Cover well with water, add flavourings such as onion, celery, carrot, whole peppercorns and a bouquet garni made of a bay leaf, sprigs of thyme and parsley. Garlic may also be used sparingly. Too much may overpower the subtle stock flavour.

Simmer stock gently, uncovered, for up to 2 hours, being careful not to boil.

If making chicken stock, the back and neck can be used or the whole bird simmered, the liquid kept and the meat used separately.

Fish stock is easy to make using fish trimmings. It should not be cooked longer than the amount of time given in the recipe because the taste will become bitter.

Leftover fresh stock can be frozen for future use. Freeze in 1-cup quantities in plastic bags. These can be used for making soups or casseroles.

Ready-made stocks

When you don't have time to make your own stock, ready-made stock is now available. Chicken specialty stores sell frozen stock which is very convenient and good to have on hand. Many Asian grocery stores sell good stock in cans. Some butchers and fish retailers all sell stock made on the premises. Supermarkets sell a wide variety of stocks, in both dry and liquid form, which can be used instead of freshly made stock. Some commercial stocks are quite salty so if using them, don't add salt to the recipe until you have tasted the food.

After browning the bones, add them to your stockpot.

Lemongrass and makrut leaves can be used in Asian dishes.

Italian or French dishes would suit a bouquet garni.

Flavourings

Suitable flavours can be added to the stock for recipes from different countries to give them their distinctive regional character. Typical seasonings used in Chinese dishes could be ginger, spring onion, soy sauce and rice wine. Southeast Asian dishes would suit aromatics such as galangal, makrut (kaffir lime) leaves, coriander (cilantro) and fish sauce. Italian or French dishes would suit a bouquet garni or some fresh herbs, such as parsley or marjoram.

Herb bundle Wrap the green part of a leek loosely around a bay leaf, sprig of thyme, some celery leaves and a few stalks of parsley, then tie with kitchen string. Leave enough string for easy removal.

Bouquet garni Place a mixture of fresh herbs such as parsley, lemon thyme and a bay leaf on a square of muslin (cheesecloth), tie into a bundle with string. The herbs will add flavour and can be easily removed.

Freezing stock

Once you are making stock you may as well make a large amount and freeze some for another time. Simply pour the stock into a measuring jug lined with a plastic bag, so you can measure how much you have, and then divide it up and freeze it in convenient portions. Remove the bag from the jug, label, seal securely and freeze.

Alternatively, keep simmering the stock until it is reduced, pour into ice cube trays and freeze. You will now have quite concentrated stock 'cubes' that can be diluted to use.

Beef stock

2 kg (4 lb 8 oz) beef bones
2 unpeeled carrots, chopped
2 unpeeled onions, quartered
2 tablespoons tomato paste (concentrated purée)
2 celery stalks, leaves included, chopped
1 bouquet garni
12 black peppercorns

Preheat the oven to 210°C (425°F/Gas 6–7). Put the bones in a baking dish and bake for 30 minutes, turning occasionally. Add the carrot and onion and cook for a further 20 minutes. Allow to cool.

Put the bones, carrot and onion in a large, heavy-based pan. Drain the excess fat from the baking dish and pour 250 ml (9 fl oz/1 cup) of water into the dish. Stir to dissolve any pan juices; add the liquid to the pan.

Add the tomato paste, celery and 2.5 litres (87 fl oz/10 cups) of water. Bring to the boil, skimming the surface as required and add the bouquet garni and peppercorns. Reduce the heat to low and simmer gently for 4 hours. Skim the froth from the surface regularly.

Ladle the stock in batches into a fine sieve sitting over a bowl. Gently press the solids with a ladle to extract all the liquid. Discard the bones and vegetables and set aside to cool. Refrigerate until cold and spoon off any fat that has set on the top.

Makes 1.75 litres (61 fl oz/7 cups).

Chicken stock

2 kg (4 lb 8 oz) chicken bones
2 unpeeled onions, quartered
2 unpeeled carrots, chopped
2 celery stalks, leaves included, chopped
1 bouquet garni
12 black peppercorns

Put the chicken bones, onion, carrot, celery and 3.5 litres (122 fl oz/14 cups) of water in a large, heavy-based pan. Bring slowly to the boil. Skim the surface as required and add the bouquet garni and peppercorns. Reduce the heat to low and simmer gently for 3 hours. Skim the froth from the surface regularly.

Ladle the stock in batches into a fine sieve sitting over a bowl. Gently press the solids with a ladle to extract all the liquid. Let the stock cool, then refrigerate until cold and spoon off any fat that has set on the top.

Makes 2.5 litres (87 fl oz/10 cups).

Fish stock

2 kg (4 lb 8 oz) chopped fish bones, heads and tails
1 celery stalk, leaves included, roughly chopped
1 onion, chopped
1 unpeeled carrot, chopped
1 leek, sliced
1 bouquet garni
12 black peppercorns

Place the fish bones, celery, onion, carrot, leek and 2 litres (70 fl oz/8 cups) of water in a large, heavy-based pan. Bring slowly to the boil. Skim the surface as required and add the bouquet garni and peppercorns. Reduce the heat to low and simmer very gently for 20 minutes. Skim off any froth regularly.

Ladle the stock in batches into a sieve lined with damp muslin (cheesecloth) sitting over a bowl. To keep a clear fish stock, do not press the solids, but simply allow the stock to strain undisturbed. Allow to cool.

Makes 1.75 litres (61 fl oz/7 cups).

Vegetable stock

1 tablespoon oil
1 onion, chopped
2 leeks, chopped
4 carrots, chopped
2 parsnips, chopped
4 celery stalks, leaves included, chopped
2 bay leaves
1 bouquet garni
4 unpeeled garlic cloves (see Note)
8 black peppercorns

Heat the oil in a large, heavy-based pan and add the onion, leek, carrot, parsnip and celery. Cover and cook for 5 minutes without colouring. Add 3 litres (105 fl oz/12 cups) of water. Bring to the boil. Skim the surface if required and add the bay leaves, bouquet garni, garlic and peppercorns. Reduce the heat to low and simmer for 1 hour. Skim the froth from the surface of the stock regularly.

Ladle the stock in batches into a fine sieve sitting over a bowl. Gently press the solids to extract all the liquid. Allow the stock to cool, then refrigerate until cold and spoon off any fat that has set on the top.

Makes 2 litres (70 fl oz/8 cups).

Note Like bouquet garni, unpeeled garlic added to a stock adds a subtle flavour and will not cloud the soup.

asian soups

Hot and sour soup with chicken and mushrooms

preparation 40 minutes + overnight refrigeration + 10 minutes standing
cooking 4 hours
serves 6

stock
1.5 kg (3 lb 5 oz) chicken bones (chicken necks, backs, wings), washed
2 slices fresh ginger, 1 cm (½ inch) thick
4 spring onions (scallions), white part only

200 g (7 oz) boneless, skinless chicken breasts, cut into 2 cm (¾ inch) pieces
2 tablespoons garlic and red chilli paste
60 ml (2 fl oz/¼ cup) light soy sauce
¾ teaspoon ground white pepper
115 g (4 oz) baby corn, quartered lengthways
80 ml (2½ fl oz/⅓ cup) Chinese black vinegar
4 fresh shiitake mushrooms, stems removed, caps thinly sliced
100 g (3½ oz) enoki mushrooms, trimmed and separated
65 g (2 oz) fresh black wood fungus, cut into 1 cm (½ inch) strips
200 g (7 oz) fresh Shanghai noodles
200 g (7 oz) firm tofu, cut into 2.5 cm (1 inch) cubes
30 g (1 oz/¼ cup) cornflour (cornstarch)
3 eggs, lightly beaten
1 teaspoon sesame oil
2 spring onions (scallions), thinly sliced on the diagonal, to garnish

To make the stock, place the bones and 3.5 litres (121 fl oz/ 14 cups) water in a large saucepan to simmer—do not boil. Cook for 30 minutes, removing the surface scum. Add the ginger and spring onion, and cook, partially covered, at a low simmer for 3 hours. Strain and cool. Cover and refrigerate overnight. Remove the fat from the surface.

Bring 2 litres (70 fl oz/8 cups) of stock to the boil in a saucepan over high heat (freeze any remaining stock). Reduce the heat to medium, add the chicken, garlic and chilli paste, soy sauce and white pepper, and stir to combine.

Simmer, covered, for 10 minutes, or until the chicken is cooked. Add the corn, vinegar, mushrooms, wood fungus, noodles and tofu. Season with salt, and gently simmer for 5 minutes—do not stir.

Combine the cornflour and 60 ml (2 fl oz/¼ cup) water. Slowly stir into soup until combined and just thickened. Simmer, then slowly pour the egg over the surface. Turn off the heat, allow to stand for 10 minutes, then stir in the sesame oil. Garnish with spring onion and serve.

Cut the ends off the enoki mushrooms, then separate the stems.

Thai lemongrass broth with mussels

preparation 20 minutes
cooking 25 minutes
serves 4

1.5 kg (3 lb 5 oz) black mussels
1 tablespoon vegetable oil
5 spring onions (scallions), thinly sliced
2 garlic cloves, crushed
750 ml (26 fl oz/3 cups) chicken or fish stock
2½ tablespoons sliced fresh galangal or ginger
4 lemongrass stems, white part only, bruised
2 long red chillies, halved lengthways
6 makrut (kaffir lime) leaves, crushed
2 tablespoons roughly chopped coriander (cilantro) leaves

Scrub the mussels with a stiff brush and pull out the hairy beards. Discard any broken mussels, or open ones that don't close when tapped on the bench. Rinse well.

Heat a wok over medium heat, add the oil and swirl to coat the side of the wok. Cook the spring onion and garlic for 1 minute, or until softened. Add the stock, galangal, lemongrass, chilli, makrut leaves and 750 ml (26 fl oz/3 cups) water and rapidly simmer for 15 minutes.

Add the mussels, cover with a lid, bring to the boil over high heat and cook for 7–8 minutes, or until the mussels open, tossing occasionally. Discard any unopened mussels.

Stir in half the coriander, then divide the broth and mussels among four large serving bowls. Sprinkle with the remaining coriander, then serve immediately.

Pumpkin, prawn and coconut soup

preparation 15 minutes
cooking 20 minutes
serves 4–6

500 g (1 lb 2 oz) pumpkin (winter squash), diced
80 ml (2½ fl oz/⅓ cup) lime juice
1 kg (2 lb 4 oz) raw large prawns (shrimp)
2 onions, chopped
1 small fresh red chilli, finely chopped
1 lemongrass stem, white part only, chopped
1 teaspoon shrimp paste
1 teaspoon sugar
375 ml (13 fl oz/1½ cups) coconut milk
1 teaspoon tamarind purée
125 ml (4 fl oz/½ cup) coconut cream
1 tablespoon fish sauce
2 tablespoons Thai basil leaves, plus extra, to serve

Combine the pumpkin with half the lime juice in a bowl. Peel the prawns and gently pull out the dark vein from each prawn back, starting at the head end.

Process the onion, chilli, lemongrass, shrimp paste, sugar and 60 ml (2 fl oz/¼ cup) coconut milk in a food processor until a paste forms.

Combine the paste with the remaining coconut milk, tamarind purée and 250 ml (9 fl oz/1 cup) water in a large saucepan and stir until smooth. Add the pumpkin and lime juice to the pan and bring to the boil. Reduce the heat and simmer, covered, for about 10 minutes, or until the pumpkin is just tender.

Add the prawns and coconut cream, then simmer for 3 minutes, or until the prawns are just pink and cooked through. Stir in the fish sauce, the remaining lime juice and the Thai basil leaves.

To serve, pour the soup into warmed bowls and garnish with basil leaves.

Bottom: Pumpkin, prawn and coconut soup. Top: Thai lemongrass broth with mussels.

Vietnamese beef noodle soup

preparation 15 minutes + 40 minutes freezing +
5 minutes soaking
cooking 30 minutes
serves 4

400 g (14 oz) rump steak, trimmed
1 litre (35 fl oz/4 cups) beef stock
½ onion
1 star anise
1 cinnamon stick
1 tablespoon fish sauce
pinch ground white pepper
200 g (7 oz) fresh thin round rice noodles
2 spring onions (scallions), thinly sliced
30 mint leaves
90 g (3 oz/1 cup) bean sprouts, trimmed
1 small white onion, thinly sliced
1 small red chilli, thinly sliced

Wrap the meat in plastic wrap and freeze for 30–40 minutes, or until partially frozen, then thinly slice across the grain.

Place the stock in a large heavy-based saucepan with the onion half, star anise, cinnamon stick, fish sauce, white pepper and 500 ml (17 fl oz/2 cups) water, and bring to the boil over high heat. Reduce the heat to low–medium and simmer, covered, for 20 minutes. Discard the onion, star anise and cinnamon stick.

Meanwhile, cover the noodles with boiling water and gently separate. Drain and refresh with cold water. Divide the noodles and spring onion among the serving bowls. Top with equal amounts of beef, mint leaves, bean sprouts, onion slices and chilli. Ladle the simmering broth into the bowls, and serve.

Note It is important that the broth is kept hot as the heat will cook the slices of beef.

Won ton noodle soup

preparation 25 minutes
cooking 25 minutes
serves 4

70 g (2½ oz) raw prawns (shrimp)
70 g (2½ oz) minced (ground) veal
60 ml (2 fl oz/¼ cup) soy sauce
1 tablespoon finely chopped spring onion (scallion)
1 tablespoon finely chopped water chestnuts
1 teaspoon finely chopped fresh ginger
2 garlic cloves, finely chopped
24 gow gee wrappers
1.25 litres (44 fl oz/5 cups) chicken stock
2 tablespoons mirin (sweet rice wine)
500 g (1 lb 2 oz) baby bok choy (pak choy), finely shredded
8 spring onions (scallions), sliced

Peel the prawns and gently pull out the dark vein from each prawn back, starting at the head end. Finely chop the prawns. Mix with the minced veal, 2 teaspoons of the soy sauce, the spring onion, water chestnuts, ginger and garlic. Lay the round wrappers out on a work surface and place a teaspoon of mixture in the middle of each.

Moisten the edges of the wrappers and bring up the sides to form a pouch. Pinch together to seal. Cook in batches in a large saucepan of rapidly boiling water for 4–5 minutes. Drain and divide among soup bowls.

Bring the stock, remaining soy sauce and mirin to the boil in a large saucepan. Add the bok choy, cover and simmer for 2 minutes, or until the bok choy has just wilted. Add the sliced spring onion and season. Ladle the stock, bok choy and spring onion over the won tons.

Thinly slice the partially frozen steak across the grain with a sharp knife.

Use your finger or a pastry brush to moisten the edges of the wrappers, then pinch together.

Bottom: Won ton noodle soup. Top: Vietnamese beef noodle soup.

Prawn laksa

preparation 45 minutes + 5 minutes soaking
cooking 50 minutes
serves 4

1 kg (2 lb 4 oz) raw prawns (shrimp)
80 ml (2½ fl oz/⅓ cup) oil
2–6 small red chillies, seeded
1 onion, roughly chopped
3 garlic cloves, halved
2 cm x 2 cm (¾ inch x ¾ inch) piece fresh ginger or galangal, chopped
3 lemongrass stems, white part only, chopped
1 teaspoon ground turmeric
1 tablespoon ground coriander
2 teaspoons shrimp paste
625 ml (21½ fl oz/2½ cups) coconut cream
2 teaspoons grated palm sugar (jaggery) or soft brown sugar
4 makrut (kaffir lime) leaves, crushed
1–2 tablespoons fish sauce
200 g (7 oz) packet fish balls
190 g (7 oz) fried tofu puffs
250 g (9 oz) dried rice vermicelli
125 g (4½ oz) bean sprouts, trimmed
mint leaves, to serve
coriander (cilantro) leaves, to serve

Peel the prawns and gently pull out the dark vein from each prawn back, starting at the head end. Reserve the heads, shells and tails. Cover and refrigerate the prawn meat.

Heat 2 tablespoons of the oil in a wok or large saucepan and add the prawn shells, tails and heads. Stir over medium heat for 10 minutes, or until orange, then add 1 litre (35 fl oz/ 4 cups) water. Bring to the boil, then reduce the heat and simmer for 15 minutes. Strain the stock through a fine sieve and reserve the liquid. Discard the shells and clean the pan.

Finely chop the chillies (use two for mild flavour, increase for hot), and process with the onion, garlic, ginger, lemongrass, turmeric, coriander and 60 ml (2 fl oz/¼ cup) of the prawn stock in a food processor.

Heat the remaining oil in the pan, add the chilli mixture and shrimp paste, and stir over medium heat for 3 minutes, or until fragrant. Pour in the remaining stock and simmer for 10 minutes. Add the coconut cream, palm sugar, makrut leaves and fish sauce, and simmer for 5 minutes. Add the prawns and simmer for 2 minutes, or until firm and light pink. Add the fish balls and fried tofu puffs, and simmer gently until just heated through.

Soak the rice vermicelli in a bowl of boiling water for 2 minutes, then drain and divide among serving bowls. Top with the bean sprouts and ladle the soup over the top. Garnish with the mint and coriander.

Stir and toss the prawn heads, shells and tails until the heads turn bright orange.

Process the chilli, onion, garlic, ginger, lemongrass, spices and stock.

Tom yam goong

preparation 25 minutes
cooking 45 minutes
serves 6

500 g (1 lb 2 oz) raw prawns (shrimp)
1 tablespoon oil
2 tablespoons tom yam curry paste
2 tablespoons tamarind purée
2 teaspoons ground turmeric
1 teaspoon chopped small red chillies
4 makrut (kaffir lime) leaves, shredded, plus extra, to garnish
2 tablespoons fish sauce
2 tablespoons lime juice
2 teaspoons grated palm sugar (jaggery) or soft brown sugar

Peel the prawns, leaving the tail intact, and gently pull out the dark vein from each prawn back, starting at the head end. Reserve the shells and heads. Cover and refrigerate the prawn meat. Heat the oil in a wok or large saucepan and cook the shells and heads over medium heat, stirring frequently, for 10 minutes, or until the shells turn orange.

Add 250 ml (9 fl oz/1 cup) water and the tom yam paste to the pan. Bring to the boil and cook for 5 minutes, or until reduced slightly. Add another 2 litres (70 fl oz/8 cups) water, bring to the boil, reduce the heat and simmer for 20 minutes. Strain, discarding the shells and heads, and return the stock to the pan.

Add the tamarind purée, turmeric, chilli and makrut leaves to the pan, bring to the boil and cook for 2 minutes. Add the prawn meat and cook for 5 minutes, or until pink. Stir in the fish sauce, lime juice and sugar. Garnish with shredded makrut leaves.

Thai-style chicken and baby corn soup

preparation 30 minutes
cooking 15 minutes
serves 4

150 g (5½ oz) whole baby corn (see Note)
1 tablespoon oil
2 lemongrass stems, white part only, very thinly sliced
2 tablespoons finely grated fresh ginger
6 spring onions (scallions), chopped
1 red chilli, finely chopped
1 litre (35 fl oz/4 cups) chicken stock
375 ml (13 fl oz/1½ cups) coconut milk
2 boneless, skinless chicken breasts, thinly sliced
130 g (4½ oz) creamed corn
1 tablespoon soy sauce
2 tablespoons finely snipped chives, to serve
1 red chilli, thinly sliced, to serve

Cut the baby corn in half or quarters lengthways, depending on their size.

Heat the oil in a saucepan over medium heat. Cook the lemongrass, ginger, spring onion and chilli for 1 minute, stirring. Add the stock and coconut milk and bring to the boil—do not cover or the coconut milk will curdle.

Stir in the corn, chicken and creamed corn and simmer for 8 minutes, or until the corn and chicken are just tender. Add the soy sauce, season well and serve garnished with the chives and chilli.

Note *Tinned baby corn can be substituted for fresh corn. Add during the last 2 minutes of cooking.*

Cook the prawn shells and tom yam paste until the liquid has reduced and thickened slightly.

Grate the peeled ginger, using the fine side of the grater or a specialist ginger grater.

Bottom: Thai-style chicken and baby corn soup. Top: Tom yam goong.

Spicy lamb soup

preparation 40 minutes
cooking 1 hour 30 minutes
serves 4–6

2 large onions, roughly chopped
3 red chillies, seeded and chopped (or 2 teaspoons dried chilli)
3–4 garlic cloves
2.5 cm (1 inch) piece fresh ginger, peeled and chopped
5 cm (2 inch) lemongrass, white part only, finely chopped
½ teaspoon ground cardamom
2 teaspoons ground cumin
½ teaspoon ground cinnamon
1 teaspoon ground turmeric
2 tablespoons peanut oil
1.5 kg (3 lb 5 oz) lamb neck chops
2–3 tablespoons vindaloo paste
600 ml (21 fl oz) coconut cream
55 g (2 oz/¼ cup firmly packed) soft brown sugar
2–3 tablespoons lime juice
4 makrut (kaffir lime) leaves

Put the onion, chilli, garlic, ginger, 1 teaspoon ground black pepper, the lemongrass, cardamom, cumin, cinnamon and turmeric in a food processor and process to a paste. Heat half the oil in a large frying pan and brown the chops in batches. Drain on paper towels.

Add the remaining oil to the pan and cook the spice and vindaloo pastes for 2–3 minutes. Add the chops and 1.75 litres (61 fl oz/7 cups) water, cover and bring to the boil. Reduce the heat and simmer, covered, for 1 hour. Remove the chops from the pan and stir in the coconut cream. Remove the meat from the bones, shred and return to the pan.

Add the sugar, lime juice and makrut leaves. Simmer, uncovered, over low heat for 20–25 minutes, until the soup is slightly thickened.

Crab dumpling soup

preparation 25 minutes
cooking 20 minutes
serves 4

170 g (6 oz) tin crabmeat, well drained
2 tablespoons finely chopped spring onions (scallions)
2 garlic cloves, finely chopped
2 teaspoons sesame oil
3 teaspoons chopped fresh ginger
12 small round gow gee (egg) or won ton wrappers
3 spring onions (scallions), extra
1.25 litres (44 fl oz/5 cups) chicken stock
1 tablespoon soy sauce
1 tablespoon mirin (sweet rice wine)
1 teaspoon sugar

To make the crab filling, mix the crab with the chopped spring onion, half the garlic, 1 teaspoon of sesame oil and 1 teaspoon of the ginger.

Place 2 teaspoons of the filling on one half of each wrapper. Moisten the edge with some water and fold over to form a crescent. Press the edges together firmly. Lay the dumplings on a lightly floured surface.

Cut the extra spring onions into thin strips and set aside. Heat the remaining sesame oil in a saucepan, add the remaining garlic and ginger and cook over medium heat for 3–4 minutes, or until the garlic is lightly golden. Add the stock, soy sauce, mirin and sugar. Bring to the boil, add the spring onion strips (reserving some to garnish) and simmer for 2–3 minutes.

Bring a large saucepan of water to the boil, add three to four dumplings at a time and cook for 5 minutes, or until just cooked. Place in bowls, ladle the stock over the dumplings, garnish with the spring onion strips and serve.

Process the onion with the chilli, garlic and spices to make a paste.

Fold over the wrapper to enclose the filling, then press firmly to seal.

Bottom: Crab dumpling soup. Top: Spicy lamb soup.

Chicken mulligatawny

preparation 25 minutes
cooking 4 hours
serves 6

stock
1.5 kg (3 lb 5 oz) chicken
1 carrot, chopped
2 celery stalks, chopped
4 spring onions (scallions), chopped
2 cm (¾ inch) piece of fresh ginger, sliced

2 tomatoes, peeled
20 g (¾ oz) ghee
1 large onion, finely chopped
3 garlic cloves, crushed
8 curry leaves
55 g (2 oz/¼ cup) Madras curry paste
250 g (9 oz/1 cup) red lentils, washed and drained
70 g (2½ oz/⅓ cup) short-grain rice
250 ml (9 fl oz/1 cup) coconut cream
2 tablespoons coriander (cilantro) leaves, chopped
mango chutney, to serve

To make the stock, put all the ingredients and 4 litres (140 fl oz/16 cups) cold water in a large stockpot or saucepan. Bring to the boil, removing any scum that rises to the surface. Reduce the heat to low and simmer, partly covered, for 3 hours. Continue to remove any scum from the surface. Carefully remove the chicken and cool. Strain the stock into a bowl and cool. Cover and refrigerate overnight. Discard the skin and bones from the chicken and shred the flesh into small pieces. Cover and refrigerate overnight.

Score a cross in the base of the tomatoes. Put in a heatproof bowl and cover with boiling water. Leave for 30 seconds then transfer to a bowl of cold water and peel the skin away from the cross. Cut the tomatoes in half, scoop out the seeds and chop the flesh.

Melt the ghee in a large saucepan over medium heat. Cook the onion for 5 minutes, or until softened but not browned. Add the garlic and curry leaves and cook for 1 minute. Add the curry paste, cook for 1 minute, then stir in the lentils. Pour in the stock and bring to the boil over high heat, removing any scum from the surface. Reduce the heat, add the tomato and simmer for 30 minutes, or until the lentils are soft.

Meanwhile, bring a large saucepan of water to the boil. Add the rice and cook for 12 minutes, stirring once or twice. Drain. Stir the rice into the soup with the chicken and coconut cream until warmed through—don't allow it to boil or it will curdle. Season. Sprinkle with the coriander and serve with the mango chutney.

Corn and crab soup

preparation 15 minutes
cooking 10 minutes
serves 4

1½ tablespoons oil
6 garlic cloves, chopped
6 red Asian shallots, chopped
2 lemongrass stems, white part only, chopped
1 tablespoon grated fresh ginger
1 litre (35 fl oz/4 cups) chicken stock
250 ml (9 fl oz/1 cup) coconut milk
375 g (13 oz/2½ cups) corn kernels
350 g (12 oz) tinned crabmeat, drained
2 tablespoons fish sauce
2 tablespoons lime juice
1 teaspoon grated palm sugar (jaggery) or soft brown sugar
coriander (cilantro) leaves, to garnish
sliced chilli (optional), to serve

Heat the oil in a large saucepan. Add the garlic, shallots, lemongrass and ginger and stir over medium heat for 2 minutes. Add the stock and coconut milk and bring to the boil. Add the corn and cook for 5 minutes. Add the crabmeat, fish sauce, lime juice and sugar and stir. Serve topped with coriander leaves, and sliced chillies, if desired.

Udon noodle soup

preparation 20 minutes
cooking 16 minutes
serves 4

400 g (14 oz) dried udon noodles
3 teaspoons dashi granules
2 leeks, white part only, thinly sliced
200 g (7 oz) pork loin, cut into thin strips
125 ml (4 fl oz/½ cup) Japanese soy sauce
2 tablespoons mirin (sweet rice wine)
4 spring onions (scallions), finely chopped
shichimi togarashi (see Note), to serve

Cook the noodles in a large saucepan of rapidly boiling water for 5 minutes, or until tender. Drain; keep warm.

Combine 1 litre (35 fl oz/4 cups) water and the dashi in a large saucepan and bring to the boil. Add the leek, reduce the heat and simmer for 5 minutes. Add the pork, soy sauce, mirin and spring onion and simmer for 2 minutes. Divide the noodles among four serving bowls and ladle on the soup. Top with spring onion and shichimi togarashi.

Note *Shichimi togarashi is a spice mix; buy it in Asian stores.*

Tom kha gai

preparation 20 minutes
cooking 20 minutes
serves 4

5 cm (2 inch) piece fresh galangal, thinly sliced
500 ml (17 fl oz/2 cups) coconut milk
250 ml (9 fl oz/1 cup) chicken stock
600 g (1 lb 5 oz) boneless, skinless chicken breasts, sliced
1–2 teaspoons finely chopped red chilli
2 tablespoons fish sauce
1 teaspoon soft brown sugar
10 g (¼ oz) coriander (cilantro) leaves, plus extra, to garnish

Combine the galangal, coconut milk and stock in a saucepan. Bring to the boil, then reduce the heat and simmer over low heat for 10 minutes, stirring occasionally. Add the chicken and chilli and simmer for 8 minutes. Add the fish sauce and sugar and stir. Add the coriander leaves and serve immediately, garnished with extra coriander.

Fragrant corn, coconut and chicken noodle soup

preparation 20 minutes
cooking 20 minutes
serves 4

100 g (3½ oz) dried rice vermicelli
250 ml (9 fl oz/1 cup) coconut cream
500 ml (17 fl oz/2 cups) coconut milk
250 ml (9 fl oz/1 cup) chicken stock
125 g (4½ oz) tinned creamed corn
500 g (1 lb 2 oz) boneless, skinless chicken thighs, diced
200 g (7 oz) baby corn, halved lengthways
5 cm (2 inch) piece of galangal, sliced
6 makrut (kaffir lime) leaves, shredded
2 lemongrass stems, white part only, bruised, cut into pieces
2 tablespoons fish sauce
2 tablespoons lime juice
1 tablespoon grated palm sugar (jaggery) or soft brown sugar
15 g (½ oz) coriander (cilantro) leaves

Soak the vermicelli in boiling water for 6–7 minutes, or until soft. Drain and set aside.

Put the coconut cream and milk, stock and creamed corn in a large saucepan and bring to the boil; reduce the heat and simmer for 5 minutes. Add the chicken, baby corn, galangal, lime leaves and lemongrass and simmer for 10 minutes. Add the fish sauce, lime juice and sugar. Stir through half the coriander and serve topped with the rest.

Top left: Corn and crab soup. Top right: Tom kha gai. Bottom right: Fragrant corn, coconut and chicken noodle soup. Bottom left: Udon noodle soup.

Shanghai chicken and noodle soup

preparation 10 minutes
cooking 35 minutes
serves 4–6

2 litres (70 fl oz/8 cups) ready-made stock diluted with
500 ml (17 fl oz/2 cups) water
1 star anise
4 thin slices fresh ginger
600 g (1 lb 5 oz) boneless, skinless chicken breasts
375 g (13 oz) Shanghai noodles
200 g (7 oz) fresh asparagus, woody ends trimmed,
cut into 3 cm (1¼ inch) pieces
1 tablespoon thinly sliced fresh ginger
1½ tablespoons light soy sauce
1 tablespoon Chinese rice wine
½ teaspoon sugar
4 spring onions (scallions), thinly sliced on the diagonal
50 g (2 oz) watercress tips (optional)
¼ teaspoon sesame oil, to drizzle
soy sauce, extra, to serve (optional)

Pour the stock into a non-stick wok and bring to the boil. Reduce to medium–low heat, add the star anise and ginger slices. Add the chicken and poach for 15–20 minutes, or until cooked through. Remove the chicken with a slotted spoon and set aside to cool. Leave the stock in the wok.

Meanwhile, bring 2 litres (70 fl oz/8 cups) water to the boil in a large saucepan and cook the noodles for 3 minutes. Drain and refresh under cold water.

Cut the chicken across the breast into 5 mm (¼ inch) slices. Return the stock to the boil and add the asparagus, ginger, soy sauce, rice wine, sugar and ½ teaspoon salt. Reduce the heat, add the noodles and simmer for 2 minutes. Return the chicken to the wok and cook for 1 minute, or until heated through.

Remove the noodles from the liquid with tongs and evenly divide among serving bowls. Divide the chicken, asparagus, spring onion and watercress (if using) among the bowls, then ladle the broth on top. Drizzle with sesame oil and serve with extra soy sauce, if desired.

Scallop and eggflower soup

preparation 30 minutes
cooking 45 minutes
serves 4

300 g (10½ oz) scallops
1 tablespoon dry sherry
¼ teaspoon ground white pepper
1 teaspoon grated fresh ginger
7 spring onions (scallions), thinly sliced, white and
green parts separated
2 tablespoons oil
1 tablespoon cornflour (cornstarch)
750 ml (26 fl oz/3 cups) chicken stock
2 tablespoons soy sauce
70 g (2½ oz) tinned straw mushrooms, cut into halves
(see Note)
50 g (2 oz/⅓ cup) frozen peas
1 egg, lightly beaten
dry sherry, extra, to taste
2 teaspoons soy sauce, extra

Slice or pull off any vein, membrane or hard white muscle from the scallops, leaving any roe attached. Combine with the sherry, pepper and ginger in a bowl and refrigerate for 10 minutes.

Heat the oil in a wok or heavy-based frying pan, swirling gently to coat the base and side. Add the white part of the spring onion and cook for 30 seconds. Add the scallops and their liquid and cook over high heat, turning occasionally, until the scallops turn milky white. Remove the scallops with a slotted spoon and set aside.

Blend the cornflour with a little of the stock until smooth, add to the wok with the remaining stock and soy sauce and bring to the boil, stirring until the mixture boils and thickens. Add the straw mushrooms and peas and cook for a further 2 minutes. Return the scallops to the wok, stirring the soup constantly.

Pour in the egg and cook, stirring until it turns opaque. Stir the spring onion greens through and add a little more sherry and soy sauce, to taste.

Note Drain and rinse straw mushrooms before using. Leftover tinned mushrooms can be kept chilled, covered with water, for up to 3 days. They can be used in dishes such as stir-fries.

Bottom: Scallop and eggflower soup. Top: Shanghai chicken and noodle soup.

Chicken laksa

preparation 30 minutes + 10 minutes soaking
cooking 35 minutes
serves 4–6

1½ tablespoons coriander seeds
1 tablespoon cumin seeds
1 teaspoon ground turmeric
1 onion, roughly chopped
1 tablespoon roughly chopped fresh ginger
3 garlic cloves
3 lemongrass stems, white part only, sliced
6 candlenuts or macadamias (see Notes)
4–6 small red chillies, sliced
2–3 teaspoons shrimp paste, roasted (see Notes)
1 litre (35 fl oz/4 cups) chicken stock
60 ml (2 fl oz/¼ cup) oil
400 g (14 oz) boneless, skinless chicken thighs, cut into 2 cm (¾ inch) pieces
750 ml (26 fl oz/3 cups) coconut milk
4 makrut (kaffir lime) leaves
2½ tablespoons lime juice
2 tablespoons fish sauce
2 tablespoons grated palm sugar (jaggery) or soft brown sugar
250 g (9 oz) dried rice vermicelli
90 g (3 oz/1 cup) bean sprouts, trimmed
4 fried tofu puffs, cut into matchsticks
1 very large handful mint leaves
2 large handfuls coriander (cilantro) leaves
lime wedges, to serve

Dry-fry (no oil) the coriander and cumin seeds in a frying pan over medium heat for 1–2 minutes, or until fragrant, tossing to prevent burning. Grind finely in a mortar with a pestle.

Place all the spices, onion, ginger, garlic, lemongrass, nuts, chillies and shrimp paste in a food processor or blender. Add 125 ml (4 fl oz/½ cup) of the stock and blend to a fine paste.

Heat the oil in a large saucepan over low heat and cook the paste for 3–5 minutes, stirring. Add the remaining stock and bring to the boil over high heat. Reduce the heat to medium and simmer for 15 minutes, or until reduced slightly. Add the chicken and simmer for 4–5 minutes, or until cooked.

Add the coconut milk, makrut leaves, lime juice, fish sauce and sugar, and simmer for 5 minutes over low–medium heat. Do not allow to boil, as the coconut milk will split.

Meanwhile, place the vermicelli in a heatproof bowl, cover with boiling water and soak for 6–7 minutes, or until soft. Drain and divide among large serving bowls with the sprouts. Ladle the hot soup over the top and garnish with tofu strips, mint and coriander. Serve with a wedge of lime.

Notes *Raw candlenuts are slightly toxic so must be cooked before use. To roast the shrimp paste, wrap the paste in foil and place under a hot grill (broiler) for 1 minute.*

Dry-fry the coriander and cumin seeds over medium heat, tossing constantly.

Place the spices, onion, ginger, garlic, chillies, nuts, lemongrass and shrimp paste in a food processor.

Hot and sour lime soup with beef

preparation 20 minutes
cooking 30 minutes
serves 4

1 litre (35 fl oz/4 cups) beef stock
2 lemongrass stems, white part only, halved
3 garlic cloves, halved
2.5 cm (1 inch) piece fresh ginger, sliced
3 very large handfuls coriander (cilantro), leaves
and stalks separated
4 spring onions (scallions), thinly sliced
2 strips lime zest
2 star anise
3 small fresh red chillies, seeded and finely chopped
500 g (1 lb 2 oz) fillet steak, trimmed
2 tablespoons fish sauce
1 tablespoon grated palm sugar (jaggery)
2 tablespoons lime juice, or to taste
coriander (cilantro) leaves, to garnish

Put the stock, lemongrass, garlic, ginger, coriander stalks, half the spring onion, lime zest, star anise, 1 teaspoon chopped chilli and 1 litre (35 fl oz/4 cups) water in a saucepan. Bring to the boil and simmer, covered, for 25 minutes. Strain and return the liquid to the pan.

Heat a chargrill pan or barbecue flat plate until very hot. Brush lightly with olive oil and sear the steak on both sides until browned but very rare in the centre.

Reheat the soup, adding the fish sauce and palm sugar. Season with salt and black pepper. Add the lime juice to taste (you may want more than 2 tablespoons) to achieve a hot and sour flavour.

Add the remaining spring onion and the chopped coriander leaves to the soup. Slice the beef across the grain into thin strips. Curl the strips into a decorative pattern, then place in the centre of four deep wide serving bowls. Pour the soup over the beef and garnish with the remaining chilli and a few extra coriander leaves.

Slice the beef along the grain and curl the strips into a decorative pattern.

Chicken and coconut milk soup

preparation 30 minutes + 5 minutes soaking
cooking 15 minutes
serves 8

150 g (5½ oz) dried rice vermicelli
1 lime
4 small red chillies, seeded and chopped
1 onion, chopped
2 garlic cloves, crushed
4 thin slices fresh ginger, finely chopped
2 lemongrass stems, white part only, chopped
1 tablespoon chopped coriander (cilantro) leaves
1 tablespoon peanut oil
750 ml (26 fl oz/3 cups) chicken stock
685 ml (23½ fl oz/2¾ cups) coconut milk
500 g (1 lb 2 oz) chicken tenderloins, cut into thin strips
4 spring onions (scallions), chopped
150 g (5½ oz) fried tofu puffs, sliced
90 g (3 oz/1 cup) bean sprouts
3 teaspoons soft brown sugar

Soak the vermicelli in boiling water for 5 minutes. Drain, then cut into short lengths. Remove the lime zest with a vegetable peeler and cut it into long, thin strips.

Place the chilli, onion, garlic, ginger, lemongrass and coriander into a food processor and process in short bursts for 20 seconds, or until smooth.

Heat the oil in a large heavy-based saucepan over medium heat. Add the chilli mixture and cook, stirring frequently, for 3 minutes, or until fragrant. Add the stock, coconut milk and lime zest strips, and bring to the boil. Add the chicken and cook, stirring, for 4 minutes, or until tender.

Add the spring onion, tofu, bean sprouts and brown sugar, and season with salt. Stir over medium heat for 3 minutes, or until the spring onion is tender. Divide the noodles among eight bowls and pour the soup over the top. Garnish with chilli and coriander.

Remove the lime zest with a vegetable peeler, and cut it into long, thin strips.

Bottom: Chicken and coconut milk soup. Top: Hot and sour lime soup with beef.

Miso with ramen

preparation 15 minutes + 15 minutes soaking
cooking 15 minutes
serves 4

1 teaspoon finely chopped dried wakame
180 g (6 oz) fresh ramen noodles
100 g (3½ oz) silken firm tofu, cut into 1.5 cm (⅝ inch) cubes
2 spring onions (scallions), thinly sliced on the diagonal
1¾ teaspoons dashi granules
2–3 tablespoons red miso (see Notes)
2 teaspoons mirin (sweet rice wine)
2 teaspoons Japanese soy sauce

Soak the wakame in a bowl of warm water for 15 minutes. Drain and set aside.

Cook the noodles in a large saucepan of boiling salted water for 2 minutes, or until cooked through. Drain and rinse, then divide among warmed serving bowls. Place the tofu and spring onion on top.

Meanwhile, bring 1.25 litres (44 fl oz/5 cups) water to the boil in a large saucepan. Reduce the heat to low and add the dashi granules, stirring for 30 seconds, or until the dashi is dissolved.

In a bowl, combine the miso with 250 ml (9 fl oz/1 cup) of the dashi stock, whisking until smooth. Return the miso mixture to the pan of stock and stir until combined—be careful not to boil the broth as this will diminish the flavour of the miso. Add the mirin, soy sauce and wakame, and gently heat for 1 minute, then stir to combine. Ladle the broth over the noodles, tofu and spring onion, and serve immediately.

Note *Shiro (white) miso can be used instead of red miso, however the flavour will not be as strong—adjust to taste.*

Soba noodle and vegetable soup

preparation 15 minutes + 5 minutes soaking
cooking 10 minutes
serves 4

250 g (9 oz) soba noodles
2 dried shiitake mushrooms
2 litres (70 fl oz/8 cups) vegetable stock
120 g (4 oz) snow peas (mangetout), cut into thin strips
2 small carrots, cut into thin 5 cm (2 inch) strips
2 garlic cloves, finely chopped
6 spring onions (scallions), cut into 5 cm (2 inch) lengths and thinly sliced lengthways
3 cm (1¼ inch) piece fresh ginger, cut into matchsticks
80 ml (2½ fl oz/⅓ cup) soy sauce
60 ml (2 fl oz/¼ cup) mirin (sweet rice wine) or sake (dry rice wine)
90 g (3 oz/1 cup) bean sprouts, trimmed
coriander (cilantro) leaves, to garnish

Cook the noodles according to the packet instructions, then drain well.

Soak the mushrooms in 125 ml (4 fl oz/½ cup) boiling water until soft. Drain, reserving the liquid. Discard the stems and slice the caps.

Combine the vegetable stock, mushrooms, reserved liquid, snow peas, carrot, garlic, spring onion and ginger in a large saucepan. Bring slowly to the boil, then reduce the heat to low and simmer for 5 minutes, or until the vegetables are tender. Add the soy sauce, mirin and bean sprouts. Cook for a further 3 minutes.

Divide the noodles among serving bowls. Ladle the soup and vegetables over the noodles. Garnish with coriander.

With a very sharp knife, chop the dried wakame into fine pieces.

Simmer the vegetables for 5 minutes, or until they are tender.

Bottom: Soba noodle and vegetable soup. Top: Miso with ramen.

Beef pho

preparation 15 minutes
cooking 35 minutes
serves 4

2 litres (70 fl oz/8 cups) beef stock
1 star anise
4 cm (1½ inch) piece fresh ginger, sliced
2 pigs' trotters, halved
½ onion, studded with 2 whole cloves
2 lemongrass stems, bruised
2 garlic cloves, crushed
¼ teaspoon ground white pepper
1 tablespoon fish sauce, plus extra, to serve
200 g (7 oz) fresh thin rice noodles
300 g (10½ oz) beef fillet, partially frozen, thinly sliced
90 g (3 oz/1 cup) bean sprouts, trimmed
2 spring onions (scallions), thinly sliced,
25 g (1 oz) chopped coriander (cilantro) leaves,
plus extra, to serve
4 tablespoons chopped Vietnamese mint, plus extra, to serve
1 red chilli, thinly sliced, plus extra, to serve
2 limes, quartered

Put the beef stock, star anise, ginger, pigs' trotters, onion, lemongrass, garlic and white pepper in a wok and bring to the boil. Reduce the heat to very low and simmer, covered, for 30 minutes. Strain, return the liquid to the wok and stir in the fish sauce.

Meanwhile, put the noodles in a heatproof bowl, cover with boiling water and gently separate. Drain well then refresh under cold running water.

Divide the noodles among four deep soup bowls then top with beef strips, bean sprouts, spring onion, coriander, mint and chilli. Ladle over the hot broth.

Place the extra chilli, mint and coriander, the lime quarters and fish sauce in small bowls on a platter, serve with the soup and allow your guests to help themselves.

Meat dumpling soup

preparation 45 minutes
cooking 35 minutes
serves 4–6

1 tablespoon white sesame seeds
2 tablespoons oil
2 garlic cloves, finely chopped
150 g (5½ oz) lean minced (ground) pork
200 g (7 oz) lean minced (ground) beef
200 g (7 oz) Chinese cabbage (wong bok), finely shredded
100 g (3½ oz) bean sprouts, trimmed and chopped
100 g (3½ oz) mushrooms, finely chopped
3 spring onions (scallions), finely chopped
150 g (5½ oz) gow gee (egg) dumpling wrappers

soup
2.5 litres (87 fl oz/10 cups) beef stock
2 tablespoons soy sauce
3 cm (1¼ inch) piece fresh ginger, very thinly sliced
4 spring onions (scallions), chopped, to serve

To make the filling, toast the sesame seeds in a dry frying pan over medium heat for 3–4 minutes, shaking the pan gently, until the seeds are golden brown. Remove from the pan at once to prevent burning. Crush the seeds in a food mill or using a mortar and pestle.

Heat the oil in a saucepan. Cook the garlic and mince over medium heat until the meat changes colour, breaking up any lumps with a fork. Add the cabbage, sprouts, mushrooms and 80 ml (2½ fl oz/⅓ cup) water. Cook, stirring occasionally, for 5–6 minutes, or until the water evaporates and the vegetables soften. Add the spring onion, crushed sesame seeds and season to taste. Set aside.

Work with one gow gee wrapper at a time and keep the extra wrappers covered with a damp tea towel (dish towel). Place 1 teaspoon of filling on a wrapper, just off-centre, and gently smooth out the filling a little. Brush the edges of the wrapper with a little water and fold it over the filling to form a semi-circle. Press the edges together to seal. Repeat with the extra wrappers and filling.

To make the soup, combine the beef stock, soy sauce, ginger and half the spring onion in a large saucepan. Bring to the boil and simmer for 15 minutes.

Drop the dumplings into the soup and cook gently for 5 minutes, or until they change colour and look plump. Garnish with the remaining spring onion and serve.

Bottom: Meat dumpling soup. Top: Beef pho.

Chinese pork and noodle soup

preparation 25 minutes + overnight refrigeration + 1 hour refrigeration
cooking 4 hours
serves 4–6

stock
1.5 kg (3 lb 5 oz) chicken bones (chicken necks, backs, wings), washed
3 garlic cloves, sliced
2 slices fresh ginger, 1 cm (½ inch) thick
4 spring onions (scallions), white part only

150 g (5½ oz) Chinese cabbage (wong bok), shredded
1 tablespoon peanut oil
2 teaspoons sesame oil
4 garlic cloves, crushed
1 tablespoon grated fresh ginger
300 g (10½ oz) minced (ground) pork
1 egg white
¼ teaspoon ground white pepper
2 tablespoons light soy sauce
1 tablespoon Chinese rice wine
1½ tablespoons cornflour (cornstarch)
1 very large handful coriander (cilantro) leaves, finely chopped
6 spring onions (scallions), extra, thinly sliced
200 g (7 oz) fresh thin egg noodles

To make the stock, place the bones and 3.5 litres (122 fl oz/ 14 cups) water in a large saucepan and bring to a simmer— do not boil. Cook for 30 minutes, removing any scum that rises to the surface. Add the garlic, ginger and spring onion, and cook, partially covered, at a low simmer for 3 hours. Strain through a fine sieve, then cool. Cover and refrigerate overnight. Remove the layer of fat from the surface once it has solidified.

Bring a large saucepan of water to the boil and cook the cabbage for 2 minutes, or until soft. Drain the cabbage, cool and squeeze out the excess water.

Heat the peanut oil and 1 teaspoon of the sesame oil in a small frying pan, and cook the garlic and ginger for 1 minute, or until the garlic just starts to brown; cool.

Combine the pork, cabbage, garlic mixture, egg white, white pepper, soy sauce, rice wine, cornflour, half the coriander and half the spring onion. Cover and refrigerate for 1 hour. Shape tablespoons of the mixture into balls.

Bring 1.5 litres (52 fl oz/6 cups) of the stock (freeze the leftover stock) to the boil in a wok over high heat. Reduce the heat to medium and simmer for 1–2 minutes. Add the pork balls and cook, covered, for 8–10 minutes, or until they rise to the surface and are cooked through.

Bring a large saucepan of water to the boil. Cook the noodles for 1 minute, then drain and rinse. Divide among serving bowls and ladle the soup and pork balls on top. Garnish with the remaining spring onion, coriander leaves and sprinkle over remaining sesame oil.

Place all the meatball ingredients in a bowl and combine with your hands.

Once the pork balls have been shaped, add them to the wok one by one.

Vietnamese fish and noodle soup

preparation 30 minutes + 5 minutes soaking
cooking 20 minutes
serves 4

1 teaspoon shrimp paste
150 g (5½ oz) mung bean vermicelli
2 tablespoons peanut oil
6 garlic cloves, finely chopped
1 small onion, thinly sliced
2 long red chillies, chopped
2 lemongrass stems, white part only, thinly sliced
1.25 litres (44 fl oz/5 cups) chicken stock
60 ml (2 fl oz/¼ cup) fish sauce
1 tablespoon rice vinegar
4 ripe tomatoes, peeled, seeded and chopped
500 g (1 lb 2 oz) firm white fish fillets (snapper or blue-eye cod),
cut into 3 cm (1¼ inch) pieces
1 large handful mint, torn, plus extra, to garnish
1 very large handful coriander (cilantro) leaves, plus extra,
to garnish
90 g (3 oz/1 cup) bean sprouts, trimmed
2 long red chillies, extra, sliced
lemon wedges, to serve

Wrap the shrimp paste in foil and place under a hot grill (broiler) for 1 minute. Set aside.

Soak the noodles in boiling water for 3–4 minutes. Rinse under cold water, drain and cut into 15 cm (6 inch) lengths.

Heat the oil in a heavy-based saucepan over medium heat. Add the garlic and cook for 1 minute, or until golden. Add the onion, chilli, lemongrass and paste, and cook, stirring, for a further minute. Add the stock, fish sauce, vinegar and tomato. Bring to the boil, then reduce the heat to medium and simmer for 10 minutes. Add the fish and simmer gently for 3 minutes, or until cooked. Stir in the herbs.

Divide the noodles and sprouts among bowls and ladle on the soup. Top with extra mint, coriander and chilli. Serve with lemon wedges.

Roast duck and noodle broth

preparation 25 minutes + 25 minutes soaking
cooking 10 minutes
serves 4–6

3 dried shiitake mushrooms
1 Chinese roast duck (1.5 kg/3 lb 5 oz)
500 ml (17 fl oz/2 cups) chicken stock
2 tablespoons light soy sauce
1 tablespoon Chinese rice wine
2 teaspoons sugar
400 g (14 oz) fresh flat rice noodles
2 tablespoons oil
3 spring onions (scallions), thinly sliced
1 teaspoon finely chopped fresh ginger
400 g (14 oz) bok choy (pak choy), leaves separated
¼ teaspoon sesame oil

Soak the mushrooms in 250 ml (9 fl oz/1 cup) boiling water for 20 minutes. Drain, reserving the liquid and squeezing the excess liquid from the mushrooms. Discard the stems and thinly slice the caps.

Remove the skin and flesh from the duck. Discard the fat and carcass. Finely slice the duck meat and the skin (you need about 400 g/14 oz of duck meat).

Place the stock, soy sauce, rice wine, sugar and the reserved mushroom liquid in a saucepan over medium heat. Bring to a simmer and cook for 5 minutes.

Meanwhile, place the rice noodles in a heatproof bowl, cover with boiling water and soak briefly. Gently separate the noodles with your hands and drain well. Divide evenly among large soup bowls.

Heat the oil in a wok over high heat. Add the spring onion, ginger and mushroom, and cook for several seconds. Transfer to the broth with the bok choy and duck meat, and simmer for 1 minute, or until the duck has warmed through and the bok choy has wilted. Ladle the soup on the noodles and drizzle sesame oil on each serving. Serve immediately.

Gently simmer the fish pieces in the soup until they are cooked.

Once the shiitake mushrooms have been soaked, thinly slice the caps.

Bottom: Roast duck and noodle broth. Top: Vietnamese fish and noodle soup.

Cambodian sour chicken soup

preparation 20 minutes
cooking 40 minutes
serves 4

800 g (1 lb 12 oz) chicken quarters (leg and thigh), skin
removed, cut into 5 cm (2 inch) pieces on the bone
1 tablespoon tamarind pulp, soaked in 60 ml (2 fl oz/¼ cup)
boiling water
60 ml (2 fl oz/¼ cup) fish sauce
½ teaspoon sugar
200 g (7 oz) fresh pineapple, cut into 2 cm (¾ inch) cubes
2 small tomatoes, cut into wedges
3 spring onions (scallions), finely chopped
1 teaspoon vegetable oil
4 garlic cloves, finely chopped
2 tablespoons chopped coriander (cilantro) leaves
3 tablespoons chopped basil
1 red chilli, thinly sliced
2 tablespoons lime juice
90 g (3 oz/1 cup) bean sprouts, trimmed

Pour 1.25 litres (44 fl oz/5 cups) water into a non-stick wok,
then bring to the boil over medium heat. Add the chicken
pieces and cook for 30 minutes, or until the stock is clear,
occasionally skimming any scum from the surface. Remove
the chicken from the wok with a slotted spoon, then take
the meat off the bones and discard any fat and bones. Cool
the meat slightly, then shred the chicken meat, keeping the
stock simmering while you do this.

Strain the tamarind liquid to remove the seeds, then add
the strained liquid to the stock. Return the shredded chicken
meat to the wok, add the fish sauce, sugar, pineapple,
tomato and spring onion and season to taste with salt,
then cook for 1–2 minutes over medium heat, or until the
chicken, tomato and pineapple are heated through.

Heat the oil in a small frying pan over medium heat and
add the garlic. Cook for 2 minutes, or until golden. Remove
the garlic with a slotted spoon and add it to the soup.
Remove the wok from the heat and stir in the coriander,
basil, chilli and lime juice. To serve, divide the bean sprouts
in the bottom of four bowls and ladle the soup over the top.
Serve immediately.

Scallops with soba noodles and dashi broth

preparation 10 minutes
cooking 15 minutes
serves 4

250 g (9 oz) dried soba noodles
60 ml (2 fl oz/¼ cup) mirin (sweet rice wine)
60 ml (2 fl oz/¼ cup) light soy sauce
2 teaspoons rice vinegar
1 teaspoon dashi granules
2 spring onions (scallions), sliced
1 teaspoon finely chopped fresh ginger
24 large scallops (without roe)
5 fresh black fungus, chopped (see Note)
1 sheet nori, shredded

Add the noodles to a large saucepan of boiling water and
stir to separate. Return to the boil, adding 250 ml (9 fl oz/
1 cup) cold water and repeat this step three times, as it
comes to the boil. Drain and rinse under cold water.

Put the mirin, soy sauce, vinegar, dashi and 875 ml (30 fl oz/
3½ cups) water in a non-stick wok. Bring to the boil, then
reduce the heat and simmer for 3–4 minutes. Add the
spring onion and ginger and keep at a gentle simmer.

Heat a chargrill pan or plate until very hot and sear the
scallops in batches for 30 seconds each side. Remove from
the pan. Divide the noodles and black fungus among four
deep serving bowls. Pour 185 ml (6 fl oz/¾ cup) of the broth
into each bowl and top with six scallops each. Garnish with
the shredded nori and serve immediately.

Note If fresh black fungus is not available, use dried and soak it
in warm water for 20 minutes.

Bottom: Scallops with soba noodles and dashi broth. Top: Cambodian sour chicken soup.

Rainbow congee

preparation 15 minutes
cooking 2 hours 15 minutes
serves 6

200 g (7 oz) short-grain rice
2 dried Chinese mushrooms
85 g (3 oz) snow peas (mangetout), trimmed
2 Chinese sausages (lap cheong) (see Note)
2 tablespoons oil
¼ red onion, finely diced
1 carrot, cut into 1 cm (½ inch) cubes
3 teaspoons light soy sauce
2 litres (70 fl oz/8 cups) chicken stock

Put the rice in a bowl and, using your fingers as a rake, rinse under cold running water to remove any dust. Drain the rice in a colander. Soak the dried mushrooms in boiling water for 30 minutes then drain and squeeze out any excess water. Remove and discard the stems and chop the caps into 5 mm (¼ inch) cubes. Cut the snow peas into 1 cm (½ inch) pieces.

Place the sausages on a plate in a steamer. Cover and steam over simmering water in a wok for 10 minutes, then cut them into 1 cm (½ inch) pieces.

Heat the oil in a wok over medium heat. Stir-fry the sausage until it is brown and the fat has melted out of it. Remove with a wire sieve or slotted spoon and drain. Pour the oil from the wok, leaving 1 tablespoon.

Reheat the reserved oil over high heat until very hot. Stir-fry the red onion until soft and transparent. Add the mushrooms and carrot and stir-fry for 1 minute, or until fragrant.

Put the mushroom mixture in a clay pot, casserole dish or saucepan and stir in the soy sauce, rice, chicken stock and ¼ teaspoon salt. Bring to the boil, then reduce the heat and simmer very gently, stirring occasionally, for 1¾–2 hours, or until it has a porridge-like texture and the rice is breaking up. If it is too thick, add some water and return to the boil.

Toss in the snow peas and sausage, cover and stand for 5 minutes before serving.

Note *Lap cheong is a type of dried pork sausage that is quite red in colour. It needs to be cooked before being eaten.*

Pork, corn and noodle soup

preparation 15 minutes
cooking 30 minutes
serves 4

2 small fresh corn cobs
200 g (7 oz) dried ramen noodles
2 teaspoons peanut oil
1 teaspoon grated fresh ginger
1.5 litres (52 fl oz/6 cups) chicken stock
2 tablespoons mirin (sweet rice wine)
200 g (7 oz) piece Chinese barbecued pork (char siu),
thinly sliced
3 spring onions (scallions), sliced on the diagonal
20 g (¾ oz) unsalted butter (optional, see Note)

Remove the corn kernels from the cob using a sharp knife.

Cook the ramen noodles in a large saucepan of boiling water for 4 minutes, or until tender. Drain, then rinse in cold water.

Heat the oil in a large saucepan over high heat. Stir-fry the ginger for 1 minute. Add the chicken stock and mirin and bring to the boil. Reduce the heat and simmer for 8 minutes.

Add the pork slices and cook for 5 minutes, then add the corn kernels and two-thirds of the spring onion, and cook for a further 4–5 minutes, or until the corn is tender.

Separate the noodles by running them under hot water, then divide them among four deep bowls. Ladle on the soup, then place 1 teaspoon of butter on top of each serving. Garnish with the remaining spring onion and serve immediately.

Note *This soup is traditionally served with the butter on top. However, for a healthier option, it can be omitted.*

Eight-treasure noodle soup

preparation 20 minutes + 20 minutes soaking
cooking 20 minutes
serves 4

10 g (¼ oz) dried shiitake mushrooms
375 g (13 oz) fresh thick hokkien (egg) noodles
1.2 litres (42 fl oz/5 cups) chicken stock
60 ml (2 fl oz/¼ cup) light soy sauce
2 teaspoons Chinese rice wine
200 g (7 oz) boneless, skinless chicken breasts, cut into 1 cm
(½ inch) strips on the diagonal
200 g (7 oz) Chinese barbecued pork (char siu), cut into 5 mm
(¼ inch) slices
¼ onion, finely chopped
1 carrot, cut into 1 cm (½ inch) sliced on the diagonal
120 g (4 oz) snow peas (mangetout), cut in half on the diagonal
4 bulb spring onions (scallions), thinly sliced

Soak the mushrooms in boiling water for 20 minutes, or until soft. Drain and squeeze out any excess liquid. Discard the stems and thinly slice the caps.

Bring a large saucepan of water to the boil and cook the noodles for 1 minute, or until cooked through. Drain, then rinse with cold water. Divide evenly among four deep warmed serving bowls.

Meanwhile, bring the stock to the boil in a large saucepan over high heat. Reduce the heat to medium and stir in the soy sauce and rice wine. Simmer for 2 minutes. Add the chicken and pork and cook for 2 minutes, or until the chicken is cooked and the pork is heated through. Add the onion, carrot, snow peas, mushrooms and half the spring onion, and cook for 1 minute, or until the carrot is tender.

Divide the vegetables and meat among the serving bowls and ladle on the hot broth. Garnish with the remaining spring onion.

Cut the barbecued pork into thin slices, using a small sharp knife.

Add the meat to the stock and cook until the chicken is cooked and pork is warmed through.

vegetable soups

French onion soup

preparation 30 minutes
cooking 1 hour 30 minutes
serves 4

55 g (2 oz) butter
1 tablespoon olive oil
1 kg (2 lb 4 oz) onions, thinly sliced into rings
800 ml (28 fl oz) vegetable stock
125 ml (4 fl oz/½ cup) dry sherry
½ baguette
35 g (1 oz/⅓ cup) grated parmesan cheese
125 g (4½ oz/1 cup) finely grated cheddar or gruyère cheese
chopped parsley, to serve

Heat the butter and oil in a large saucepan, then add the onion and cook, stirring frequently, over low heat for 45 minutes, or until softened and golden brown. It is important not to rush this stage—cook the onion thoroughly so that it caramelises and the flavours develop.

Add the vegetable stock, sherry and 250 ml (9 fl oz/1 cup) water. Bring to the boil, then reduce the heat and simmer for 30 minutes. Season to taste.

Meanwhile, slice the bread into four thick slices and arrange them in a single layer under a hot grill (broiler). Toast one side, turn and sprinkle with parmesan, and toast until crisp and golden and the cheese has melted.

Put bread slices into serving bowls. Ladle in the hot soup, sprinkle with the cheese and parsley and serve.

58

Heat the oil and butter in a large saucepan and then add the onion.

Stir frequently over low heat until the onion is softened and golden brown.

Curried sweet potato soup

preparation 20 minutes
cooking 40 minutes
serves 6

1 tablespoon oil
1 large onion, chopped
2 garlic cloves, crushed
3 teaspoons curry powder
1.25 kg (2 lb 12 oz) orange sweet potato, peeled and cubed
1 litre (35 fl oz/4 cups) chicken stock
1 large apple, peeled, cored and grated
125 ml (4 fl oz/½ cup) light coconut milk

Heat the oil in a large saucepan over medium heat and cook the onion for 10 minutes, stirring occasionally, until very soft. Add the garlic and curry powder and cook for a further 1 minute.

Add the sweet potato, stock and apple. Bring to the boil, reduce the heat and simmer, partially covered, for 30 minutes, until very soft.

Cool the soup a little before processing in batches until smooth. Return to the pan, stir in the coconut milk and reheat gently without boiling. Serve with warm pitta bread.

Note *This soup can be kept in the fridge for 1 day without the coconut milk: add this when you reheat.*

Mexican bean chowder

preparation 20 minutes + overnight soaking
cooking 1 hour 20 minutes
serves 6

155 g (5½ oz/¾ cup) dried red kidney beans
165 g (6 oz/¾ cup) dried Mexican black beans (see Note)
1 tablespoon oil
1 onion, chopped
2 garlic cloves, crushed
½–1 teaspoon chilli powder
1 tablespoon ground cumin
2 teaspoons ground coriander
2 x 400 g (14 oz) tins chopped tomatoes
750 ml (26 fl oz/3 cups) vegetable stock
1 red capsicum (pepper), chopped
1 green capsicum (pepper), chopped
440 g (15½ oz) tin corn kernels
2 tablespoons tomato paste (concentrated purée)
grated cheddar cheese, to serve
sour cream, to serve

Put the kidney beans and black beans in separate bowls, cover with cold water and soak overnight.

Drain the beans and rinse under cold water. Place them in a large saucepan, cover with water and bring to the boil. Reduce the heat and simmer for 45 minutes, or until tender. Drain well.

Heat the oil in a large saucepan, add the onion and cook over medium heat until soft. Add the garlic, chilli powder, cumin and coriander, and cook for 1 minute. Stir in the tomato, stock, capsicum, corn and tomato paste. Cook, covered, for 25–30 minutes. Add the beans during the last 10 minutes of cooking. Stir occasionally.

Serve topped with the grated cheddar and a spoonful of sour cream.

Note *Mexican black beans are also known as black turtle beans.*

Add the garlic and curry powder to the softened onion and cook for another minute.

Add the tinned tomato, stock, capsicum, corn and the tomato paste.

Bottom: Mexican bean chowder. Top: Curried sweet potato soup.

Chunky vegetable soup

preparation 20 minutes + overnight soaking
cooking 1 hour 5 minutes
serves 6

100 g (3½ oz/½ cup) dried red kidney beans or borlotti
(cranberry) beans (see Note)
1 tablespoon olive oil
1 leek, halved lengthways, chopped
1 small onion, diced
2 carrots, chopped
2 celery stalks, chopped
1 large zucchini (courgette), chopped
1 tablespoon tomato paste (concentrated purée)
1 litre (35 fl oz/4 cups) vegetable stock
400 g (14 oz) pumpkin (winter squash), cut into
2 cm (¾ inch) cubes
2 potatoes, cut into 2 cm (¾ inch) cubes
crusty wholemeal bread, to serve

Put the beans in a large bowl, cover with cold water and soak overnight.

Drain the beans and rinse under cold water. Transfer to a saucepan, cover with cold water and cook on medium–high for 45 minutes, or until just tender. Drain and set aside.

Meanwhile, heat the oil in a large saucepan. Add the leek and onion, and cook over medium heat for 2–3 minutes without browning, or until they start to soften. Add the carrot, celery and zucchini, and cook for 3–4 minutes. Add the tomato paste and stir for a further 1 minute. Pour in the stock and 1.25 litres (44 fl oz/5 cups) water, and bring to the boil. Reduce the heat to low and simmer for 20 minutes.

Add the pumpkin, potato and beans, and simmer on low–medium heat for a further 20 minutes, or until the vegetables are tender and the beans are cooked. Season to taste. Serve immediately with crusty bread.

Note *To save time, use a 400 g (14 oz) tin of red kidney beans instead of dried beans. Rinse well and leave out Step 1.*

Spiced lentil soup

preparation 10 minutes + 20 minutes standing
cooking 50 minutes
serves 4

1 eggplant (aubergine)
60 ml (2 fl oz/¼ cup) olive oil
1 onion, finely chopped
2 teaspoons brown mustard seeds
2 teaspoons ground cumin
1 teaspoon garam masala
¼ teaspoon cayenne pepper (optional)
2 large carrots, cut into cubes
1 celery stalk, diced
400 g (14 oz) tin chopped tomatoes
100 g (3½ oz/1 cup) puy or small blue-green lentils
1 litre (35 fl oz/4 cups) chicken stock
2 large handfuls coriander (cilantro) leaves, roughly chopped
125 g (4½ oz/½ cup) plain yoghurt

Cut the eggplant into cubes, place in a colander, sprinkle with salt and leave for 20 minutes. Rinse well and pat the eggplant dry with paper towels.

Heat the oil in a large saucepan over medium heat. Add the onion and cook for 5 minutes, or until softened. Add the eggplant, stir to coat in the oil and cook for 3 minutes, or until softened.

Add the spices and the cayenne pepper (if using) and cook, stirring, for 1 minute, or until fragrant and the mustard seeds begin to pop. Add the carrot and celery and cook for 1 minute. Stir in the tomato, lentils and stock and bring to the boil. Reduce the heat and simmer for 40 minutes, or until the lentils are tender and the liquid is reduced to a thick stew-like soup. Season to taste with salt and freshly ground black pepper.

Stir the coriander into the soup just before serving. Ladle the soup into four warmed bowls and serve with a dollop of the yoghurt on top.

Add the vegetables and beans, and simmer until the vegetables are cooked.

Simmer the mixture until it is thick and the lentils are tender.

Bottom: Spiced lentil soup. Top: Chunky vegetable soup.

Cannellini bean soup

preparation 20 minutes + overnight soaking
cooking 1 hour 15 minutes
serves 8

500 g (1 lb 2 oz) dried cannellini beans
450 g (1 lb) ripe tomatoes
2 tablespoons olive oil
2 onions, chopped
2 garlic cloves, crushed
60 g (2 oz/¼ cup) tomato passata (puréed tomatoes)
2 large carrots, diced
2 celery stalks, trimmed and diced
1.7 litres (59 fl oz) vegetable or chicken stock
2 bay leaves
2 tablespoons lemon juice
1 large handful flat-leaf (Italian) parsley, chopped

Put the beans in a large bowl, cover with cold water and soak overnight.

Score a cross in the base of each tomato. Put in a heatproof bowl and cover with boiling water. Leave for 30 seconds then transfer to cold water and peel the skin away from the cross and roughly chop the flesh.

Drain the beans and rinse under cold water. Heat the oil in a 5 litre (175 fl oz/20 cup) saucepan. Add the onion, reduce the heat and cook gently for 10 minutes, stirring occasionally. Stir in the garlic and cook for 1 minute. Add the cannellini beans, chopped tomato, passata, carrot, celery and stock. Add the bay leaves and stir. Bring to the boil, then reduce the heat to medium–low and simmer, covered, for 45–60 minutes, or until the beans are cooked and tender.

Just before serving, stir in the lemon juice and season to taste with salt and pepper. Stir in some of the parsley and use the rest as a garnish.

Risoni and mushroom broth

preparation 15 minutes
cooking 20–25 minutes
serves 4

90 g (3 oz) butter
2 garlic cloves, sliced
2 large onions, sliced
375 g (13 oz) mushrooms, thinly sliced
1.25 litres (44 fl oz/5 cups) chicken stock
125 g (4½ oz) risoni
310 ml (11 fl oz/1¼ cups) pouring (whipping) cream

Melt the butter in a large saucepan over low heat. Add the garlic and onion and cook for 1 minute. Add the mushrooms and cook gently for 5 minutes. (Set aside a few slices for garnish.) Add the stock and cook for 10 minutes. Cool slightly before blending smooth in a food processor.

Meanwhile, cook the risoni in a large saucepan of rapidly boiling salted water until al dente. Drain and set aside.

Return the soup to a clean pan and stir in the risoni and cream. Heat through. Garnish with mushroom slices.

Spicy tomato and pea soup

preparation 15 minutes
cooking 20–25 minutes
serves 6

5 large very ripe tomatoes, chopped
2 tablespoons ghee or butter
1 large onion, thinly sliced
1 garlic clove, crushed
2 teaspoons ground coriander
2 teaspoons ground cumin
½ teaspoon fennel seeds
2 bay leaves
1 green chilli, seeded and sliced
375 ml (13 fl oz/1½ cups) coconut cream
235 g (8½ oz/1½ cups) frozen peas
1 tablespoon sugar
1 tablespoon chopped mint

Cook the tomato in 500 ml (17 fl oz/2 cups) water until soft. Allow to cool slightly before blending in a food processor.

Heat the ghee in a large saucepan, add the onion and garlic and cook over medium heat until very soft. Add the spices, bay leaves and chilli, and cook, stirring, for 1 minute. Add the coconut cream and tomato purée, and bring to the boil. Reduce the heat, add the peas and cook until tender. Remove the bay leaves and add the sugar and mint.

Top left: Cannellini bean soup. Top right: Risoni and mushroom broth. Bottom left: Spicy tomato and pea soup.

Minestrone with pesto

preparation 25 minutes + overnight soaking
cooking 2 hours
serves 6

125 g (4½ oz) dried borlotti (cranberry) beans
60 ml (2 fl oz/¼ cup) olive oil
1 large onion, finely chopped
2 garlic cloves, crushed
60 g (2 oz) pancetta, finely chopped
1 celery stalk, halved lengthways and cut into thin slices
1 carrot, halved lengthways and cut into thin slices
1 potato, diced
2 teaspoons tomato paste (concentrated purée)
400 g (14 oz) tinned crushed tomatoes
6 basil leaves, roughly torn
2 litres (70 fl oz/8 cups) chicken or vegetable stock
2 zucchini (courgettes), cut into thin slices
115 g (4 oz/¾ cup) fresh peas, shelled
60 g (2 oz) green beans, cut into short lengths
80 g (3 oz) silverbeet (Swiss chard) leaves, shredded
3 tablespoons chopped flat-leaf (Italian) parsley
70 g (2½ oz) ditalini or other small pasta

pesto
30 g (1 oz) basil leaves
20 g (¾ oz) pine nuts, lightly toasted
2 garlic cloves
100 ml (3½ fl oz) olive oil
25 g (1 oz/¼ cup) freshly grated parmesan cheese

Put the borlotti beans in a large bowl, cover with cold water and soak overnight.

Drain the beans and rinse under cold water.

Heat the oil in a large, deep saucepan, add the onion, garlic and pancetta and cook over low heat, stirring occasionally, for 8–10 minutes, or until softened. Add the celery, carrot and potato and cook for 5 minutes. Stir in the tomato paste, tomatoes, basil and drained borlotti beans. Season to taste with freshly ground black pepper.

Add the stock and bring slowly to the boil. Cover and simmer, stirring occasionally, for 1½ hours. Add the zucchini, peas, green beans, silverbeet, parsley and the pasta. Simmer for 8–10 minutes, or until the vegetables and pasta are al dente. Check for seasoning and adjust if necessary.

To make the pesto, combine the basil, pine nuts and garlic with a pinch of salt in a food processor. Process until finely chopped. With the motor running, slowing add the olive oil. Transfer to a bowl and stir in the parmesan and some ground black pepper to taste. Serve with the soup.

Gazpacho

preparation 40 minutes + 3 hours refrigeration
cooking nil
serves 4–6

750 g (1 lb 10 oz) ripe tomatoes
1 Lebanese (short) cucumber, chopped
1 green capsicum (pepper), chopped
2–3 garlic cloves, crushed
1–2 tablespoons finely chopped black olives
80 ml (2½ fl oz/⅓ cup) red or white wine vinegar
60 ml (2 fl oz/¼ cup) olive oil
1 tablespoon tomato paste (concentrated purée)

accompaniments

1 onion, finely chopped
1 red capsicum (pepper), finely chopped
2 spring onions (scallions), finely chopped
1 Lebanese (short) cucumber, finely chopped
2 hard-boiled eggs, chopped
1 small handful mint or parsley, chopped
croutons

To peel the tomatoes, score a cross in the base of each tomato. Cover with boiling water for 30 seconds, then plunge into cold water. Drain and peel away the tomato skin from the cross. Chop the flesh so finely that it is almost a purée.

Mix together the tomato, cucumber, capsicum, garlic, olives, vinegar, oil and tomato paste, and season to taste with salt and freshly ground black pepper. Cover and refrigerate for 2–3 hours.

Use 750 ml (26 fl oz/3 cups) chilled water to thin the soup to your taste. Serve chilled, with the chopped onion, capsicum, spring onion, cucumber, boiled egg, herbs and croutons served separately for diners to add to their own bowls as they wish.

Halve the cucumber lengthways, cut into strips, then chop finely.

Lentil and silverbeet soup

preparation 20 minutes + overnight refrigeration
cooking 3 hours 20 minutes
serves 6

chicken stock

1 kg (2 lb 4 oz) chicken bones (chicken necks, backs, wings), washed
1 small onion, roughly chopped
1 bay leaf
3–4 flat-leaf (Italian) parsley sprigs
1–2 oregano or thyme sprigs

280 g (10 oz/1½ cups) brown lentils, washed
850 g (1 lb 14 oz) silverbeet (Swiss chard)
60 ml (2 fl oz/¼ cup) olive oil
1 large onion, finely chopped
4 garlic cloves, crushed
2 large handfuls finely chopped coriander (cilantro) leaves
80 ml (2½ fl oz/⅓ cup) lemon juice
lemon wedges, to serve
crusty bread, to serve

To make the stock, place all the stock ingredients in a large saucepan, add 3 litres (105 fl oz/12 cups) water and bring to the boil. Skim any scum from the surface. Reduce the heat and simmer for 2 hours. Strain the stock, discarding the bones, onion and herbs. Chill overnight.

Skim any fat from the stock. Place the lentils in a large saucepan and add the stock and 1 litre (35 fl oz/4 cups) water. Bring to the boil, then reduce the heat and simmer, covered, for 1 hour.

Meanwhile, remove the stems from the silverbeet and shred the leaves. Heat the oil in a saucepan over medium heat and cook the onion for 2–3 minutes, or until transparent. Add the garlic and cook for 1 minute. Add the silverbeet and toss for 2–3 minutes, or until wilted. Stir the mixture into the lentils. Add the coriander and lemon juice, season, and simmer, covered, for 15–20 minutes. Serve with the lemon wedges and crusty bread.

Add the coriander and lemon juice to the silverbeet and lentil mixture.

Bottom: Lentil and silverbeet soup. Top: Gazpacho.

Carrot and orange soup

preparation 20 minutes
cooking 35 minutes
serves 4

500 g (1 lb 2 oz) carrots, peeled and sliced
30 g (1 oz) butter
125 ml (4 fl oz/½ cup) orange juice
1–1.25 litres (35–44 fl oz/4–5 cups) vegetable stock
1 small onion, roughly chopped
3–4 teaspoons chopped thyme
sour cream, to serve
freshly grated nutmeg, to serve

Put the carrots and butter in a large heavy-based saucepan and cook over medium heat for 10 minutes, stirring occasionally. Add the orange juice, vegetable stock and onion. Bring to the boil, add the thyme and season. Reduce the heat, cover and cook for 20 minutes, or until the carrots are tender. Allow to cool.

Process the mixture in a food processor or blender, in batches, until smooth. When ready to serve, return the mixture to the pan and reheat.

Spoon into individual bowls. Top each with a dollop of sour cream and sprinkle with nutmeg. Garnish with a small sprig of thyme, if desired.

Pasta soup

preparation 10 minutes
cooking 10 minutes
serves 4

1 tablespoon oil
2 spring onions (scallions), chopped
150 g (5½ oz) snow peas (mangetout), trimmed and cut into pieces
200 g (7 oz) mushrooms, sliced
2 garlic cloves, crushed
1 teaspoon grated fresh ginger
1 litre (35 fl oz/4 cups) vegetable stock
150 g (5½ oz) angel hair pasta

Heat the oil in a saucepan over medium heat and stir-fry the spring onion, snow peas and mushrooms for a few minutes, or until just tender.

Add the garlic and grated fresh ginger and stir for a further minute. Pour in the vegetable stock and bring to the boil. Once boiling, add the pasta and cook for 3 minutes, or until just tender. Serve immediately.

Broccoli soup

preparation 15 minutes
cooking 20 minutes
serves 4

2 tablespoons olive oil
1 large onion, thinly sliced
50 g (2 oz) diced prosciutto or smoked ham
1 garlic clove, crushed
1.25 litres (44 fl oz/5 cups) chicken stock
50 g (2 oz) stellini or other small pasta shapes
250 g (9 oz) broccoli, tops cut into small florets and the tender stems cut into thin batons
freshly grated parmesan cheese, to serve

Heat the oil in a large saucepan over low heat, add the onion, prosciutto and garlic and cook for 4–5 minutes. Add the chicken stock, bring to the boil, reduce the heat slightly and simmer for 10 minutes with the lid three-quarters on.

Add the stellini and broccoli and cook until the pasta is al dente and the broccoli is crisp but tender. Season to taste. Serve in warm bowls with the grated parmesan.

Spinach and lentil soup

preparation 10 minutes
cooking 1 hour 25 minutes
serves 4–6

375 g (13 oz/2 cups) brown lentils
2 teaspoons olive oil
1 onion, finely chopped
2 garlic cloves, crushed
20 English spinach leaves, stalks removed, leaves finely shredded
1 teaspoon ground cumin
1 teaspoon finely grated lemon zest
500 ml (17 fl oz/2 cups) vegetable stock
2 tablespoons finely chopped coriander (cilantro)

Put the lentils in a large saucepan with 1.25 litres (44 fl oz/ 5 cups) water. Bring to the boil and then simmer, uncovered, for 1 hour. Rinse and drain, then set aside.

In a separate saucepan heat the oil. Add the onion and garlic. Cook over medium heat until golden. Add the spinach and cook for a further 2 minutes.

Add the lentils, cumin, lemon zest, vegetable stock and 500 ml (17 fl oz/2 cups) water to the pan. Simmer, uncovered, for 15 minutes. Add the coriander and stir through. Serve immediately.

Top left: Carrot and orange soup. Top right: Broccoli soup. Bottom right: Spinach and lentil soup. Bottom left: Pasta soup.

Cream of asparagus soup

preparation 20 minutes
cooking 55 minutes
serves 4–6

1 kg (2 lb 4 oz) asparagus spears
30 g (1 oz) butter
1 onion, finely chopped
1 litre (35 fl oz/4 cups) vegetable stock
1 small handful basil leaves, chopped
1 teaspoon celery salt
250 ml (9 fl oz/1 cup) pouring (whipping) cream

Break off the woody ends from the asparagus (hold both ends of the spear and bend it gently—the woody end will snap off and can be thrown away) and trim off the tips. Blanch the tips in boiling water for 1–2 minutes, refresh in cold water and set aside. Chop the asparagus stems into large pieces.

Melt the butter in a large saucepan and cook the onion for 3–4 minutes over low–medium heat, or until soft and golden. Add the chopped asparagus stems and cook for 1–2 minutes, stirring continuously.

Add the stock, basil and celery salt. Bring to the boil, reduce the heat and simmer, covered, for 30 minutes.

Check that the asparagus is cooked and soft. If not, simmer for a further 10 minutes. Set aside and allow to cool slightly.

Pour into a food processor and process in batches until smooth. Then sieve into a clean saucepan. Return to the heat, pour in the cream and gently reheat. Do not allow the soup to boil. Season to taste with salt and white pepper. Add the asparagus tips and serve immediately.

Note If you are not using home-made stock, always taste the soup before adding any seasoning—ready-made stock can be very salty.

The woody end from the asparagus spear will snap off when you bend the spear.

Test whether the asparagus is well cooked by piercing it with a fork.

Roast pumpkin soup

preparation 20 minutes
cooking 55 minutes
serves 6

1.25 kg (2 lb 12 oz) pumpkin (winter squash), peeled and
cut into chunks
2 tablespoons olive oil
1 large onion, chopped
2 teaspoons ground cumin
1 large carrot, chopped
1 celery stalk, chopped
1 litre (35 fl oz/4 cups) vegetable stock
sour cream, to serve
finely chopped parsley, to serve
freshly grated nutmeg, to serve

Preheat the oven to 180°C (350°F/Gas 4). Put the pumpkin
on a greased baking tray and lightly brush with half the
olive oil. Bake for 25 minutes, or until softened and slightly
browned around the edges.

Heat the remaining oil in a large saucepan. Cook the onion
and cumin for 2 minutes, then add the carrot and celery
and cook for 3 minutes more, stirring frequently. Add the
roasted pumpkin and stock. Bring to the boil, then reduce
the heat and simmer for 20 minutes.

Allow to cool a little then purée in batches in a blender
or food processor. Return the soup to the pan and gently
reheat without boiling. Season to taste with salt and freshly
ground black pepper. Top with sour cream and sprinkle with
chopped parsley and ground nutmeg before serving.

*Note If the soup is too thick, thin it down with a little more
stock or water.*

Potato, broccoli and coriander soup

preparation 15 minutes
cooking 30 minutes
serves 6

500 g (1 lb 2 oz) broccoli
cooking oil spray
2 onions, finely chopped
2 garlic cloves, finely chopped
2 teaspoons ground cumin
1 teaspoon ground coriander
750 g (1 lb 10 oz) potatoes, cubed
2 small chicken stock (bouillon) cubes
375 ml (13 fl oz/1½ cups) skim milk
3 tablespoons finely chopped coriander (cilantro)

Cut the broccoli into small pieces. Lightly spray the base
of a large saucepan with oil, then place over medium heat
and add the onion and garlic. Add 1 tablespoon water to
prevent sticking. Cover and cook, stirring occasionally, over
low heat for 5 minutes, or until the onion has softened and
is lightly golden. Add the ground cumin and coriander and
cook for 2 minutes.

Add the potato and broccoli to the pan, stir well and add
the stock cubes and 1 litre (35 fl oz/4 cups) water. Slowly
bring to the boil, reduce the heat, cover and simmer over
low heat for 20 minutes, or until the vegetables are tender.
Allow to cool slightly.

Blend the soup in batches in a food processor or blender
until smooth. Return to the pan and stir in the milk. Slowly
reheat, without boiling. Stir the chopped coriander through
and season well before serving.

Lightly brush the pumpkin chunks with oil and bake
until softened.

Stir the ground cumin and coriander into the onion and
cook for about 2 minutes.

Bottom: Potato, broccoli and coriander soup. Top: Roast pumpkin soup.

Roasted red capsicum soup

preparation 50 minutes
cooking 1 hour
serves 6

4 large red capsicums (peppers)
4 ripe tomatoes
2 tablespoons oil
1 red onion, chopped
1 garlic clove, crushed
1 litre (35 fl oz/4 cups) vegetable stock
1 teaspoon sweet chilli sauce
parmesan cheese, to serve
pesto, to serve (optional)

Cut the capsicums into large flat pieces, removing the seeds and membrane. Place, skin side up, under a hot grill (broiler) until blackened. Leave in a plastic bag until cool, then peel away the skin and chop the flesh.

Score a small cross in the base of each tomato, put them in a large heatproof bowl and cover with boiling water. Leave for 1 minute, then plunge into cold water and peel the skin from the cross. Cut in half, scoop out the seeds and roughly chop the flesh.

Heat the oil in a large heavy-based saucepan and add the onion. Cook over medium heat for 10 minutes, stirring frequently, until very soft. Add the garlic and cook for a further 1 minute. Add the capsicum, tomato and stock; bring to the boil, reduce the heat and simmer for about 20 minutes.

Purée the soup in a food processor or blender until smooth (in batches if necessary). Return to the pan to reheat gently and stir in the chilli sauce. Serve topped with shavings of parmesan and a little pesto, if desired.

Chickpea and herb dumpling soup

preparation 30 minutes
cooking 35 minutes
serves 4

1 tablespoon oil
1 onion, chopped
2 garlic cloves, crushed
2 teaspoons ground cumin
1 teaspoon ground coriander
¼ teaspoon chilli powder
2 x 300 g (10½ oz) tins chickpeas
875 ml (30 fl oz/3½ cups) vegetable stock
2 x 400 g (14 oz) tins chopped tomatoes
1 tablespoon chopped fresh coriander (cilantro) leaves
125 g (4½ oz/1 cup) self-raising flour
30 g (1 oz) butter, chopped
2 tablespoons grated parmesan cheese
2 tablespoons mixed chopped herbs (chives, parsley, coriander)
60 ml (2 fl oz/¼ cup) milk

Heat the oil in a large saucepan, and cook the onion over medium heat for 2–3 minutes, or until soft. Add the garlic, cumin, ground coriander and chilli and cook for 1 minute, or until fragrant. Add the chickpeas, stock and tomato. Bring to the boil, then reduce the heat and simmer, covered, for 10 minutes. Stir in the coriander.

To make the dumplings, sift the flour into a bowl and add the chopped butter. Rub together with your fingertips until the mixture resembles fine breadcrumbs. Stir in the parmesan and herbs. Make a well in the centre, add the milk and mix with a flat-bladed knife until just combined. Bring together into a rough ball, divide into eight portions and roll into small balls.

Add the dumplings to the soup, cover and simmer for 20 minutes, or until a skewer comes out clean when inserted into the centre of a dumpling.

Scoring a cross in the base of the tomato makes it easier to remove the skin.

Add the milk to the dumpling mixture and mix with a flat-bladed knife.

Bottom: Chickpea and herb dumpling soup. Top: Roasted red capsicum soup.

Pappa al pomodoro

preparation 25 minutes
cooking 25 minutes
serves 4

750 g (1 lb 10 oz) vine-ripened tomatoes
1 loaf (about 450 g/1 lb) day-old crusty Italian bread
1 tablespoon olive oil
3 garlic cloves, crushed
1 tablespoon tomato paste (concentrated purée)
1.25 litres (44 fl oz/5 cups) hot vegetable stock or water
1 tablespoon torn basil leaves
2–3 tablespoons extra virgin olive oil, plus extra, to serve

Score a cross in the base of the tomatoes. Put in a heatproof bowl and cover with boiling water. Leave for 30 seconds, then transfer to cold water and peel the skin away from the cross. Cut the tomatoes in half, scoop out the seeds and chop the flesh.

Discard most of the crust from the bread and tear the bread into 3 cm (1¼ inch) pieces.

Heat the oil in a large saucepan. Add the garlic, tomato and tomato paste, then reduce the heat and simmer, stirring occasionally, for 10–15 minutes, or until reduced. Add the stock and bring to the boil, stirring for about 3 minutes. Reduce the heat to medium, add the bread pieces and cook, stirring, for 5 minutes, or until the bread softens and absorbs most of the liquid. Add more stock or water if the soup is too thick. Remove from the heat.

Stir in the basil leaves and extra virgin olive oil, and leave for 5 minutes so the flavours have time to develop. Serve drizzled with a little extra virgin olive oil.

Wild rice soup

preparation 15 minutes
cooking 1 hour
serves 6

95 g (3 oz/½ cup) wild rice
1 tablespoon oil
1 onion, finely chopped
2 celery stalks, finely chopped
1 green capsicum (pepper), seeded, membrane removed and finely chopped
4 back bacon slices, finely chopped
4 open cap mushrooms, thinly sliced
1 litre (35 fl oz/4 cups) chicken stock
125 ml (4 fl oz/½ cup) pouring (whipping) cream
1 tablespoon finely chopped flat-leaf (Italian) parsley

Put the wild rice in a saucepan with 500 ml (17 fl oz/2 cups) water and bring to the boil. Cook for 40 minutes, or until the rice is tender. Drain and rinse well.

Heat the oil in a large saucepan and add the onion, celery, capsicum and bacon. Fry for 8 minutes, or until the onion has softened and the bacon has browned. Add the mushrooms and cook for 1–2 minutes. Pour in the chicken stock and bring to the boil, then add the rice, stir, and cook the mixture for 2 minutes. Remove from the heat.

Stir in the cream and parsley, then reheat until the soup is almost boiling. Serve in deep bowls.

Green pea soup

preparation 20 minutes + 2 hours soaking
cooking 1 hour 40 minutes
serves 4–6

335 g (12 oz/1½ cups) dried green split peas
2 tablespoons oil
1 onion, finely chopped
1 celery stalk, thinly sliced
1 carrot, thinly sliced
1 tablespoon ground cumin
1 tablespoon ground coriander
2 teaspoons grated fresh ginger
1.25 litres (44 fl oz/5 cups) vegetable stock
310 g (11 oz/2 cups) frozen green peas
1 tablespoon chopped mint
yoghurt or sour cream, to serve

Soak the split peas in cold water for 2 hours. Drain well.

Heat the oil in a large heavy-based saucepan and add the onion, celery and carrot. Cook over medium heat for 3 minutes, stirring occasionally, until soft but not browned. Stir in the cumin, coriander and ginger, then cook for 1 minute. Add the split peas and stock to pan. Bring to the boil, then reduce the heat to low. Simmer, covered, for 1½ hours, stirring occasionally. Add the frozen peas to the pan and stir to combine.

Allow to cool slightly before transferring to a food processor and blending, in batches, until smooth. Return to a clean pan and gently reheat. Season to taste and then stir in the mint. Serve the soup in bowls with a swirl of yoghurt or sour cream.

Top left: Pappa al pomodoro. Top right: Green pea soup. Bottom left: Wild rice soup.

Barley soup with golden parsnips

preparation 30 minutes + overnight soaking
cooking 2 hours 20 minutes
serves 6

200 g (7 oz) pearl barley
1 tablespoon oil
2 onions, chopped
2 garlic cloves, finely chopped
2 carrots, chopped
2 potatoes, chopped
2 celery stalks, chopped
2 bay leaves, torn in half
2 litres (70 fl oz/8 cups) chicken stock
125 ml (4 fl oz/½ cup) full-cream (whole) milk
40 g (1½ oz) butter
3 parsnips, cubed
1 teaspoon soft brown sugar
chopped flat-leaf (Italian) parsley, to serve

Soak the barley in water overnight. Drain. Place in a saucepan with 2 litres (70 fl oz/8 cups) water. Bring to the boil, then reduce the heat and simmer, partially covered, for 1¼ hours, or until tender. Drain the barley.

Heat the oil in a large saucepan, add the onion, garlic, carrot, potato and celery, and cook for 3 minutes. Stir well and cook, covered, for 15 minutes over low heat, stirring occasionally.

Add the barley, bay leaves, stock, milk, 2 teaspoons of salt and 1 teaspoon of pepper. Bring to the boil, then reduce the

heat and simmer the soup, partially covered, for around 35 minutes. If the soup is too thick, add about 250 ml (9 fl oz/ 1 cup) cold water, a little at a time, until it reaches your preferred consistency.

While the soup is simmering, melt the butter in a frying pan, add the parsnip and toss in the butter. Sprinkle with the sugar and cook until golden brown and tender. Serve the parsnip on top of the soup and sprinkle with the parsley and, if desired, season with cracked black pepper.

Using a sharp knife, chop the carrots, potatoes and the celery.

Add the drained barley to the cooked vegetables and stir through.

Pasta and bean soup

preparation 15 minutes + overnight soaking
+ 10 minutes resting
cooking 1 hour 45 minutes
serves 4

200 g (7 oz) dried borlotti (cranberry) beans (see Note)
60 ml (2 fl oz/¼ cup) olive oil
90 g (3 oz) piece pancetta, finely diced
1 onion, finely chopped
2 garlic cloves, crushed
1 celery stalk, thinly sliced
1 carrot, diced
1 bay leaf
1 rosemary sprig
1 flat-leaf (Italian) parsley sprig
400 g (14 oz) tin chopped tomatoes, drained
1.6 litres (56 fl oz) vegetable stock
2 tablespoons finely chopped flat-leaf (Italian) parsley
150 g (5½ oz) ditalini or other small dried pasta
extra virgin olive oil, to serve
grated parmesan cheese, to serve

Place the beans in a large bowl, cover with cold water and soak overnight.

Drain the beans and rinse under cold water.

Heat the oil in a large saucepan, add the pancetta, onion, garlic, celery and carrot, and cook over medium heat for 5 minutes, or until golden. Season. Add the bay leaf, rosemary, parsley sprig, tomato, stock and beans. Bring to the boil. Reduce heat and simmer for 1½ hours, or until tender. Add boiling water if needed.

Discard the bay leaf, rosemary and parsley sprigs. Scoop out 250 ml (9 fl oz/1 cup) of the mixture and purée in a food processor. Return to the pan, season, and add chopped parsley and pasta. Simmer for 6 minutes, or until al dente. Remove from heat and set aside for 10 minutes. Serve drizzled with olive oil, sprinkled with parmesan if desired.

Note If you prefer, you can use three 400 g (14 oz) tins drained borlotti beans. Simmer with the vegetables for 30 minutes.

Purée 250 ml (9 fl oz/1 cup) of the bean mixture in a food processor.

Chilli, corn and red capsicum soup

preparation 20 minutes
cooking 45 minutes
serves 4

1 coriander (cilantro) sprig
4 corn cobs
30 g (1 oz) butter
2 red capsicums (peppers), diced
1 small onion, finely chopped
1 small red chilli, finely chopped
1 tablespoon plain (all-purpose) flour
500 ml (17 fl oz/2 cups) vegetable stock
125 ml (4 fl oz/½ cup) pouring (whipping) cream

Trim the leaves off the coriander and finely chop the root and stems. Cut the kernels off the corn cobs.

Heat the butter in a large saucepan over medium heat. Add the corn kernels, capsicum, onion and chilli and stir to coat the vegetables in the butter. Cook, covered, over low heat, stirring occasionally, for 10 minutes, or until the vegetables are soft. Increase the heat to medium and add the coriander root and stem. Cook, stirring, for 30 seconds, or until fragrant. Sprinkle with the flour and stir for a further minute. Remove from the heat and gradually add the vegetable stock, stirring together. Add 500 ml (17 fl oz/2 cups) water and return to the heat. Bring to the boil, reduce the heat to low and simmer, covered, for 30 minutes, or until the vegetables are tender. Cool slightly.

Ladle about 500 ml (17 fl oz/2 cups) of the soup into a blender and purée until smooth. Return the purée to the soup in the saucepan, pour in the cream and gently heat until warmed through. Season to taste with salt. Sprinkle with the coriander leaves to serve. Delicious with grilled (broiled) cheese on pitta bread.

Using a sharp knife, carefully cut all the kernels from the corn cob.

Bottom: Chilli, corn and red capsicum soup. Top: Pasta and bean soup.

meat *and* seafood soups

Clear soup with salmon quenelles

preparation 20 minutes
cooking 25 minutes
serves 4

400 g (14 oz) salmon cutlets
1 litre (35 fl oz/4 cups) fish stock
125 ml (4 fl oz/½ cup) dry white wine
2 teaspoons lemon juice
1 small carrot, finely chopped
2 spring onions (scallions), sliced
2 dill sprigs
2 parsley sprigs
3 black peppercorns
1 egg white, chilled
ground white pepper, to taste
125 ml (4 fl oz/½ cup) pouring (whipping) cream, chilled
2 tablespoons chervil leaves

Remove the skin and bones from the salmon and set aside. Weigh 150 g (5½ oz) of the fish, chop roughly, cover and chill until needed.

To make the soup, combine the fish skin and bones in a large saucepan with the remaining salmon, fish stock, wine, lemon juice, carrot, spring onion, dill, parsley and peppercorns. Slowly bring to the boil, then reduce the heat, cover and simmer for 15 minutes. Strain the soup and discard the vegetables. (You won't be using the cooked salmon for this recipe, but you can use it as a sandwich filling. When cool, flake the salmon and mix with a little mayonnaise and some chopped herbs.)

Pour the soup into a clean saucepan, bring to the boil, then reduce the heat to just simmering. Season to taste.

To make the quenelles, process the reserved salmon in a food processor until finely chopped. Gradually add the egg white and process until very smooth. Transfer to a chilled bowl and season well with salt and ground white pepper. Whip the cream and quickly fold into the salmon. Shape quenelles using 2 teaspoons dipped in cold water. Add to the soup in two batches and poach for 2 minutes, or until cooked. Transfer the quenelles to warm soup bowls.

Heat the soup to almost boiling and carefully ladle over the quenelles. Sprinkle with chervil leaves and serve.

Notes *Ocean trout can be used instead of salmon. To make light fluffy quenelles, the ingredients used should be almost ice cold. The mixture will make about 24 quenelles.*

Garlic, pasta and fish soup

preparation 30 minutes
cooking 40 minutes
serves 4–6

80 ml (2½ fl oz/⅓ cup) olive oil
1 leek, white part only, trimmed and sliced
20–30 garlic cloves, thinly sliced
2 potatoes, chopped
2 litres (70 fl oz/8 cups) fish stock
70 g (2½ oz/½ cup) small pasta shapes
10 baby (pattypan) squash, halved
2 zucchini (courgettes), cut into thick slices
300 g (10½ oz) ling fillets, chopped into large pieces
1–2 tablespoons lemon juice
2 tablespoons shredded basil

Heat the oil in a large saucepan, add the leek, garlic and potato and cook over medium heat for 10 minutes. Add 500 ml (17 fl oz/2 cups) of the stock and cook for 10 minutes. Allow to cool slightly before transferring to a food processor or blender and blending, in batches, until smooth.

Pour the remaining stock into the pan and bring to the boil. Add the pasta, squash and zucchini. Add the purée, and simmer for 15 minutes. When the pasta is soft, add the fish pieces and cook for 5 minutes, or until tender. Add the lemon juice and basil, and season to taste.

Lemon-scented broth with tortellini

preparation 10 minutes
cooking 20 minutes
serves 4–6

1 lemon
125 ml (4 fl oz/½ cup) dry white wine
500 ml (17 fl oz/2 cups) ready-made chicken consommé
375 g (13 oz) fresh or dried veal or chicken tortellini
4 tablespoons chopped flat-leaf (Italian) parsley

Using a vegetable peeler, peel wide strips from the lemon. Remove the white pith with a small sharp knife. Cut three of the wide pieces into thin strips and set aside for garnishing.

Combine the remaining wide lemon strips, white wine, consommé and 750 ml (26 fl oz/3 cups) water in a large saucepan. Cook for 10 minutes over low heat. Remove the lemon zest from the pan and bring the mixture to the boil. Add the tortellini and parsley and season with black pepper. Cook for 6–7 minutes, or until the pasta is al dente. Garnish with thin strips of lemon zest.

Lamb and fusilli soup

preparation 25 minutes
cooking 40 minutes
serves 6–8

2 tablespoons oil
500 g (1 lb 2 oz) lean lamb meat, cubed
2 onions, finely chopped
2 carrots, diced
4 celery stalks, diced
400 g (14 oz) tinned chopped tomatoes
2 litres (70 fl oz/8 cups) beef stock
500 g (1 lb 2 oz) fusilli
chopped flat-leaf (Italian) parsley, to serve

Heat the oil in a large saucepan and cook the lamb in batches until golden. Drain on paper towel and set aside.

Add the onion to the pan and cook for 2 minutes or until softened. Return the meat to the pan, add the carrot, celery, tomato and stock. Stir to combine and bring to the boil. Reduce the heat to low and simmer, covered, for 15 minutes. Add the fusilli and stir well. Simmer, uncovered, for a further 10 minutes, or until the lamb and pasta are tender. Sprinkle with parsley before serving.

Lemon chicken soup

preparation 10 minutes
cooking 10 minutes
serves 4

2 boneless, skinless chicken breasts
1 lemon
1 litre (35 fl oz/4 cups) chicken stock
2 lemon thyme sprigs, plus extra, to serve

Trim any excess fat from the chicken. Using a vegetable peeler, cut 3 strips of zest from the lemon and remove the pith. Place the stock, 2 strips of zest and the thyme in a shallow pan and slowly bring almost to the boil. Reduce the heat to simmering point, add the chicken and cook, covered, for 7 minutes, or until the meat is cooked through. Meanwhile, cut the remaining zest into thin strips.

Remove the chicken from the pan, transfer to a plate and cover with foil.

Strain the stock into a clean pan through a sieve lined with two layers of damp muslin (cheesecloth). Finely shred the chicken and return to the soup. Reheat gently and season to taste with salt and black pepper. Serve immediately, garnished with the extra sprigs of lemon thyme and thin strips of lemon zest.

Top left: Garlic, pasta and fish soup. Top right: Lamb and fusilli soup. Bottom right: Lemon chicken soup. Bottom left: Lemon-scented broth with tortellini.

Soupe de poisson

preparation 30 minutes
cooking 45 minutes
serves 6

1 large ripe tomato
1.5 kg (3 lb 5 oz) chopped fish bones from firm white fish
1 leek, white part only, chopped
1 carrot, chopped
1 celery stalk, chopped
1 garlic clove, chopped
1 bay leaf
3 parsley stalks
6 black peppercorns
250 ml (9 fl oz/1 cup) dry white wine
1 tablespoon lemon juice
250 g (9 oz) skinless firm white fish fillets (such as snapper, perch, cod),
cut into bite-sized pieces
ground white pepper, to taste
2 tablespoons chervil leaves
¼ lemon, cut into very fine slices

Score a cross in the base of the tomato. Put in a heatproof bowl and cover with boiling water. Leave for 30 seconds, then transfer to cold water and peel the skin away from the cross. Cut the tomato in half, scoop out the seeds and chop the flesh. Set aside.

Rinse the fish bones well in cold water and combine in a large saucepan with the leek, carrot, celery, garlic, bay leaf, parsley, peppercorns, wine, lemon juice and 2 litres (70 fl oz/8 cups) water. Slowly bring to the boil, skimming off any scum from the surface. Reduce the heat and simmer for 20 minutes.

Strain and discard the fish bones and vegetables. Strain the stock again, through a sieve lined with dampened muslin (cheesecloth), into a clean saucepan. Simmer, uncovered, for 10 minutes.

Add the fish pieces to the fish stock and simmer for 2 minutes, or until tender. Season to taste with salt and ground white pepper.

Divide the chopped tomato and chervil among six warm soup bowls and ladle the hot soup over them. Float some lemon slices on top and serve immediately.

Note *The straining muslin is dampened before use so it won't absorb too much of the cooking liquid.*

Portuguese chicken broth with rice

preparation 15 minutes
cooking 1 hour
serves 6

2.5 litres (87 fl oz/10 cups) chicken stock
1 onion, cut into thin wedges
1 teaspoon finely grated lemon zest
1 mint sprig
500 g (1 lb 2 oz) potatoes, chopped
1 tablespoon olive oil
2 boneless, skinless chicken breasts
200 g (7 oz/1 cup) long-grain rice
2 tablespoons lemon juice
mint leaves, to garnish

Combine the chicken stock, onion, lemon zest, mint sprig, potato and olive oil in a large saucepan. Slowly bring to the boil, then reduce the heat, add the chicken breasts and simmer gently for 20–25 minutes, or until the chicken is cooked through.

Remove the chicken breasts and discard the mint sprig. Cool the chicken, then cut it into thin slices.

Meanwhile, add the rice to the saucepan and simmer for 25–30 minutes, or until the rice is tender. Return the sliced chicken to the saucepan, add the lemon juice and stir for 1–2 minutes, or until the chicken is warmed through. Season, and serve garnished with mint leaves.

Note *Rice and potato absorb liquid on standing, so serve the broth immediately.*

Smoked haddock chowder

preparation 20 minutes
cooking 35 minutes
serves 4–6

500 g (1 lb 2 oz) smoked haddock
1 potato, diced
1 celery stalk, diced
1 onion, finely chopped
50 g (2 oz) butter
1 bacon slice, rind removed, finely chopped
2 tablespoons plain (all-purpose) flour
½ teaspoon mustard powder
½ teaspoon worcestershire sauce
250 ml (9 fl oz/1 cup) full-cream (whole) milk
2 very large handfuls chopped flat-leaf (Italian) parsley
cream (optional), to serve

To make the fish stock, put the fish in a frying pan, cover with water and bring to the boil. Reduce the heat and simmer for 8 minutes, or until the fish flakes easily. Drain, reserving the fish stock, then peel, bone and flake the fish.

Put the potato, celery and onion in a medium saucepan, and pour over enough of the reserved fish stock to cover the vegetables. Bring to the boil, then reduce the heat and simmer for 8 minutes, or until the vegetables are tender.

Melt the butter in a large saucepan over low heat. Increase the heat to medium–high, add the bacon and cook, stirring, for 3 minutes. Add the flour, mustard and worcestershire sauce, and stir until combined. Cook for 1 minute. Remove from the heat and gradually pour in the milk, stirring continuously until smooth. Return to the heat and stir for 5 minutes, until the mixture comes to the boil and has thickened. Stir in the vegetables and remaining stock, then add the parsley and fish. Simmer over low heat for 5 minutes, or until heated through. Season to taste, and serve with cream, if desired.

Simmer the chicken for 20–25 minutes, or until cooked through.

Lay the fish on paper towels to drain well, then peel, bone and flake into small pieces.

meat *and* **seafood soups**

Bottom: Smoked haddock chowder. Top: Portuguese chicken broth with rice.

Chicken gumbo

preparation 15 minutes
cooking 2 hours 30 minutes
serves 4–6

80 ml (2½ fl oz/⅓ cup) vegetable oil
30 g (1 oz/¼ cup) plain (all-purpose) flour
450 g (1 lb) tomatoes
600 g (1 lb 5 oz) boneless, skinless chicken thighs
60 g (2 oz) unsalted butter
100 g (3½ oz) smoked ham, diced
150 g (5½ oz) chorizo, thinly sliced
2 onions, chopped
2 garlic cloves, finely chopped
2 celery stalks, thinly sliced
1 red capsicum (pepper), seeded, membrane removed and finely chopped
500 ml (17 fl oz/2 cups) chicken stock
1 bay leaf
2 teaspoons thyme
Tabasco sauce, to taste
350 g (12 oz) okra, cut into 1 cm (½ inch) slices
2 spring onions (scallions), sliced (optional)
2 tablespoons chopped parsley (optional)

Heat 60 ml (2 fl oz/¼ cup) of the oil in a small, heavy-based saucepan, add the flour and stir to make a smooth paste. Stir over very low heat for 1 hour, or until the roux turns very dark brown, but is not burnt. This requires a great deal of patience and stirring but provides the gumbo with its dark look and rich flavour—when it is done, the roux should be the colour of dark chocolate. Remove from the heat.

Score a cross in the base of each tomato. Put in a heatproof bowl and cover with boiling water. Leave for 30 seconds then transfer to cold water and peel the skin away from the cross. Cut the tomatoes in half, scoop out the seeds and roughly chop the flesh.

Pat the chicken thighs dry with paper towels, cut into quarters and lightly season with salt and pepper. Heat the remaining oil and half the butter in a heavy-based frying pan over medium heat. Cook the chicken for about 5 minutes, or until golden brown. Remove the chicken with a slotted spoon. Add the ham and chorizo and cook for 4–5 minutes, or until lightly golden. Remove, leaving as much rendered fat in the pan as possible.

Add the remaining butter to the same pan and cook the onion, garlic, celery and capsicum over medium heat for 5–6 minutes, or until the vegetables have softened but not browned. Transfer the vegetables to a heavy-based, flameproof casserole dish. Add the tomatoes and the roux to the vegetables and stir well. Gradually stir the stock into the casserole dish.

Add the herbs and season with the Tabasco. Bring to the boil, stirring constantly. Reduce the heat, add the chicken, ham and chorizo to the casserole dish and simmer, uncovered, for 1 hour. Add the okra and cook for a further hour. Skim the surface as the gumbo cooks because a lot of oil will come out of the chorizo. The gumbo should thicken considerably in the last 20 minutes as the okra softens. Remove the bay leaf and serve. Garnish with spring onion and parsley, if desired.

Note Gumbo is a speciality of Cajun cuisine and is a cross between a soup and a stew. Traditionally, gumbo is served in deep bowls, each containing a few tablespoons of cooked rice in the bottom.

Avgolemono with chicken

preparation 30 minutes
cooking 30 minutes
serves 4

1 onion, halved
2 cloves
1 carrot, cut into chunks
1 bay leaf
500 g (1 lb 2 oz) boneless, skinless chicken breasts
75 g (2½ oz/⅓ cup) short-grain rice
3 eggs, separated
60 ml (2 fl oz/¼ cup) lemon juice
2 tablespoons chopped flat-leaf (Italian) parsley
4 thin lemon slices, to garnish

Stud the onion halves with the cloves and then place in a large saucepan with 1.5 litres (52 fl oz/6 cups) water. Add the carrot, bay leaf and chicken. Season with salt and freshly ground black pepper. Slowly bring to the boil, reduce the heat and simmer for 10 minutes, or until chicken is cooked.

Strain the stock into a clean saucepan, reserving the chicken and discarding the vegetables. Add the rice to the stock, bring to the boil, then reduce the heat and simmer for 15 minutes, or until tender. Tear the chicken into shreds.

Whisk the egg whites until stiff peaks form, then beat in the yolks. Slowly beat in the lemon juice. Gently stir in 150 ml (5 fl oz) of the hot (not boiling) soup and beat thoroughly. Add the egg mixture to the soup and stir gently over low heat until thickened slightly. It should still be quite thin. Do not let it boil or the eggs may scramble. Add the shredded chicken, and season to taste.

Set aside for 3–4 minutes to allow the flavours to develop, then sprinkle with the parsley. Garnish with lemon slices and serve.

Cock-a-leekie

preparation 10 minutes + 2 hours refrigeration
cooking 1 hour 40 minutes
serves 4–6

1.5 kg (3 lb 5 oz) chicken
250 g (9 oz) chicken giblets (optional)
1 onion, sliced
2 litres (70 fl oz/8 cups) chicken stock
4 leeks, white part only, thinly sliced
¼ teaspoon ground coriander
pinch nutmeg
bouquet garni
12 pitted prunes
pinch cayenne pepper
3 thyme sprigs, plus extra, to serve

Put the chicken in a large saucepan and add the giblets (if using), onion and stock. Bring to the boil, skimming the surface as required. Add the leek, coriander, nutmeg and bouquet garni. Reduce the heat, cover and simmer for 1¼ hours.

Remove the chicken and bouquet garni from the pan and lift out the giblets with a slotted spoon. Cool the stock, then refrigerate for 2 hours. Spoon off the fat from the surface and discard. Remove the chicken meat from the bones and shred. Discard the skin and carcass.

Return the chicken to the soup with the prunes, cayenne pepper and thyme. Simmer for 20 minutes. Season to taste and garnish with the extra thyme sprigs.

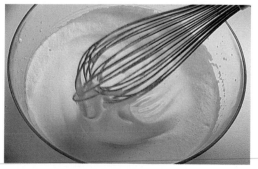

Whisk the egg whites until stiff peaks form, then beat in the yolks, then the lemon juice.

Wrap the thyme, parsley and bay leaves in a small square of muslin (cheesecloth).

Bottom: Cock-a-leekie. Top: Avgolemono with chicken.

Lamb hotpot

preparation 40 minutes + 1 hour refrigeration
cooking 2 hours
serves 4

2 tablespoons olive oil
8 lamb shanks
2 onions, sliced
4 garlic cloves, finely chopped
3 bay leaves, torn in half
1–2 teaspoons hot paprika
2 teaspoons sweet paprika
1 tablespoon plain (all-purpose) flour
60 g (2 oz/¼ cup) tomato paste (concentrated purée)
1.5 litres (52 fl oz/6 cups) vegetable stock
4 potatoes, chopped
4 carrots, sliced
3 celery stalks, thickly sliced
3 tomatoes, seeded and chopped

To make the lamb stock, heat 1 tablespoon of the oil in a large heavy-based saucepan over medium heat. Brown the shanks well in two batches, then drain on paper towels.

Add the remaining oil to the pan and cook the onion, garlic and bay leaves over low heat for 10 minutes, stirring regularly. Add the paprikas and flour and cook, stirring, for 2 minutes. Gradually add the combined tomato paste and vegetable stock. Bring to the boil, stirring continuously, and return the shanks to the pan. Reduce the heat to low and simmer, covered, for 1½ hours, stirring occasionally.

Remove and discard the bay leaves. Remove the shanks, allow to cool slightly and then cut the meat from the bone. Discard the bone. Cut the meat into pieces and refrigerate. Refrigerate the stock for about 1 hour, or until fat forms on the surface and it can be spooned off.

Return the meat to the stock along with the potato, carrot and celery, turn the heat up to medium–high and bring to the boil. Reduce the heat and simmer for 15 minutes. Season, and add the chopped tomato to serve.

Brown the shanks in two batches, remove with tongs and drain on paper towels.

Spoon off the layer of fat that forms on the surface of the soup.

meat *and* **seafood soups**

Creamy fish soup

preparation 10 minutes
cooking 35 minutes
serves 4–6

¼ teaspoon saffron threads
2 tablespoons boiling water
1 litre (35 fl oz/4 cups) fish stock
125 ml (4 fl oz/½ cup) dry white wine
1 onion, finely chopped
1 small carrot, finely chopped
1 celery stalk, chopped
1 bay leaf
50 g (2 oz) butter
2 tablespoons plain (all-purpose) flour
300 g (10½ oz) skinless firm white fish fillets (such as snapper,
orange roughy, bream), cut into bite-sized pieces
250 ml (9 fl oz/1 cup) pouring (whipping) cream
2 teaspoons snipped chives, to garnish

In a small bowl, soak the saffron threads in the small amount of boiling water.

Put the fish stock, wine, onion, carrot, celery and bay leaf in a large saucepan and slowly bring to the boil. Cover and simmer for 20 minutes. Strain and discard the vegetables. Stir the saffron (with the liquid) into the hot stock.

In a clean saucepan, melt the butter and stir in the flour for 2 minutes, or until pale and foaming. Remove from the heat and gradually stir in the fish stock. Return to the heat and stir until the mixture boils and thickens. Add the fish and simmer for 2 minutes, or until the fish is cooked. Stir in the cream and heat through without boiling. Season to taste. Serve garnished with the chives.

New England clam chowder

preparation 35 minutes
cooking 45 minutes
serves 4

1.5 kg (3 lb 5 oz) clams (vongole) or pipis, in the shell
2 teaspoons oil
3 bacon slices, chopped
1 onion, chopped
1 garlic clove, crushed
750 g (1 lb 10 oz) potatoes, diced
310 ml (11 fl oz/1¼ cups) fish stock
500 ml (17 fl oz/2 cups) milk
125 ml (4 fl oz/½ cup) pouring (whipping) cream
3 tablespoons chopped flat-leaf (Italian) parsley

Discard any clams that are broken, already open or do not close when tapped on the bench. If necessary, soak in cold water for 1–2 hours to remove any grit. Drain and put in a large heavy-based saucepan with 250 ml (9 fl oz/1 cup) water. Cover and simmer over low heat for 5 minutes, or until open. Discard any that do not open. Strain and reserve the liquid. Remove the clam meat from the shells.

Heat the oil in a clean saucepan. Add the bacon, onion and garlic and cook, stirring, over medium heat until the onion is soft and the bacon golden. Add the potato and stir well.

Measure the reserved clam liquid and add water to make 310 ml (11 fl oz/1¼ cups). Add to the pan with the stock and milk. Bring to the boil, reduce the heat, cover and simmer 20 minutes, or until the potato is tender. Uncover and simmer for 10 minutes, or until slightly thickened. Add the cream, clam meat and parsley and season to taste. Heat through gently before serving, but do not allow to boil or the liquid may curdle.

Bottom: New England clam chowder. Top: Creamy fish soup.

Bourride

preparation 25 minutes
cooking 1 hour 10 minutes
serves 8

1 tablespoon butter
1 tablespoon olive oil
4 slices white bread, crusts removed and cut into 1.5 cm (⅝ inch) cubes
2 kg (4 lb 8 oz) assorted firm white fish fillets (such as bass,
whiting and cod)
5 egg yolks
4 garlic cloves, crushed
3–5 teaspoons lemon juice
250 ml (9 fl oz/1 cup) olive oil

stock
80 ml (2½ fl oz/⅓ cup) olive oil
1 large onion, chopped
1 carrot, sliced
1 leek, white part only, chopped
420 ml (14½ fl oz/1⅔ cups) dry white wine
1 teaspoon dried fennel seeds
2 garlic cloves, bruised
2 bay leaves
1 large strip orange zest
2 thyme sprigs

To make the croutons, heat the butter and oil in a heavy-based frying pan. When the butter begins to foam, add the bread cubes and cook for 5 minutes, or until golden. Drain on crumpled paper towel. Set aside.

Fillet the fish (or ask your fishmonger to do it), reserving the heads and bones for the stock.

To make the aïoli, put 2 of the egg yolks, garlic and 3 teaspoons lemon juice in a food processor and blend until creamy. With the motor still running, slowly drizzle in the oil. Season and add the remaining lemon juice, to taste. Set aside until needed.

To make the stock, heat the olive oil in large saucepan or stockpot and add the onion, carrot and leek. Cook over low heat for 12–15 minutes, or until the vegetables are soft. Add the fish heads and bones, wine, fennel seed, garlic, bay leaves, orange zest, thyme, black pepper and ½ teaspoon salt. Cover with 2 litres (70 fl oz/8 cups) water. Bring to the boil and skim off the froth. Reduce the heat and simmer for 30 minutes. Strain into a pot, crushing the bones well to release as much flavour as possible. Return to the heat.

Preheat the oven to 120°C (235°F/Gas ½). Cut the fish fillets into large pieces about 9 cm (3½ inches) long. Add to the stock and bring to a simmer, putting the heavier pieces in first and adding the more delicate pieces later. Poach for 6–8 minutes, until the flesh starts to become translucent and begins to flake easily. Transfer the fish pieces to a serving platter and moisten with a little stock. Cover with foil and keep warm in the oven.

Place 8 tablespoons of the aïoli in a large bowl and slowly add the remaining 3 egg yolks, stirring constantly. Ladle a little stock into the aïoli mixture, blend well and return slowly to the rest of the stock. Stir continuously with a wooden spoon for 8–10 minutes over low heat, or until the soup has thickened and coats the back of a spoon. Do not boil or the mixture will curdle.

To serve, scatter the croutons and fish pieces into individual bowls and ladle the stock over the top.

Hot beef borscht

preparation 30 minutes
cooking 2 hours 50 minutes
serves 4–6

500 g (1 lb 2 oz) stewing beef, cut into cubes
500 g (1 lb 2 oz) beetroot (beet)
1 onion, finely chopped
1 carrot, cut into short strips
1 parsnip, cut into short strips
75 g (2½ oz/1 cup) finely shredded cabbage
sour cream, to serve
snipped chives, to serve

Put the beef and 1 litre (35 fl oz/4 cups) water in a large heavy-based saucepan, and bring slowly to the boil. Reduce the heat, cover and simmer for 1 hour. Skim the surface of the stock to remove the fat as required.

Cut the stems from the beetroot, wash well and place in a large, heavy-based saucepan with 1 litre (35 fl oz/4 cups) water. Bring to the boil, then reduce the heat and simmer for 40 minutes, or until tender. Drain, reserving 250 ml (9 fl oz/1 cup) of the liquid. Allow to cool, then peel and grate the beetroot.

Remove the meat from the stock and cool. Skim any remaining fat from the surface of the stock. Return the meat to the stock and add the onion, carrot, parsnip, beetroot and reserved beetroot liquid. Bring to the boil, reduce the heat, cover and simmer for 45 minutes.

Stir in the cabbage and simmer for a further 15 minutes. Season to taste. Serve with the sour cream and chives.

Clam chowder

preparation 25 minutes
cooking 45 minutes
serves 4

30 g (1 oz) butter
2 bacon slices, finely chopped
1 large onion, finely chopped
4 potatoes, cut into small cubes
500 ml (17 fl oz/2 cups) fish stock
1 bay leaf
125 ml (4 fl oz/½ cup) full-cream (whole) milk
4 x 105 g (3½ oz) tins baby clams (vongole), drained and chopped
2 tablespoons finely chopped parsley, plus extra, to serve
250 ml (9 fl oz/1 cup) pouring (whipping) cream

Heat the butter in a large saucepan. Cook the bacon and onion for 2–3 minutes, or until softened. Stir in the potato. Cook for a further 2–3 minutes, then gradually pour on the stock. Add the bay leaf.

Bring the mixture to the boil, then reduce the heat and simmer, covered, for 20 minutes, or until the potato is cooked. Simmer for 10 minutes, or until the soup is reduced and slightly thickened. Discard the bay leaf.

Add the milk, clams, parsley and cream. Stir to gently reheat, but do not allow the soup to boil. Season with salt and freshly ground black pepper. Sprinkle with extra parsley to serve.

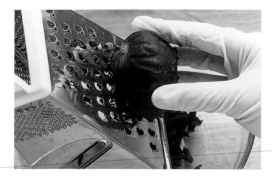

To avoid stains, wear rubber gloves to grate the cooled beetroot.

Add the milk, chopped clams and parsley, and pour in the cream.

Bottom: Clam chowder. Top: Hot beef borscht.

Bean soup with sausage

preparation 25 minutes
cooking 40 minutes
serves 4–6

4 Italian sausages
2 teaspoons olive oil
2 leeks, white part only, sliced
1 garlic clove, crushed
1 large carrot, chopped into small cubes
2 celery stalks, sliced
2 tablespoons plain (all-purpose) flour
2 beef stock (bouillon) cubes, crumbled
2 litres (70 fl oz/8 cups) boiling water
125 ml (4 fl oz/½ cup) white wine
125 g (4½ oz) conchiglie (shell pasta)
440 g (15½ oz) tinned mixed beans, drained
chopped parsley, to serve (optional)

Cut the sausages into small pieces. Heat the oil in a large heavy-based saucepan and add the sausage pieces. Cook over medium heat for 5 minutes, or until golden, stirring regularly. Remove from the pan, set aside and drain on paper towel.

Add the leek, garlic, carrot and celery to the pan and cook for 2–3 minutes or until soft, stirring occasionally. Add the flour and stir for 1 minute. Gradually stir in the combined stock cubes, water and the wine. Bring to the boil, reduce the heat and simmer for 10 minutes.

Add the pasta and beans to the pan. Increase the heat and cook for 8–10 minutes, or until the pasta is al dente. Return the sausage to the pan and season to taste. Serve with chopped fresh parsley, if desired.

Note *Use dried beans, if preferred. Put them in a bowl, cover with water and soak overnight. Drain and add to a large saucepan with enough water to cover the beans well. Bring to the boil, reduce the heat and simmer for 1 hour. Drain well before adding to the soup.*

Harira

preparation 15 minutes
cooking 2 hours 25 minutes
serves 4

2 tablespoons olive oil
2 small brown onions, chopped
2 large garlic cloves, crushed
500 g (1 lb 2 oz) lamb shoulder steaks, trimmed of excess fat and sinew, and cut into small chunks
1½ teaspoons ground cumin
2 teaspoons paprika
½ teaspoon ground cloves
1 bay leaf
2 tablespoons tomato paste (concentrated purée)
1 litre (35 fl oz/4 cups) beef stock
900 g (2 lb) tinned chickpeas, rinsed and drained
800 g (1 lb 12 oz) tinned diced tomatoes
30 g (1 oz) finely chopped coriander (cilantro) leaves, plus extra, to garnish
small black olives, to serve

Heat the oil in a large heavy-based saucepan or stockpot, add the onion and garlic and cook for 5 minutes, or until softened. Add the meat in batches and cook over high heat until browned on all sides. Return all the meat to the pan.

Add the spices and bay leaf to the pan and cook until fragrant. Add the tomato paste and cook for about 2 minutes, stirring constantly. Add the stock, stir well and bring to the boil. Add the chickpeas, tomato and chopped coriander to the pan. Stir, then bring to the boil. Reduce the heat and simmer for 2 hours, or until the meat is tender. Stir occasionally. Season to taste.

Serve garnished with coriander leaves and small black olives. This dish can also be served with toasted pitta bread drizzled with a little extra virgin olive oil.

Bottom: Harira. Top: Bean soup with sausage.

Bouillabaisse

preparation 30 minutes + 5 minutes soaking
cooking 1 hour 15 minutes
serves 6

60 ml (2 fl oz/¼ cup) olive oil
1 large onion, chopped
2 leeks, sliced
4 garlic cloves, crushed
500 g (1 lb 2 oz) ripe tomatoes, peeled and roughly chopped
1–2 tablespoons tomato paste (concentrated purée)
6 flat-leaf (Italian) parsley sprigs
2 bay leaves
2 thyme sprigs
1 fennel sprig
¼ teaspoon saffron threads
2 kg (4 lb 8 oz) seafood trimmings (fish heads, bones, shellfish remains)
1 tablespoon Pernod or Ricard liqueur
4 potatoes, cut into 1.5 cm (⅝ inch) slices
1.5 kg (3 lb 5 oz) fish fillets, such as blue-eye cod, bream, red fish and snapper, cut into large chunks

toasts
½ baguette, cut into twelve 1.5 cm (⅝ inch) slices
2 large garlic cloves, halved

rouille
3 slices day-old Italian white bread, crusts removed
1 red capsicum (pepper), seeded and quartered
1 small red chilli, seeded and chopped
3 garlic cloves, crushed
1 tablespoon chopped basil leaves
80 ml (2½ fl oz/⅓ cup) olive oil

Heat the oil in a large saucepan over low heat. Cook the onion and leek for 5 minutes without browning. Add the garlic, tomato and 1 tablespoon of the tomato paste. Simmer for 5 minutes. Stir in 2 litres (70 fl oz/8 cups) cold water, then add the parsley sprigs, bay leaves, thyme, fennel, saffron and seafood trimmings. Bring to the boil, then reduce the heat and simmer for 30–40 minutes.

Strain the stock into a large saucepan, pressing out the juices and discarding the solids. Set aside 60 ml (2 fl oz/¼ cup) stock. Add the Pernod to pan and stir in extra tomato paste if needed to enrich the colour. Season with salt and pepper. Bring to the boil and add potato, then reduce the heat and simmer for 5 minutes.

Add the blue-eye cod and bream, cook for 2–3 minutes, then add the red fish and snapper, and cook for 5–6 minutes, or until cooked.

To make the toasts, toast the bread until golden on both sides. While still warm, rub with the garlic.

To make the rouille, soak the bread in enough cold water to cover, for 5 minutes. Cook the capsicum, skin side up, under a hot grill (broiler) until the skin blackens and blisters. Place in a sealable plastic bag and leave to cool, then peel away the skin. Roughly chop the flesh. Squeeze bread dry and place in a food processor with capsicum, chilli, garlic and basil. Process to a smooth paste. While processing, gradually add the oil until the consistency resembles mayonnaise. Thin the sauce with 1–2 tablespoons of reserved fish stock. Season.

To serve, place two pieces of toast in the base of six soup bowls. Ladle in the hot soup and fish pieces and serve with the rouille.

Chicken and couscous soup

preparation 25 minutes
cooking 30 minutes
serves 6

1 tablespoon olive oil
1 onion, sliced
½ teaspoon ground cumin
½ teaspoon paprika
1 teaspoon grated fresh ginger
1 garlic clove, crushed
2 celery stalks, sliced
2 small carrots, sliced
2 zucchini (courgettes), sliced
1.25 litres (44 fl oz/5 cups) chicken stock
2 boneless, skinless chicken breasts, sliced
pinch saffron threads (optional)
95 g (3 oz/½ cup) instant couscous
2 tablespoons chopped flat-leaf (Italian) parsley

Heat the oil in a large heavy-based saucepan. Add the onion and cook over medium heat for 10 minutes, or until very soft, stirring occasionally. Add the cumin, paprika, ginger and garlic and cook, stirring, for 1 minute further.

Add the celery, carrot and zucchini and stir to coat with the spices. Stir in the stock. Bring to the boil, then reduce the heat and simmer, partially covered, for about 15 minutes, or until the vegetables are tender.

Add the chicken and saffron to the pan and cook for about 5 minutes, or until the chicken is just tender; do not overcook the chicken. Stir in the couscous and chopped parsley and serve.

Note *Add the couscous to the soup just before serving because it absorbs liquid quickly and becomes very thick.*

Creamy spinach and chicken soup

preparation 40 minutes
cooking 55 minutes
serves 6

1 tablespoon oil
1 kg (2 lb/4 oz) chicken pieces
1 carrot, chopped
2 celery stalks, chopped
1 onion, chopped
6 black peppercorns
2 garlic cloves, chopped
bouquet garni
800 g (1 lb 12 oz) orange sweet potato, chopped
500 g (1 lb/2 oz) English spinach
125 ml (4 fl oz/½ cup) pouring (whipping) cream

Heat the oil in a large saucepan, add the chicken pieces in batches and brown well. Drain on paper towels. Pour off the excess fat, leaving 1 tablespoon in the pan. Return the chicken to the pan with the carrot, celery, onion, peppercorns, garlic, bouquet garni and 1.5 litres (52 fl oz/ 6 cups) of water.

Bring the soup to the boil, reduce the heat and simmer for 40 minutes. Strain, discarding the vegetables, peppercorns and bouquet garni. Return the stock to the pan. Pull the chicken meat from the bones, shred and set aside.

Add the sweet potato to the stock in the pan. Bring to the boil, then reduce the heat and simmer until tender. Add the spinach leaves and cook until wilted. Process the spinach in batches in a food processor until finely chopped.

Return the spinach to the pan, add the shredded chicken and stir in the cream. Season to taste. Reheat gently before serving but do not allow the soup to boil.

Do not stir in the parsley and couscous until just before the soup is served.

To make a bouquet garni, tie parsley, thyme and a bay leaf with string.

Bottom: Creamy spinach and chicken soup. Top: Chicken and couscous soup.

casseroles

Navarin of lamb

preparation 25 minutes
cooking 1 hour 35 minutes
serves 4

8 lamb noisettes (see Notes)
seasoned plain (all-purpose) flour
2 tablespoons oil
2 celery stalks, sliced thinly
12 baby carrots, peeled (see Notes)
12 new potatoes, halved
6 thyme sprigs
1 large handful flat-leaf (Italian) parsley, chopped
2 onions, chopped
2 garlic cloves, crushed
40 g (1½ oz/⅓ cup) plain (all-purpose) flour
625 ml (21½ fl oz/2½ cups) chicken stock
250 ml (9 fl oz/1 cup) red wine
60 g (2 oz/¼ cup) tomato paste (concentrated purée)
chopped flat-leaf (Italian) parsley, extra, to garnish

Toss the lamb in the seasoned flour, shaking off the excess. Preheat the oven to 180°C (350°F/Gas 4).

Heat the oil in a heavy-based saucepan. In batches, brown the lamb well on both sides over medium–high heat. Remove from the heat, drain well on paper towels, then transfer to a greased, 3 litre (105 fl oz/12 cup) casserole dish. Top the lamb with the celery, carrots, potatoes, thyme sprigs and parsley.

Cook the onion and garlic in the same saucepan, stirring over medium heat for 5–10 minutes, or until the onion is soft and tender.

Add the flour and stir for 1 minute, or until the onion is coated. Add the stock, wine and tomato paste and stir until the sauce boils and thickens. Pour the sauce over the lamb and vegetables. Bake, covered, for 1¼ hours, or until the lamb is tender. Carefully remove the string from the lamb, and sprinkle with extra parsley to serve.

Notes *A noisette is a round slice of meat, cut from a boned loin and tied with string to hold its shape. For this recipe you could also use a boned leg of lamb, cut into 3 cm (1¼ inch) cubes. If baby carrots are not available, use four sliced carrots instead.*

Add the lightly floured lamb to the hot oil and brown well all over.

Add the stock, wine and tomato paste to the softened onion mixture.

Creamy apricot chicken

preparation 10 minutes
cooking 1 hour
serves 6

6 chicken thigh cutlets
425 ml (15 fl oz) apricot nectar
40 g (1½ oz) packet French onion soup mix
425 g (15 oz) tinned apricot halves in natural juice, drained
60 g (2 oz/¼ cup) sour cream

Preheat the oven to 180°C (350°F/Gas 4). Remove the skin from the chicken thigh cutlets. Put the chicken in an ovenproof dish. Mix the apricot nectar with the French onion soup mix until well combined, then pour the mixture over the chicken.

Bake, covered, for 50 minutes, then add the apricot halves and bake for a further 5 minutes. Stir in the sour cream just before serving. This is delicious served with creamy mashed potato or rice to soak up the juices.

Note *If you are looking for a healthy alternative, you can use low-fat sour cream in place of the full-fat version.*

Chicken chasseur

preparation 20 minutes
cooking 1 hour 30 minutes
serves 4

1 kg (2 lb 4 oz) boneless, skinless chicken thighs
2 tablespoons olive oil
1 garlic clove, crushed
1 large onion, sliced
100 g (3½ oz) button mushrooms, sliced
1 teaspoon thyme leaves
400 g (14 oz) tinned chopped tomatoes
60 ml (2 fl oz/¼ cup) chicken stock
60 ml (2 fl oz/¼ cup) dry white wine
1 tablespoon tomato paste (concentrated purée)

Preheat the oven to 180°C (350°F/Gas 4). Trim the chicken of excess fat and sinew. Heat the oil in a heavy-based frying pan and brown the chicken in batches over medium heat. Drain on paper towels, then transfer to a casserole dish.

Add the garlic, onion and sliced mushrooms to the pan and cook over medium heat for about 5 minutes, or until soft. Add to the chicken with the thyme and tomatoes.

Combine the stock, wine and tomato paste and pour over the chicken. Bake, covered, for 1¼ hours, or until the chicken is cooked through and tender.

Chicken and red wine casserole

preparation 15 minutes
cooking 1 hour 50 minutes
serves 4–6

30 g (1 oz) butter
125 g (4½ oz) bacon, roughly chopped
1.5 kg (3 lb 5 oz) skinless chicken pieces
350 g (12 oz) baby onions (see Note)
2 tablespoons plain (all-purpose) flour
750 ml (26 fl oz/3 cups) red wine
250 g (9 oz) mushrooms, sliced

Preheat the oven to 180°C (350°F/Gas 4). Melt the butter in a large flameproof casserole dish over medium heat. Add the bacon and cook, stirring constantly, until golden, then remove from the dish and set aside. Add the chicken pieces in batches and cook, turning, for 4–5 minutes, or until browned all over. Add to the bacon. Add the onions to the dish and cook, stirring, for 2–3 minutes, or until browned, then remove from the dish, keeping them separate from the bacon and chicken.

Stir the flour into the juices in the casserole dish, then remove the dish from the heat and slowly pour in the red wine, while stirring continuously. Return the dish to the heat, bring the liquid to the boil and return the bacon and chicken to the dish.

Cover with the casserole dish with a lid and bake for 1 hour. Return the onions to the dish and add the mushrooms. Cook in the oven for a further 30 minutes. Season to taste with salt and freshly ground black pepper. This dish is delicious served with mashed potato.

Note *Baby onions are sometimes called pickling onions.*

Top left: Creamy apricot chicken. Top right: Chicken and red wine casserole. Bottom left: Chicken chasseur.

Lamb with borlotti beans

preparation 20 minutes + overnight soaking
cooking 2 hours
serves 6

200 g (7 oz/1 cup) dried borlotti (cranberry) beans
1 tablespoon olive oil
12 lamb loin chops
1 onion, finely chopped
1 celery stalk, chopped
1 carrot, chopped
3 garlic cloves, finely chopped
½ teaspoon dried chilli flakes
1 teaspoon cumin seeds
500 ml (17 fl oz/2 cups) lamb or chicken stock
2 bay leaves
60 ml (2 fl oz/¼ cup) lemon juice
2 large handfuls parsley, chopped
1 tablespoon shredded mint

Put the beans in a large bowl, cover with cold water and soak overnight.

Drain the beans and rinse under cold water. Preheat the oven to 180°C (350°F/Gas 4). Heat the oil in a large heavy-based saucepan. Brown the lamb over high heat in batches, then transfer to a casserole dish.

Add the onion, celery and carrot to the pan, and cook over low heat for 10 minutes, or until soft and golden. Add the garlic, chilli and cumin seeds, and cook for 1 minute, then transfer to the casserole dish.

Add the stock, beans and bay leaves. Cover tightly and bake for 1½–1¾ hours, or until the lamb is very tender and the beans are cooked. Season with salt and freshly ground black pepper. Stir in the lemon juice, parsley and mint just before serving.

Veal and fennel casserole

preparation 20 minutes
cooking 2 hours 15 minutes
serves 4–6

1 tablespoon oil
30 g (1 oz) butter
4 veal shanks, cut into 4 cm (1½ inch) pieces (see Note)
1 large onion, sliced
1 garlic clove, crushed
2 celery stalks, thickly sliced
3 carrots, thickly sliced
2 small fennel bulbs, quartered
30 g (1 oz/¼ cup) plain (all-purpose) flour
400 g (14 oz) tin chopped tomatoes
80 ml (2½ fl oz/⅓ cup) dry white wine
250 ml (9 fl oz/1 cup) chicken stock
1 tablespoon chopped thyme plus extra, to garnish
12 black olives

Preheat the oven to 180°C (350°F/Gas 4). Heat the oil and butter in a large heavy-based saucepan and brown the meat quickly in batches on both sides over high heat. Transfer to a large, shallow casserole dish.

Add the onion and garlic to the pan, and cook over medium heat until soft. Add the celery, carrot and fennel, and cook for 2 minutes. Add the flour, stir until golden, then add the tomato, wine, stock and thyme. Bring to the boil, reduce the heat and simmer for 5 minutes, or until thickened. Season with salt and freshly ground black pepper.

Add the sauce to the veal; cover and bake for 1½–2 hours, or until tender. Scatter with extra thyme and olives to serve.

Note *Many butchers sell veal shanks already cut into pieces. You will need 12 medium pieces for this recipe.*

When the oil is hot, brown the lamb over high heat in batches.

Trim the leaves and base from the celery stalks, then cut into thick slices.

Bottom: Veal and fennel casserole. Top: Lamb with borlotti beans.

Cioppino

preparation 30 minutes
cooking 1 hour
serves 4

2 dried Chinese mushrooms
1 kg (2 lb 4 oz) skinless firm white fish fillets, such as hake, snapper, ocean perch or red mullet
375 g (13 oz) raw large prawns (shrimp)
1 raw lobster tail (about 400 g/14 oz)
12–15 black mussels
60 ml (2 fl oz/¼ cup) olive oil
1 large onion, finely chopped
1 green capsicum (pepper), seeded and membrane removed, finely chopped
2–3 garlic cloves, crushed
400 g (14 oz) tinned chopped tomatoes
250 ml (9 fl oz/1 cup) dry white wine
250 ml (9 fl oz/1 cup) tomato juice
250 ml (9 fl oz/1 cup) fish stock
1 bay leaf
2 flat-leaf (Italian) parsley sprigs
2 teaspoons chopped basil
1 tablespoon chopped flat-leaf (Italian) parsley, extra, to garnish

Place the mushrooms in a small bowl, cover with boiling water and soak for 20 minutes. Cut the fish into bite-size pieces, removing any bones.

Peel the prawns, leaving the tails intact. Gently pull out the dark vein from each prawn back, starting at the head end.

Starting at the end where the head was, cut down the sides of the lobster shell on the underside of the lobster with kitchen scissors. Pull back the flap, remove the meat from the shell and cut into small pieces.

Scrub the mussels with a stiff brush and pull out the hairy beards. Discard any broken mussels, or open ones that don't close when tapped on the bench. Rinse well.

Drain the mushrooms, squeeze dry and chop finely. Heat the oil in a heavy-based saucepan, add the onion, capsicum and garlic and stir over medium heat for about 5 minutes, or until the onion is soft. Add the mushrooms, tomato, wine, tomato juice, stock, bay leaf, parsley sprigs and basil. Bring to the boil, reduce the heat, then cover and simmer for 30 minutes.

Layer the fish and prawns in a large frying pan. Add the sauce, then cover and leave on low heat for 10 minutes, or until the prawns are pink and the fish is cooked. Add the lobster and mussels and simmer for a further 4–5 minutes. Season with salt and pepper. Discard any unopened mussels. Sprinkle with parsley.

Chicken paprika with dumplings

preparation 20 minutes
cooking 1 hour 10 minutes
serves 4–6

2 tablespoons oil
1.6 kg (3 lb 8 oz) chicken, cut into 10 pieces
1 large onion, chopped
1 garlic clove, crushed
1 teaspoon sweet paprika
1 teaspoon dried thyme
2 tablespoons plain (all-purpose) flour
125 ml (4 fl oz/½ cup) chicken stock
400 g (14 oz) tin chopped tomatoes
2 carrots, cut into 2 cm (¾ inch) pieces

dumplings
125 g (4½ oz/1 cup) self-raising flour
20 g (1 oz) butter, chopped
2 teaspoons finely chopped flat-leaf (Italian) parsley
2 teaspoons snipped chives
½ teaspoon mixed dried herbs
80 ml (2½ fl oz/⅓ cup) buttermilk (see Note)

Heat the oil in a frying pan. Brown the chicken in batches over medium–high heat, and place in a very deep 3 litre (105 fl oz/12 cup) casserole dish.

Add the onion and garlic to the dish, stirring until soft. Reduce the heat to low. Add the paprika, thyme and flour, and cook, stirring, for 2 minutes. Gradually stir in the stock. Add the tomato, and season. Pour the mixture over the chicken. Add the carrot. Cover with a lid and bake for 30 minutes.

To make the dumplings, sift the flour into a bowl. Rub in the butter until fine and crumbly. Stir in the herbs and almost all the buttermilk. Mix to a soft dough, adding more buttermilk if necessary. Turn the dough out onto a floured surface and gather into a ball. Divide into eight portions and roll each into a ball. Arrange the dumplings on top of the casserole. Bake, uncovered, for 20 minutes. Serve the casserole immediately.

Note *Buttermilk is available at the supermarket. It is a low-fat milk with a slight sour taste.*

Boston baked beans

preparation 25 minutes + overnight soaking
cooking 1 hour 35 minutes
serves 4–6

350 g (12 oz/1¾ cups) dried cannellini beans (see Notes)
1 whole ham hock
2 onions, chopped
2 tablespoons tomato paste (concentrated purée)
1 tablespoon worcestershire sauce
1 tablespoon molasses
1 teaspoon French mustard
45 g (1½ oz/¼ cup) soft brown sugar
125 ml (4 fl oz/½ cup) tomato juice

Put the beans in a large bowl, cover with cold water and soak overnight.

Drain the beans and rinse under cold water. Place the beans in a large saucepan. Add the ham hock and cover with cold water. Bring to the boil, then reduce the heat and simmer, covered, for 25 minutes, or until the beans are tender. Preheat the oven to 160°C (315°F/Gas 2–3).

Remove the ham hock from the saucepan and set aside to cool. Drain the beans, reserving 250 ml (9 fl oz/1 cup) of the cooking liquid. Trim the ham of all skin, fat and sinew, then chop the meat and discard the bone.

Transfer the meat and beans to a 2 litre (70 fl oz/8 cup) casserole dish. Add the reserved liquid and all the remaining ingredients. Mix gently, then cover and bake for 1 hour. Serve with hot buttered toast.

Notes *Any type of dried bean can be used in this recipe. To quick-soak beans, place them in a pan, add hot water to cover, bring slowly to the boil, then remove from the heat. Leave to soak for 1 hour before draining and using.*

Trim the ham of all fat, skin and sinew, then roughly chop the meat.

Bottom: Boston baked beans. Top: Chicken paprika with dumplings.

Rabbit with rosemary and white wine

preparation 25 minutes
cooking 2 hours
serves 4

1 large rabbit (about 1.6 kg/3 lb 8 oz) (see Note)
30 g (1 oz/¼ cup) seasoned flour
60 ml (2 fl oz/¼ cup) olive oil
2 onions, thinly sliced
1 large rosemary sprig
1 small sage sprig
2 garlic cloves, crushed
500 ml (17 fl oz/2 cups) dry white wine
400 g (14 oz) tinned chopped tomatoes
pinch of cayenne pepper
125 ml (4 fl oz/½ cup) chicken stock
small black olives such as Niçoise or Ligurian (optional)
3 small rosemary sprigs, extra (optional)

Cut the rabbit into large pieces and dredge the pieces in the seasoned flour. Heat the oil in a large heavy-based saucepan over medium heat. Brown the rabbit pieces on all sides, then remove from the saucepan.

Reduce the heat and add the onion, rosemary and sage to the saucepan. Cook gently for 10 minutes, then stir in the garlic and return the rabbit pieces to the saucepan.

Increase the heat to high, add the wine to the pan and cook for 1 minute. Stir in the tomato, the cayenne pepper and half the stock. Reduce the heat, cover and simmer over low heat for about 1½ hours, or until the rabbit is tender. Halfway through cooking, check the sauce and if it seems too dry, add 60 ml (2 fl oz/¼ cup) water.

Discard the herb sprigs. Season to taste. Garnish with the olives and extra rosemary, if desired.

Note *Buy rabbit from your butcher; you may need to provide some notice to ensure there is one available for you. Your butcher may be happy to cut the rabbit into pieces for you.*

Chicken cacciatora

preparation 15 minutes
cooking 1 hour
serves 4

60 ml (2 fl oz/¼ cup) olive oil
1 large onion, finely chopped
3 garlic cloves, crushed
150 g (5½ oz) pancetta, finely chopped
125 g (4½ oz) button mushrooms, thickly sliced
1 large chicken (at least 1.6 kg/3 lb 8 oz), cut into 8 pieces
80 ml (2½ fl oz/⅓ cup) dry vermouth or dry white wine
800 g (1 lb 12 oz) tinned chopped tomatoes
¼ teaspoon soft brown sugar
¼ teaspoon cayenne pepper
1 oregano sprig
1 thyme sprig
1 bay leaf

Heat half the olive oil in a large flameproof casserole dish. Add the onion and garlic and cook for 6–8 minutes over low heat, stirring, until the onion is golden. Add the pancetta and mushrooms, increase the heat and cook, stirring, for 4–5 minutes. Transfer to a bowl.

Add the remaining oil to the casserole dish and brown the chicken pieces, a few at a time, over medium heat. Season as they brown. Spoon off the excess fat and return all the chicken pieces to the casserole dish. Increase the heat, add the vermouth to the dish and cook until the liquid has almost evaporated.

Add the chopped tomato, brown sugar, cayenne pepper, oregano, thyme and bay leaf, and stir in 80 ml (2½ fl oz/⅓ cup) water. Bring to the boil, then stir in the reserved onion mixture. Reduce the heat, cover and simmer for 25 minutes, or until the chicken is tender but not falling off the bone.

If the liquid is too thin, remove the chicken from the casserole dish, increase the heat and boil until the liquid has thickened. Discard the sprigs of herbs and adjust the seasoning to taste.

Bottom: Chicken cacciatora. Top: Rabbit with rosemary and white wine.

Whole fish casserole

preparation 30 minutes + 2 hours marinating
cooking 1 hour 35 minutes
serves 4–6

1.25 kg (2 lb 12 oz) whole red bream or red snapper, cleaned
2 lemons, 1 left whole, 1 sliced
60 ml (2 fl oz/¼ cup) olive oil
800 g (1 lb 12 oz) potatoes, thinly sliced
3 garlic cloves, thinly sliced
1 large handful finely chopped parsley
1 small red onion, thinly sliced
1 small dried chilli, seeded and finely chopped
1 red capsicum (pepper), cut into thin rings
1 yellow capsicum (pepper), cut into thin rings
2 bay leaves
3–4 thyme sprigs
60 ml (2 fl oz/¼ cup) dry sherry

Cut off and discard the fins from the fish and place it in a large non-metallic dish. Cut two thin slices from one end of the whole lemon and reserve. Squeeze the juice from the rest of the lemon inside the fish. Add 2 tablespoons of the oil. Refrigerate, covered, for 2 hours.

Preheat the oven to 190°C (375°F/Gas 5) and lightly oil a shallow earthenware baking dish large enough to hold the whole fish. Spread half the potato on the base and scatter the garlic, parsley, onion, chilli and capsicum on top. Season with salt and pepper. Cover with the rest of the potato. Pour in 80 ml (2½ fl oz/⅓ cup) water and sprinkle the remaining oil over the top. Cover with foil and bake for 1 hour.

Increase the oven temperature to 220°C (425°F/Gas 7).

Season the fish inside and out with salt and pepper, and place the bay leaves and thyme inside the cavity. Make three or four diagonal slashes on each side. Cut the reserved lemon slices in half and fit these into the slashes on one side of the fish, to resemble fins. Nestle the fish into the potatoes with extra lemon slices on top. Bake, uncovered, for 30 minutes, or until the fish is cooked through and the potato is golden and crusty.

Pour the dry sherry over the fish and return to the oven for 3 minutes. Serve straight from the dish.

Scatter the garlic, parsley, onion, chilli and capsicum on top of the potato.

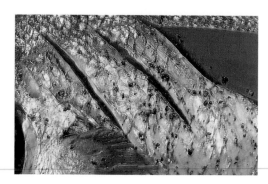

Make three or four diagonal slashes on each side of the stuffed fish.

Coq au vin

preparation 15 minutes
cooking 1 hour 40 minutes
serves 6

1 tablespoon olive oil
125 g (4½ oz) bacon, rind removed, roughly chopped
1.5 kg (3 lb 5 oz) boneless, skinless chicken pieces
350 g (12 oz) baby onions
2 tablespoons plain (all-purpose) flour
750 ml (26 fl oz/3 cups) dry red wine
250 g (9 oz) field mushrooms, sliced
1 tablespoon thyme leaves, to garnish

Preheat the oven to 180°C (350°F/Gas 4). Heat the oil in a large ovenproof casserole dish. Add the bacon and cook for 5 minutes, or until golden, then remove. Add the chicken and cook, in batches, for 4–5 minutes, or until browned. Remove. Add the onions and cook for 2–3 minutes, or until browned, then remove from the casserole dish.

Add the flour to the casserole dish and stir well, remove from the heat and slowly stir in the red wine. Return to the heat, bring to the boil and return the bacon and chicken to the dish. Cover and cook in the oven for 1 hour. Return the onions to the dish and add the mushrooms. Cook for a further 30 minutes. Season to taste and garnish with the thyme. Serve with crusty bread or pasta.

Note *Baby onions are also known as pickling onions.*

Cook the onions for a couple of minutes, or until they are browned.

Sweet and sour meatballs

preparation 20 minutes
cooking 1 hour 20 minutes
serves 4–6

1 kg (2 lb 4 oz) lean minced (ground) beef
80 g (3 oz/1 cup) fresh breadcrumbs
1 egg, lightly beaten
1 tablespoon worcestershire sauce
1 tablespoon chilli sauce
1 tablespoon chopped flat-leaf (Italian) parsley
2 tablespoons oil

sauce
2 tablespoons soft brown sugar
80 ml (2½ fl oz/⅓ cup) white vinegar
2 tablespoons barbecue sauce
2 tablespoons tomato sauce (concentrated purée)
500 ml (17 fl oz/2 cups) pineapple juice
1 tablespoon cornflour (cornstarch)
1 large cucumber, halved, seeded and cut into matchsticks
1 large carrot, cut into matchsticks
1 red capsicum (pepper), cut into matchsticks
440 g (15½ oz) tin pineapple pieces, drained

Preheat the oven to 160°C (315°F/Gas 2–3). Combine the beef, breadcrumbs, egg, sauces and parsley in a large bowl. Using your hands, mix well. Using 2 teaspoons of the mixture at a time, roll into balls.

Heat the oil in a heavy-based frying pan. Cook the meatballs in batches over medium heat for 3 minutes, or until browned. Drain.

To make the sauce, place the sugar, vinegar, sauces and juice in a medium saucepan. Cook over medium heat until the sugar has dissolved. Bring to the boil, then remove from the heat.

Blend the cornflour with 2 tablespoons water. Add to the pan. Stir over medium heat for 3 minutes, or until it boils and thickens.

Place the meatballs and remaining ingredients in a casserole dish. Pour the sauce over the top. Bake for 1 hour. Serve with rice.

Bottom: Sweet and sour meatballs. Top: Coq au vin.

Beef and vegetable casserole

preparation 40 minutes
cooking 1 hour 40 minutes
serves 6

500 g (1 lb 2 oz) lean round steak
cooking oil spray
1 onion, sliced
3 garlic cloves, crushed
2 teaspoons ground cumin
1 teaspoon dried thyme leaves
2 bay leaves
400 g (14 oz) tin chopped tomatoes
500 g (1 lb 2 oz) potatoes, chopped
2 large carrots, thickly sliced
4 zucchini (courgettes), thickly sliced
250 g (9 oz) mushrooms, halved
250 g (9 oz) yellow baby (pattypan) squash, halved
2 tablespoons tomato paste (concentrated purée)
125 ml (4 fl oz/½ cup) red wine
3 large handfuls parsley, chopped

Preheat the oven to 180°C (350°F/Gas 4). Remove any excess fat and sinew from the meat and cut into 2 cm (¾ inch) cubes. Spray a deep, non-stick frying pan with oil and fry the meat in batches until brown. Remove from the pan. Spray the pan again, add the onion and cook until lightly golden. Add the garlic, cumin, thyme and bay leaves and stir for 1 minute.

Return the meat and any juices to the pan, tossing to coat with the spices. Add 375 ml (13 fl oz/1½ cups) water and the tomato, scraping the pan. Simmer for 10 minutes, or until thickened. Mix in a large casserole dish with the vegetables, tomato paste and wine.

Bake, covered, for 1 hour. Stir well, then uncover and bake for 20 minutes. Season, remove the bay leaves and stir in the parsley.

When the onion is golden, add the garlic, cumin, thyme and bay leaves.

Beef and artichoke casserole

preparation 30 minutes
cooking 2 hours 15 minutes
serves 4–6

2 tablespoons olive oil
1 kg (2 lb 4 oz) stewing beef, cut into large cubes
2 red onions, sliced
4 garlic cloves, crushed
1 teaspoon cumin seeds
2 teaspoons ground coriander
2 teaspoons sweet paprika
1 tablespoon plain (all-purpose) flour
500 ml (17 fl oz/2 cups) beef stock
1 teaspoon finely grated lemon zest
1 tablespoon soft brown sugar
1 tablespoon tomato paste (concentrated purée)
60 ml (2 fl oz/¼ cup) lemon juice
4 globe artichokes
90 g (3 oz/½ cup) black olives

Preheat the oven to 180°C (350°F/Gas 4). Heat half the oil in a large heavy-based frying pan. Brown the meat in batches over medium–high heat, then transfer to a large casserole dish and set aside.

Add the remaining oil to the frying pan and cook the onion over medium heat for 5 minutes, or until soft. Add the garlic, cumin seeds, cumin, coriander and paprika, and cook for 1 minute.

Add the flour, cook for 30 seconds, then remove from the heat. Add the stock, return to the heat and stir until the mixture bubbles. Add to the meat with the lemon zest, sugar and tomato paste. Cover tightly and bake for 1½ hours.

Meanwhile, add the lemon juice to a bowl of water. Cut the top third from each artichoke, trim the stem to 5 cm (2 inches) and cut away the dark outer leaves. Cut the artichokes in half lengthways. Remove the prickly lavender-topped leaves in the centre and scoop out the hairy choke. Drop the artichokes into the lemon-water until ready to use.

Drain the artichokes and add to the casserole, covering them in the liquid. Cover and bake for 30 minutes, or until tender. For a thicker gravy, cook uncovered for 15 minutes more. Season, and stir in the olives to serve.

Bottom: Beef and artichoke casserole. Top: Beef and vegetable casserole.

Lamb shanks with puy lentils

preparation 25 minutes
cooking 1 hour 45 minutes
serves 4

80 ml (2½ fl oz/⅓ cup) olive oil
4 French-trimmed lamb shanks (280 g/10 oz each) (see Note)
6 garlic cloves, unpeeled
1 onion, thinly sliced
1 red capsicum (pepper), sliced
2 garlic cloves, crushed
400 g (14 oz) tin chopped tomatoes
250 ml (9 fl oz/1 cup) dry white wine
1 bay leaf
1 cinnamon stick
2 orange zest strips
320 g (11 oz) puy or tiny blue-green lentils
400 g (14 oz) tin cannellini beans, rinsed and drained
2 spring onions (scallions), sliced
pinch of saffron threads
1 teaspoon ground coriander
1 teaspoon ground cumin
2 tablespoons chopped flat-leaf (Italian) parsley

Preheat the oven to 200°C (400°F/Gas 6). Heat half the oil in a large flameproof casserole dish, add the shanks in batches and cook over medium heat for 4 minutes, or until brown on all sides. Remove from the dish.

Place the unpeeled garlic cloves on a baking tray and drizzle with half the remaining oil.

Add the onion, capsicum and crushed garlic to the dish and cook until golden. Stir in the tomato, wine, bay leaf, cinnamon stick and orange zest, return the shanks to the dish, then cover and transfer to the oven. Cook for 1 hour, then uncover and cook for a further 30 minutes, or until tender and the meat just falls off the bone. Keep warm. Add the garlic clove tray to the oven 15 minutes before the meat is ready. Cook until soft. Cool slightly, then peel.

Meanwhile, place the lentils in a saucepan, cover with 1.5 litres (52 fl oz/6 cups) water and bring to the boil.

Cook over high heat for 20 minutes, or until tender. Drain, reserving the liquid.

Place the peeled garlic cloves in a food processor with the beans and a dash of the reserved lentil cooking liquid, and process until smooth and creamy. Season to taste. Cover and keep warm. Add more liquid if the purée starts to thicken and dry out.

Heat the remaining oil in a large frying pan, add the spring onion and spices, and cook over medium heat for 3 minutes, or until fragrant. Stir in the lentils and parsley, and cook until warmed through.

Place a mound of lentils on each plate, stand the shanks in the lentils and drizzle with some of the cooking liquid. Serve a spoonful of the bean purée on the side.

Note *French-trimmed lamb shanks are lamb shanks that have the meat scraped back to make a neat lamb 'drumstick'.*

Add the onion, capsicum and garlic to the dish, and cook until golden.

Cook the lamb shanks until the meat is just falling off the bone.

Chicken, leek and sweet potato one-pot

preparation 15 minutes
cooking 1 hour 40 minutes
serves 4

600 g (1 lb 5 oz) orange sweet potato
2 tablespoons olive oil
1.5 kg (3 lb 5 oz) chicken pieces
1 leek, cut into 2 cm (¾ inch) slices
2 garlic cloves, crushed
2 tablespoons plain (all-purpose) flour
500 ml (17 fl oz/2 cups) chicken stock
2 tablespoons thyme leaves

Preheat the oven to 220°C (425°F/Gas 7). Peel the sweet potato and cut it into chunks. Heat 1 tablespoon of the oil in a large flameproof casserole dish. Cook the chicken in batches for 3–4 minutes, or until browned. Set aside. Add the remaining oil and cook the leek and garlic for 2 minutes, or until soft.

Add the flour to the dish and cook, stirring, for about 1 minute to brown the flour. Gradually add the stock, stirring until the sauce boils and thickens. Remove from the heat. Return the chicken to the dish.

Add the sweet potato and half the thyme. Bake, covered, for 1½ hours, or until the chicken is cooked through and the sweet potato is tender. Season, and scatter with the remaining thyme. Serve with steamed rice.

Cassoulet

preparation 20 minutes + overnight soaking
cooking 4 hours
serves 6

500 g (1 lb 2 oz) dried haricot beans
1.5 litres (52 fl oz/6 cups) beef stock
2 tablespoons oil
500 g (1 lb 2 oz) pork spareribs, trimmed
250 g (9 oz) diced lamb
250 g (9 oz) garlic or spiced sausage
125 g (4½ oz) bacon, cut into cubes
2 onions, chopped
2 carrots, chopped
2 garlic cloves, crushed
1 bay leaf
1 parsley sprig
1 thyme sprig
6 black peppercorns
160 g (5½ oz/2 cups) fresh breadcrumbs
60 g (2 oz) butter, chilled and grated

Put the beans in a large bowl, cover with cold water and soak overnight.

Drain the beans and rinse under cold water. Put them in a large saucepan with the stock. Bring slowly to the boil, then reduce the heat and simmer for 1 hour, or until tender. Drain the beans, reserving the liquid.

Heat the oil in a frying pan. Brown the pork, lamb, sausage and bacon in several batches. Remove and drain on paper towels. Add the onion, carrot and garlic and brown well.

Preheat the oven to 160°C (315°F/Gas 2–3). Layer the meats, beans and vegetables in a large casserole dish. Tie the herbs and peppercorns together in a small piece of muslin (cheesecloth), and add to the dish. Pour over the liquid from the beans, cover and bake for 2 hours.

Remove and discard the herb bag. Combine the breadcrumbs and butter, and sprinkle over the top of the casserole. Return to the oven for 30 minutes, or until the crust is golden and crisp.

Cook the chicken pieces, in batches, until they are browned all over.

Add the onion, carrot and garlic to the frying pan, and brown well.

Bottom: Cassoulet. Top: Chicken, leek and sweet potato one-pot.

Chicken and mushroom casserole

preparation 20 minutes + 5 minutes soaking
cooking 1 hour
serves 4

20 g (1 oz) dried porcini mushrooms
1.5 kg (3 lb 5 oz) chicken pieces
30 g (1 oz/¼ cup) seasoned plain (all-purpose) flour
2 tablespoons oil
1 large onion, chopped
2 garlic cloves, crushed
60 ml (2 fl oz/¼ cup) chicken stock
80 ml (2½ fl oz/⅓ cup) dry white wine
400 g (14 oz) tin whole peeled tomatoes
1 tablespoon balsamic vinegar
3 thyme sprigs
1 bay leaf
300 g (10½ oz) field mushrooms, thickly sliced
thyme leaves, extra, to garnish

Preheat the oven to 180°C (350°F/Gas 4). Put the porcini mushrooms in a bowl and cover with 60 ml (2 fl oz/¼ cup) boiling water. Leave for 5 minutes, or until the mushrooms are rehydrated.

Lightly toss the chicken in the seasoned flour to coat, and shake off any excess.

Heat the oil in a flameproof casserole dish, and cook the chicken over medium heat in batches until well browned all over. Set aside. Add the onion and garlic to the casserole dish, and cook for 3–5 minutes, or until the onion softens. Stir in the chicken stock.

Return the chicken to the dish with the porcini mushrooms (and any remaining liquid), wine, tomatoes, vinegar, thyme sprigs and bay leaf. Cover and bake for 30 minutes.

After 30 minutes, remove the lid and add the field mushrooms. Return to the oven and cook, uncovered, for 15–20 minutes, or until the sauce thickens slightly. Garnish with thyme leaves and serve with a salad.

Tagine of lamb with quince and lemon

preparation 25 minutes
cooking 2 hours 10 minutes
serves 4

1.5 kg (3 lb 5 oz) boned shoulder of lamb, cut into
12 even pieces
1 onion, finely chopped
2 garlic cloves, crushed
1 cinnamon stick
1 teaspoon ground ginger
½ teaspoon saffron threads
1 large quince, peeled, seeded and cut into 12 pieces
1 teaspoon ground cinnamon
90 g (3 oz/¼ cup) honey
½ preserved lemon (see Note)
1 handful chopped flat-leaf (Italian) parsley, to garnish

Trim the lamb of excess fat and place in a large saucepan. Add the onion, garlic, cinnamon stick, ginger and saffron, and enough cold water to cover. Slowly bring to the boil, stirring occasionally. Reduce the heat, cover and simmer for 45 minutes. Transfer the meat to a large casserole dish and set aside.

Add the quince, ground cinnamon and honey to the cooking liquid, and simmer for 15 minutes, or until the quince is tender. Discard the cinnamon stick; remove the quince and add to the meat, reserving the liquid.

Preheat the oven to 180°C (350°F/Gas 4). Boil the cooking liquid for 30 minutes, or until reduced by half, then pour over the meat and quince. Remove and discard the flesh from the lemon. Slice the zest thinly, then add to the meat. Cover and bake for 40 minutes, or until the meat is tender. Sprinkle with parsley and serve with couscous.

Notes *Preserved lemons are available from specialty stores. As you work, place the peeled quince in water with a little lemon juice to prevent discolouring.*

Lightly toss the chicken pieces in the flour and shake off any excess.

Remove and discard the flesh from the preserved lemon and thinly slice the zest.

Bottom: Tagine of lamb with quince and lemon. Top: Chicken and mushroom casserole.

Seafood casserole with feta and olives

preparation 20 minutes
cooking 35 minutes
serves 4

500 g (1 lb 2 oz) fresh mussels
2 tablespoons olive oil
1 large onion, sliced
2 x 400 g (14 oz) tins chopped tomatoes
2 lemon zest strips
1 tablespoon chopped lemon thyme
80 ml (2½ fl oz/⅓ cup) dry vermouth or white wine
1 teaspoon sugar
12 raw king prawns (shrimp), peeled and deveined,
leaving the tails intact
750 g (1 lb 10 oz) firm white fish fillets, cut into
bite-sized pieces
12 black olives
125 g (4½ oz) feta cheese, cubed

Discard any broken mussels, or open ones that don't close when tapped on the work surface. Scrub the rest of the mussels and remove the hairy beards. Place the mussels in a saucepan of simmering water. As soon as the shells open, place the mussels in a bowl of cold water, discarding any unopened ones. Open them up and leave the mussels on their half shells, discarding the other half.

Preheat the oven to 180°C (350°F/Gas 4). Heat the oil in a large heavy-based saucepan and cook the onion over low heat for 5 minutes, or until soft but not brown. Add the tomato, lemon zest, lemon thyme, vermouth and sugar. Bring to the boil, and season to taste. Reduce the heat, cover and simmer for 10 minutes.

Place all the seafood in a shallow ovenproof dish and cover with the hot sauce. Bake, covered, for 10 minutes. Add the olives and feta, covering the seafood with the sauce. Bake for 10 minutes, or until heated through. Serve immediately.

Scrub the mussels, remove the hairy beards, then place in a saucepan of simmering water.

Fish and lemongrass casserole

preparation 15 minutes
cooking 45 minutes
serves 4

4 fish cutlets (200 g/7 oz each)
seasoned plain (all-purpose) flour
2–3 tablespoons peanut oil
2 onions, sliced
2 lemongrass stems (white part only), finely chopped
4 makrut (kaffir lime) leaves, shredded
1 teaspoon ground cumin
1 teaspoon ground coriander
1 teaspoon finely chopped fresh red chilli
185 ml (6 fl oz/¾ cup) chicken stock
375 ml (13 fl oz/1½ cups) coconut milk
1 large handful coriander (cilantro) leaves, chopped, plus extra
leaves to garnish
2 teaspoons fish sauce
lime wedges, to serve

Preheat the oven to 180°C (350°F/Gas 4). Toss the fish lightly in the flour, and gently shake off excess. Heat half the oil in a large heavy-based frying pan and cook fish over medium heat until lightly browned on both sides. Transfer to a shallow ovenproof dish.

Heat the remaining oil in the frying pan. Cook the onion and lemongrass, stirring, for 5 minutes, or until the onion softens. Add the makrut leaves, ground spices and chilli, and stir for 2 minutes, or until fragrant.

Add the stock and coconut milk to the onion mixture, and bring to the boil. Pour over the fish, then cover and bake for 30 minutes, or until the fish is tender.

Transfer the fish to a serving plate. Stir the chopped coriander and the fish sauce into the remaining sauce, and season to taste with salt and freshly ground black pepper. Pour the sauce over the fish to serve. Garnish with extra coriander leaves and serve with lime wedges.

Finely chop the white part of the lemongrass stems, and shred the makrut leaves.

Bottom: Fish and lemongrass casserole. Top: Seafood casserole with feta and olives.

Duck with juniper berries

preparation 35 minutes
cooking 2 hours
serves 4

1.8 kg (4 lb) duck
oil, for cooking
1 granny smith apple, peeled and thinly sliced
1 leek, white part only, cut into large chunks
½ small red cabbage, shredded
2 bay leaves
2 thyme sprigs
6 juniper berries, lightly crushed
¼ teaspoon black peppercorns
375 ml (13 fl oz/1½ cups) chicken stock
250 ml (9 fl oz/1 cup) orange juice
50 g (2 oz) butter, chopped
2 tablespoons soft brown sugar
80 ml (2½ fl oz/⅓ cup) cider vinegar
1½ teaspoons cornflour (cornstarch)
chervil sprigs, to serve

Preheat the oven to 180°C (350°F/Gas 4). Cut the duck in half by cutting down both sides of the backbone and through the breastbone. Discard the backbone. Cut each duck half into four portions, removing any fat. Brown the duck portions in a lightly oiled, heavy-based frying pan over medium heat; remove the duck and set aside.

Drain the frying pan of all but 1 tablespoon of fat, reserving the excess. Cook the apple until golden all over, then remove from the pan and set aside. Add 1 tablespoon of the fat to the pan and lightly brown the leek.

Add the cabbage, bay leaves, thyme sprigs, juniper berries and peppercorns, and cook, stirring, for 10 minutes, or until the cabbage softens. Transfer to a large flameproof casserole dish. Add the stock and orange juice and bring to the boil. Add the duck, pressing gently into the liquid, then cover and bake for 1½ hours.

Remove the duck and keep warm. Drain the liquid into a saucepan. Simmer for 5 minutes, or until reduced to 250 ml (9 fl oz/1 cup). Stir in the butter, sugar and vinegar. Blend the cornflour with 1 tablespoon water and stir into the mixture until it boils and thickens.

Stir the apple and half the sauce into the cabbage mixture, and season to taste. Spoon onto a serving plate, top with the duck, drizzle with the remaining sauce and garnish with chervil. Serve immediately.

Remove the backbone and any excess fat from the inside of the duck.

Add the duck portions to the cabbage mixture, pressing them into the liquid.

Beef carbonnade

preparation 15 minutes
cooking 3 hours 25 minutes
serves 4

1 leek, green part only
1 bay leaf
1 thyme sprig
1 celery leaf sprig
4 parsley sprigs
40 g (1½ oz) butter
1 tablespoon oil
1 kg (2 lb 4 oz) chuck or stewing steak, cubed
2 onions, sliced
2 garlic cloves, crushed
2 tablespoons plain (all-purpose) flour
375 ml (13 fl oz/1½ cups) brown ale or stout
1 long baguette
2 teaspoons French mustard
2 teaspoons butter, extra, softened

To make a bouquet garni, wrap the green part of the leek around the bay leaf, thyme, celery leaf and parsley sprigs, then tie up with string. Leave a long tail for easy removal.

Preheat the oven to 180°C (350°F/Gas 4). Heat the butter and oil in a large saucepan, and cook the steak in batches for 3–4 minutes, or until browned. Remove from the pan. Reduce the heat and cook the onion and garlic for 4 minutes, or until soft. Sprinkle in the flour, stir, then cook for 1 minute. Combine the ale with 375 ml (12 fl oz/1½ cups) water, and pour into the pan. Stir well, scraping the pan to incorporate any ingredients that are stuck to the base. Bring to the boil and return the meat to the pan. Add the bouquet garni and return to the boil. Transfer to a 2.5 litre (87 fl oz/10 cup) casserole dish, cover with foil and bake for 2½ hours.

Cut the bread into 2 cm (¾ inch) slices and spread with the combined mustard and extra butter. Remove the dish from the oven, take out the bouquet garni and skim off the fat. Top the casserole with bread slices, mustard side up, and press gently to soak up the juices. Return to the oven and cook, uncovered, for 30–40 minutes, until the bread toasts.

Braised oxtail casserole

preparation 15 minutes
cooking 2 hours 20 minutes
serves 6

60 ml (2 fl oz/¼ cup) oil
16 small pieces oxtail, about 1.5 kg (3 lb 5 oz)
6 baby potatoes, halved
1 large onion, chopped
2 carrots, chopped
250 g (9 oz) button mushrooms
2 tablespoons plain (all-purpose) flour
750 ml (26 fl oz/3 cups) beef stock
1 teaspoon dried marjoram leaves
2 tablespoons worcestershire sauce

Preheat the oven to 180°C (350°F/Gas 4). Heat 2 tablespoons of the oil in a saucepan over medium–high heat. Cook the oxtail quickly in small batches and until well browned. Place in a deep casserole dish and add the potato.

Heat the remaining oil in the pan. Cook the onion and carrot, stirring, over medium heat for 5 minutes. Transfer to the casserole dish. Add the mushrooms to the pan, and cook, stirring, for 5 minutes. Stir in the flour. Reduce the heat to low, and stir for 2 minutes.

Add the stock gradually, stirring until the liquid boils and thickens. Add the marjoram and worcestershire sauce. Pour into the casserole dish. Bake, covered, for 1½ hours. Stir, then bake, uncovered, for a further 30 minutes. Sprinkle with freshly ground black pepper and serve immediately.

Leave a long tail of string on the bouquet garni for easy removal.

Cook the oxtail pieces in small batches in the hot oil until browned.

Bottom: Braised oxtail casserole. Top: Beef carbonnade.

Eggplant parmigiana

preparation 30 minutes
cooking 1 hour 10 minutes
serves 6–8

60 ml (2 fl oz/¼ cup) olive oil
1 onion, diced
2 garlic cloves, crushed
1.25 kg (2 lb 12 oz) tomatoes, peeled and chopped (see Note)
oil, for shallow-frying
1 kg (2 lb 4 oz) eggplants (aubergines), very thinly sliced
250 g (9 oz) bocconcini (fresh baby mozzarella cheese), sliced
185 g (6½ oz/1½ cups) finely grated cheddar cheese
2 very large handfuls basil leaves, torn
50 g (2 oz/½ cup) grated parmesan cheese

Heat the oil in a large frying pan over medium heat. Cook the onion until soft. Add the garlic and cook for 1 minute. Add the tomato and simmer for 15 minutes. Season with salt. Preheat the oven to 200°C (400°F/Gas 6).

Shallow-fry the eggplant in small batches for 3–4 minutes, or until golden brown. Drain on paper towels.

Place one-third of the eggplant slices in a 1.75 litre (61 fl oz/7 cup) ovenproof dish. Top with half the bocconcini and half the cheddar. Repeat the layers, finishing with a good layer of the eggplant.

Pour over the tomato mixture. Scatter with torn basil leaves, then the parmesan. Bake for 40 minutes and serve.

Variation *If you prefer not to fry the eggplant, brush it lightly with oil and brown lightly under a hot grill.*

Note *To peel the tomatoes, score a cross in the base. Put in a heatproof bowl and cover with boiling water. Leave for 30 seconds, then transfer to cold water and peel off the skin.*

Lamb shanks with garlic

preparation 20 minutes
cooking 1 hour 30 minutes
serves 6

6 large lamb shanks
1 tablespoon oil
2 leeks, white part only, sliced
1 rosemary sprig
250 ml (9 fl oz/1 cup) dry white wine
1 garlic bulb
oil, for brushing

Preheat the oven to 180°C (350°F/Gas 4). Season the lamb shanks. Heat the oil in a frying pan over medium–high heat. Cook the lamb shanks briefly in batches until well browned. Drain on paper towels, then transfer the shanks to a casserole dish.

Cook the leek in the frying pan over medium–high heat, stirring, until tender. Add to the lamb shanks with the rosemary and wine.

Cut the garlic horizontally through the centre. Brush the cut surfaces with a little oil. Place cut side up in the casserole dish, but not covered by liquid. Bake, covered, for 1 hour. Remove the lid and bake for a further 15 minutes. Discard the rosemary. Serve with steamed vegetables and crusty bread on which to spread the roasted garlic.

Shallow-fry the eggplant in batches, then drain on paper towels.

Place the cut garlic bulb on top of the lamb shanks and leek.

Bottom: Lamb shanks with garlic. Top: Eggplant parmigiana.

Beef, potato and capsicum casserole

preparation 35 minutes
cooking 2 hours 20 minutes
serves 4–6

300 g (10½ oz) French shallots (eschalots)
2 tablespoons olive oil
1 kg (2 lb 4 oz) gravy beef, cut into 4 cm (1½ inch) cubes
4 garlic cloves, crushed
3 teaspoons paprika
1 teaspoon fennel seeds
½ teaspoon ground cumin
1 tablespoon plain (all-purpose) flour
125 ml (4 fl oz/½ cup) red wine
2 tablespoons brandy
½ teaspoon dried thyme
½ teaspoon dried oregano
1 bay leaf
375 ml (13 fl oz/1½ cups) beef stock
1 tablespoon honey
400 g (14 oz) potatoes, cut into large chunks
2 red capsicums (peppers), chopped
125 g (4½ oz/½ cup) sour cream, to serve
snipped chives, to serve

Preheat the oven to 180°C (350°F/Gas 4). Place the shallots in a bowl, cover with boiling water and leave for 30 seconds. Drain and peel.

Heat the oil in a large heavy-based saucepan, then brown the meat in batches over medium–high heat, and transfer to a large casserole dish.

Add the shallots to the saucepan and cook over medium heat until soft and golden. Add the garlic, paprika, fennel seeds and cumin; cook until fragrant.

Add the flour, cook for 30 seconds, then remove from the heat. Stir in the red wine and brandy. Return to the heat and add the thyme, oregano, bay leaf and stock. Stir until the mixture bubbles, then add to the meat.

Cover and bake for 1½ hours, then add the honey, potato and capsicum. Cook, uncovered, for 30 minutes, or until the potato is tender. Season to taste. Serve with a dollop of sour cream and a sprinkling of chives.

Drain the blanched shallots, then carefully peel off the skin.

Brown the meat in batches in the hot oil over medium–high heat.

Tomato chicken casserole

preparation 45 minutes
cooking 1 hour 20 minutes
serves 4

1.5 kg (3 lb 5 oz) chicken pieces
40 g (1½ oz) butter
1 tablespoon oil
1 large onion, chopped
2 garlic cloves, chopped
1 small green capsicum (pepper), chopped
150 g (5½ oz) mushrooms, thickly sliced
1 tablespoon plain (all-purpose) flour
250 ml (9 fl oz/1 cup) dry white wine
1 tablespoon white wine vinegar
4 tomatoes, peeled, seeded and chopped
2 tablespoons tomato paste (concentrated purée)
90 g (3 oz/½ cup) small black olives
2 large handfuls flat-leaf (Italian) parsley, chopped

Preheat the oven to 180°C (350°F/Gas 4). Remove the excess fat from the chicken pieces and pat dry with paper towels. Heat 2 teaspoons of the butter and 2 teaspoons of the oil in a large flameproof casserole dish. Cook half the chicken over high heat until browned all over, then set aside. Heat another 2 teaspoons of the butter and the remaining oil, and cook the remaining chicken. Set aside.

Heat the remaining butter in the casserole dish and cook the onion and garlic for 2–3 minutes over medium–high heat. Add the capsicum and mushroom, and cook, stirring, for 3 minutes. Stir in the flour and cook for 1 minute. Add the wine, vinegar, tomato and tomato paste, and cook, stirring, for 2 minutes, or until slightly thickened.

Return the chicken to the casserole dish and make sure it is covered by the tomato and onion mixture. Place in the oven and cook, covered, for 1 hour, or until the chicken is tender. Stir in the olives and parsley. Season with salt and freshly cracked black pepper, and serve with pasta.

Mexican chicken casserole

preparation 15 minutes
cooking 1 hour
serves 4

165 g (6 oz/¾ cup) short-grain rice
300 g (10½ oz) tin red kidney beans, drained and rinsed
3½ tablespoons chopped coriander (cilantro) leaves
1 tablespoon oil
600 g (1 lb 5 oz) boneless, skinless chicken thighs
2 x 200 g (7 oz) jars spicy taco sauce
250 g (9 oz/2 cups) grated cheddar cheese
125 g (4½ oz/½ cup) sour cream

Preheat the oven to 180°C (350°F/Gas 4). Lightly grease a 7 cm (2¾ inch) deep, 21 cm (8¼ inch) round casserole dish.

Bring a large saucepan of water to the boil, add the rice and cook for 10–12 minutes, stirring occasionally. Drain well and set aside.

In the casserole dish, combine the kidney beans and 1½ tablespoons of the coriander, then add the rice and toss together. Lightly press the mixture so the beans are mixed into the rice and the mixture is flat.

Heat the oil in a large frying pan over medium–high heat. Sauté the chicken thighs for 3 minutes, then turn over. Add the spicy taco sauce, and cook for a further 3 minutes.

To assemble, spread half the cheese over the rice. Arrange the chicken and sauce on top in a star shape, sprinkle with 1½ tablespoons of the coriander, then sprinkle with the remaining cheese. Cover with foil.

Bake for 35–40 minutes, or until the mixture is bubbling and the cheese is melted and slightly browned—remove the foil for the last 5 minutes of cooking. Cut into four servings with a knife and scoop out carefully, keeping the layers intact. Serve sprinkled with the remaining coriander and a dollop of the sour cream.

Score a cross in the base of the tomatoes, soak in boiling water for 30 seconds, then drain and peel.

Arrange the chicken thighs and sauce on top of the cheese in a star shape.

Bottom: Mexican chicken casserole. Top: Tomato chicken casserole.

Fish and macaroni casserole

preparation 20 minutes
cooking 55 minutes
serves 4

155 g (5½ oz/1 cup) macaroni
30 g (1 oz) butter
1 onion, chopped
500 g (1 lb 2 oz) white fish fillets, cut into 2 cm (¾ inch) cubes (see Note)
1 tablespoon chopped thyme
100 g (3½ oz) button mushrooms, sliced
½ teaspoon hot English mustard
1 tablespoon plain (all-purpose) flour
250 ml (9 fl oz/1 cup) chicken stock
125 ml (4 fl oz/½ cup) pouring (whipping) cream
125 g (4½ oz/½ cup) sour cream
80 g (3 oz/1 cup) fresh breadcrumbs
125 g (4½ oz/1 cup) grated cheddar cheese
50 g (2 oz/½ cup) grated parmesan cheese
2 tablespoons chopped flat-leaf (Italian) parsley

Preheat the oven to 180°C (350°F/Gas 4). Cook the macaroni in a large saucepan of rapidly boiling water until it is just al dente. Drain and set aside.

Heat the butter in a heavy-based saucepan over medium heat. Cook the onion for 3 minutes, or until golden. Add the fish, thyme and mushrooms. Cook for 5 minutes, or until the fish is tender. Remove from the pan and keep warm.

Stir the mustard and flour into the pan. Add the stock and cream gradually, stirring over medium heat for 3 minutes, or until sauce boils and thickens. Boil for 1 minute, then remove from heat. Stir in sour cream.

Transfer the mixture to a large bowl, and stir in the macaroni, and fish and mushroom mixture. Spoon into a large ovenproof dish. Combine the breadcrumbs, cheeses and parsley. Sprinkle over the macaroni mixture. Bake for 30 minutes, or until golden, and serve.

Note If you prefer, you can use a drained tin of tuna instead of the fresh fish.

Add the fish, thyme and mushrooms to the pan, and cook.

Chicken and cauliflower casserole

preparation 20 minutes
cooking 1 hour
serves 6

30 g (1 oz) butter
4 boneless, skinless chicken breasts, cut into 3 cm (1¼ inch) cubes
6 spring onions (scallions), sliced
2 garlic cloves, crushed
2 tablespoons plain (all-purpose) flour
375 ml (13 fl oz/1½ cups) chicken stock
2 teaspoons dijon mustard
280 g (10 oz) cauliflower, cut into florets
1 kg (2 lb 4 oz) potatoes, quartered
2 tablespoons full-cream (whole) milk
60 g (2 oz) butter, extra
2 eggs
30 g (1 oz/⅓ cup) flaked almonds, toasted

Preheat the oven to 180°C (350°F/Gas 4). Heat half the butter in a large frying pan and cook the chicken in batches until browned and cooked through. Remove from the pan. In the same pan, melt the remaining butter and cook the spring onion and garlic for 2 minutes. Stir in the flour and mix well. Pour in the stock and cook, stirring, until the mixture boils and thickens. Add the mustard and then stir in the chicken. Season well with salt and pepper.

Meanwhile, steam or microwave the cauliflower until just tender, taking care not to overcook it. Refresh the cauliflower in iced water and drain well.

Boil the potato in salted water for 15–20 minutes, or until tender. Drain and mash well with the milk, extra butter and eggs. Put the cauliflower in a 2.5 litre (87 fl oz/10 cup) ovenproof dish and pour in the chicken mixture. Pipe or spoon the mashed potato over the top. Sprinkle with the almonds and bake for 25 minutes, or until the top is browned and cooked through. Serve straight from the dish.

Use a large sharp knife to cut the chicken breasts into cubes.

Bottom: Chicken and cauliflower casserole. Top: Fish and macaroni casserole.

Lamb and bean casserole

preparation 25 minutes + overnight soaking
cooking 2 hours 15 minutes
serves 6

300 g (10½ oz/1½ cups) borlotti (cranberry) beans or
red kidney beans
1 kg (2 lb 4 oz) boned leg of lamb
1½ tablespoons olive oil
2 bacon slices, rind removed, chopped
1 large onion, chopped
2 garlic cloves, crushed
1 large carrot, chopped
500 ml (17 fl oz/2 cups) dry red wine
1 tablespoon tomato paste (concentrated purée)
375 ml (13 fl oz/1½ cups) beef stock
2 large rosemary sprigs
2 thyme sprigs
small thyme sprigs, extra, to garnish

Put the beans in a large bowl, cover with cold water and
soak overnight.

Drain the beans and rinse under cold water. Preheat the
oven to 160°C (315°F/Gas 2–3). Trim any excess fat from the
lamb and cut the lamb into 3 cm (1¼ inch) pieces.

Heat 1 tablespoon of the oil in a large flameproof casserole
dish. Add half the meat and toss over medium–high heat
for 2 minutes, or until browned. Remove from the dish
and repeat with the remaining lamb. Heat the remaining
olive oil in the dish and add the bacon and onion. Cook
over medium heat for 3 minutes, or until the onion is
translucent. Add the garlic and carrot, and cook for
1 minute, or until aromatic.

Return the meat and any juices to the dish, increase
the heat to high and add the wine. Bring to the boil and
cook for 2 minutes. Add the beans, tomato paste, stock,
rosemary and thyme sprigs, return to the boil, then cover,
place in the oven and cook for 2 hours, or until the meat
is tender. Stir occasionally during cooking. Skim off any
excess fat, remove the sprigs of herbs. Season and garnish
with extra thyme sprigs to serve.

Remove any excess fat from the lamb, then cut it
into large pieces.

Tuna and white bean casserole

preparation 40 minutes + overnight soaking
cooking 3 hours
serves 6

400 g (14 oz/2 cups) dried cannellini beans
60 ml (2 fl oz/¼ cup) olive oil
2 red onions, chopped
2 garlic cloves, crushed
1 teaspoon ground coriander
1 teaspoon finely grated lemon zest
2 teaspoons chopped thyme
500 ml (17 fl oz/2 cups) dry white wine
500 ml (17 fl oz/2 cups) fish stock
480 g (1 lb 1 oz) tin tuna in brine, drained
1 bunch of basil, leaves only
4 large ripe tomatoes, cut into 1 cm (½ inch) slices

topping
40 g (1½ oz/½ cup) fresh breadcrumbs
1 garlic clove, crushed
30 g (1 oz/¾ cup) finely chopped flat-leaf (Italian) parsley
30 g (1 oz) butter, melted

Put the beans in a large bowl, cover with cold water and
soak overnight.

Drain the beans and rinse under cold water. Heat the oil
in a large, heavy-based saucepan. Add the onion, garlic,
coriander, lemon zest and thyme. Cook over medium heat
for 10–15 minutes, or until the onion is softened. Add the
beans and cook for 10 minutes. Add the wine and stock.
Cover and cook over low heat for 2 hours, until the beans
are tender but not mashed.

Preheat the oven to 210°C (415°F/Gas 6–7). Transfer the
bean mixture to a large casserole dish. Top with the tuna
and basil leaves. Arrange the tomato slices over the basil.

To make the topping, combine the breadcrumbs, garlic and
parsley. Sprinkle over the tomato. Drizzle with the butter.
Bake for 30 minutes, or until golden and serve.

Arrange the tuna over the bean mixture in the
casserole dish.

Bottom: Tuna and white bean casserole. Top: Lamb and bean casserole.

Beef casserole with caraway dumplings

preparation 1 hour
cooking 1 hour 30 minutes
serves 6

1.5 kg (3 lb 5 oz) round or topside steak, trimmed and
cut into 3 cm (1¼ inch) cubes
60 g (2 oz/½ cup) plain (all-purpose) flour
¼ teaspoon freshly ground black pepper
80 ml (2½ fl oz/⅓ cup) olive oil
1 garlic clove, crushed
2 onions, sliced
1 teaspoon sweet paprika
½ teaspoon ground cinnamon
80 ml (2½ fl oz/⅓ cup) red wine
125 ml (4 fl oz/½ cup) beef stock
½ teaspoon mixed dried herbs
160 g (5½ oz/⅔ cup) tomato pasta sauce
3 large red capsicums (peppers)

dumplings
185 g (6½ oz/1½ cups) self-raising flour
65 g (2¼ oz) butter
125 ml (4 fl oz/½ cup) full-cream (whole) milk
1 teaspoon caraway seeds
1 tablespoon full-cream (whole) milk, extra

Preheat the oven to 180°C (350°F/Gas 4). Toss the meat lightly in the combined flour and pepper, and shake off any excess.

Heat 2 tablespoons of the oil in a heavy-based saucepan. Cook the meat in batches over medium–high heat until browned. Drain on paper towels.

Heat the remaining oil in the saucepan. Cook the garlic and onion over medium heat, stirring, for 2 minutes, or until soft. Return the meat to the pan with the spices, wine, stock, mixed herbs and pasta sauce. Bring to the boil, then remove from the heat and transfer to a deep casserole dish. Bake, covered, for 45 minutes. Remove from the oven and uncover. Increase the oven to 240°C (475°F/Gas 8).

Cut the capsicums into large flat pieces, removing the seeds and membrane. Place, skin side up, under a hot grill (broiler) until blackened. Leave in a plastic bag until cool, then peel away the skin. Cut into 2 cm (¾ inch) wide strips. Arrange over the meat.

To make the dumplings, process the flour and butter in a food processor for 10 seconds, or until fine and crumbly. Add all the milk and process for 10 seconds, until a soft dough is formed. Turn out onto a floured surface. Add the caraway seeds and knead for 1 minute until smooth. Press out to a 1 cm (½ inch) thick round. Cut 4 cm (1½ inch) rounds using a cutter. Top the casserole with the dumplings and brush with milk. Return to the oven, uncovered, for 15 minutes, or until the dumplings are golden and puffed.

Carefully peel the blackened skin from the grilled capsicum pieces.

After pressing the dough out flat, cut into rounds with a fluted cutter.

Lamb shanks in tomato sauce on polenta

preparation 10 minutes
cooking 2 hours 30 minutes
serves 4

2 tablespoons olive oil
1 large red onion, sliced
4 French-trimmed lamb shanks (about 250 g/9 oz each)
(see Note)
2 garlic cloves, crushed
400 g (14 oz) tin chopped tomatoes
125 ml (4 fl oz/½ cup) red wine
2 teaspoons chopped rosemary
150 g (5½ oz/1 cup) instant polenta
50 g (1¾ oz) butter
50 g (2 oz/½ cup) grated parmesan cheese
rosemary, extra, to garnish

Preheat the oven to 160°C (315°F/Gas 2–3). Heat the oil in a 4 litre (140 fl oz/16 cup) flameproof casserole dish over medium heat and sauté the onion for 3–4 minutes, or until softening and becoming transparent. Add the lamb shanks and cook for 2–3 minutes, or until lightly browned. Add the garlic, tomato and wine, then bring to the boil and cook for 3–4 minutes. Stir in the rosemary. Season with ¼ teaspoon each of salt and pepper.

Cover and bake for 2 hours. Remove the lid, return to the oven and simmer for a further 15 minutes, or until the lamb just starts to fall off the bone. Check periodically that the sauce is not too dry, adding water if needed.

About 20 minutes before serving, bring 1 litre (35 fl oz/ 4 cups) water to the boil in a saucepan. Add the polenta in a thin stream, whisking continuously, then reduce the heat to very low. Simmer for 8–10 minutes, or until thick and coming away from the side of pan. Stir in the butter and parmesan. To serve, spoon the polenta onto serving plates, top with the shanks and tomato sauce. Top with rosemary.

Note *French-trimmed lamb shanks are lamb shanks with the meat scraped back to make a neat lamb 'drumstick'.*

Add the polenta to the water in a very thin stream, whisking continuously.

Middle Eastern potato casserole

preparation 10 minutes
cooking 30 minutes
serves 4

¼ teaspoon saffron threads
1 kg (2 lb 4 oz) potatoes, cut into large cubes
1 teaspoon olive oil
1 small onion, sliced
½ teaspoon ground turmeric
½ teaspoon ground coriander
250 ml (9 fl oz/1 cup) vegetable stock
1 garlic clove, crushed
30 g (1 oz/¼ cup) raisins
1 teaspoon chopped parsley
1 teaspoon chopped coriander (cilantro) leaves

Put the saffron to soak in 1 tablespoon hot water. Place the potato in a saucepan of cold, salted water. Bring to the boil and cook for 12 minutes, or until tender but still firm. Drain and set aside.

Heat the oil in a separate saucepan, add the onion, turmeric and ground coriander and cook over low heat for 5 minutes, or until the onion is soft.

Add the potato, vegetable stock and garlic. Bring to the boil, then reduce the heat and simmer for 10 minutes.

Add the saffron with its soaking water and the raisins, and cook for 10 minutes, or until the potato is soft and the sauce has reduced and thickened. Stir in the parsley and coriander. Delicious with couscous.

Soak the saffron threads in 1 tablespoon hot water while you cook the potatoes.

Bottom: Middle Eastern potato casserole. Top: Lamb shanks in tomato sauce on polenta.

Creamy fish casserole

preparation 10 minutes
cooking 1 hour
serves 4

2 large potatoes, chopped
60 ml (2 fl oz/¼ cup) full-cream (whole) milk or cream
1 egg
60 g (2¼ oz) butter
60 g (2 oz/½ cup) grated cheddar cheese
800 g (1 lb 12 oz) white fish fillets, cut into large chunks (see Note)
375 ml (13 fl oz/1½ cups) full-cream (whole) milk, extra
1 onion, finely chopped
1 garlic clove, crushed
2 tablespoons plain (all-purpose) flour
2 tablespoons lemon juice
2 teaspoons finely grated lemon zest
1 tablespoon chopped dill

Preheat the oven to 180°C (350°F/Gas 4). Boil or steam the potato for 8 minutes, or until tender. Drain and mash with the milk or cream, egg and half the butter. Mix in half the cheese, then set aside.

Put the fish in a shallow frying pan and cover with the extra milk. Bring to the boil, then reduce the heat and simmer for 2–3 minutes, or until the fish flakes easily. Drain the fish well, reserving the milk, and place in a 1.5 litre (52 fl oz/6 cup) ovenproof dish.

Melt the remaining butter over medium heat in a saucepan and cook the onion and garlic for 2 minutes. Stir in the flour and cook for 1 minute, or until golden. Remove from the heat and gradually stir in the reserved milk. Return to the heat and stir constantly until the sauce boils and thickens. Reduce the heat and simmer for 2 minutes. Add the lemon juice, lemon zest and dill, and season. Mix with the fish, cover with the potato and sprinkle with the remaining cheese. Bake for 35 minutes, or until golden.

Note You could use ling, perch, hake or snapper.

Lancashire hotpot

preparation 20 minutes
cooking 2 hours
serves 8

8 lamb forequarter chops
4 lamb kidneys
30 g (1 oz/¼ cup) plain (all-purpose) flour
50 g (1¾ oz) butter
4 potatoes, thinly sliced
2 large brown onions, sliced
1 large carrot, chopped
435 ml (15 fl oz/1¾ cups) beef or vegetable stock
2 teaspoons chopped thyme
1 bay leaf
melted butter, extra

Preheat the oven to 160°C (315°F/Gas 2–3), and grease a large casserole dish. Trim the chops of excess fat and sinew, then remove and discard the cores from the kidneys. Cut kidneys into quarters. Toss the chops and kidneys in the flour, shaking off and reserving the excess. Heat the butter in a frying pan and brown the chops quickly on both sides. Remove the chops from the pan and brown the kidneys.

Layer half the potato slices in the base of the casserole dish and top with the chops and the kidneys.

Add the onion and carrot to the pan, and cook until the carrot begins to brown. Layer on top of the chops and kidneys. Sprinkle the reserved flour over the base of the pan and fry, stirring, until dark brown. Gradually pour in the stock and bring to the boil, stirring. Season well, and add the thyme and bay leaf. Reduce the heat and simmer for 10 minutes. Pour into the casserole dish.

Layer the remaining potato over the meat and vegetables. Cover and bake for 1¼ hours. Increase the oven temperature to 180°C (350°F/Gas 4), brush the potato with the extra melted butter and cook, uncovered, for 20 minutes, or until the potato is brown. Season and serve.

Cook the fish in the simmering milk until it flakes easily when tested.

Remove the cores from the kidneys and then cut the kidneys into quarters.

Bottom: Lancashire hotpot. Top: Creamy fish casserole.

Pork sausage and soya bean casserole

preparation 25 minutes + overnight soaking
cooking 4 hours
serves 4

325 g (11½ oz/1¾ cups) dried soya beans
8 thin pork sausages
2 tablespoons oil
1 red onion, chopped
4 garlic cloves, chopped
1 large carrot, diced
1 celery stalk, diced
2 x 400 g (14 oz) tins chopped tomatoes
1 tablespoon tomato paste (concentrated purée)
250 ml (9 fl oz/1 cup) white wine
2 thyme sprigs
1 teaspoon dried oregano
1 tablespoon oregano, chopped
thyme sprigs, extra, to garnish

Put the beans in a large bowl, cover with cold water and soak overnight.

Drain the beans and rinse under cold water. Place in a large saucepan with enough fresh water to cover. Bring to the boil, then reduce the heat and slowly simmer for 1¼–2 hours—keep the beans covered with water during cooking; drain.

Meanwhile prick the sausages all over with a fork. Cook in a frying pan, turning, for 10 minutes, or until browned. Drain on paper towels.

Heat the oil in a 3.5 litre (122 fl oz/14 cup) flameproof casserole dish over medium heat. Cook the onion and garlic for 3–5 minutes, or until softened. Add the carrot and celery.

Cook, stirring, for 5 minutes. Stir in the tomato, tomato paste, wine, thyme sprigs and dried oregano, and bring to the boil. Reduce the heat and simmer, stirring often, for 10 minutes, or until reduced and thickened slightly.

Preheat the oven to 160°C (315°F/Gas 2–3). Add the sausages, beans and 250 ml (9 fl oz/1 cup) water to the casserole dish. Bake, covered, for 2 hours. Stir occasionally, adding more water to keep the beans covered.

Return the casserole dish to the stove, skim off any fat, then reduce the liquid until thickened slightly. Remove the thyme and stir in the chopped oregano. Garnish with extra thyme sprigs and serve.

Drain the soaked and cooked soya beans well in a colander.

Cook the sausages in a frying pan, turning frequently, until brown all over.

stews

Spanish meat and chickpea stew

preparation 25 minutes + overnight soaking
cooking 2 hours 45 minutes
serves 6–8

220 g (8 oz/1 cup) dried chickpeas
1 kg (2 lb 4 oz) whole chicken, trussed
500 g (1 lb 2 oz) piece lean beef brisket
250 g (9 oz) piece smoke-cured bacon
125 g (4½ oz) tocino, streaky bacon or speck
1 pig's trotter
200 g (7 oz) chorizo
1 onion, studded with 2 cloves
1 bay leaf
1 morcilla blood sausage (optional)
250 g (9 oz) green beans, trimmed and sliced lengthways
250 g (9 oz) green cabbage, cut into sections through the heart
300 g (10½ oz) silverbeet (Swiss chard) leaves, stalks removed
4 small potatoes
2 leeks, white part only, cut into 10 cm (4 inch) lengths
pinch of saffron threads
75 g (2½ oz) dried rice vermicelli

Put the chickpeas in a large bowl, cover with cold water and soak overnight

Drain the chickpeas and rinse under cold water. Tie loosely in a muslin (cheesecloth) bag.

Put 3 litres (105 fl oz/12 cups) cold water in a very large, deep saucepan. Add the chicken, beef, bacon and tocino, and bring to the boil. Add the chickpeas, pig's trotter and chorizo, return to the boil, then add the onion, bay leaf and ½ teaspoon salt. Simmer, partially covered, for 2½ hours.

After 2 hours, bring a saucepan of water to the boil, add the morcilla and gently boil for 5 minutes. Drain and set aside. Tie the green beans loosely in a muslin (cheesecloth) bag. Pour 1 litre (35 fl oz/4 cups) water into a large saucepan and bring to the boil. Add the beans, cabbage, silverbeet,

potatoes, leek and saffron with 1 teaspoon of salt. Return to the boil and simmer for 30 minutes.

Strain the stock from both the meat and vegetable saucepans, and combine them in a large saucepan. Bring to the boil, adjust the seasoning and add the vermicelli. Simmer for 6–7 minutes. Release the chickpeas and pile them in the centre of a large warm platter. Discard the trotter, then slice the meats and sausages. Arrange the meats and sausages in groups around the chickpeas at one end of the platter. Release the beans. Arrange the vegetables in groups around the other end. Spoon a little of the simmering broth (minus the vermicelli) over the meat, then pour the rest (with the vermicelli) into a soup tureen. Serve at once. It is traditional to serve the two dishes together, although the broth is eaten first.

Using a sharp knife, cut the green beans lengthways into long slices.

Add the chickpeas, pig's trotter and chorizo to the saucepan and return to the boil.

Chicken mole

preparation 25 minutes
cooking 1 hour
serves 4

8 chicken drumsticks
plain (all-purpose) flour, for dusting
cooking oil spray
1 large onion, finely chopped
2 garlic cloves, finely chopped
1 teaspoon ground cumin
1 teaspoon Mexican chilli powder
2 teaspoons unsweetened cocoa powder
250 ml (9 fl oz/1 cup) chicken stock
2 x 440 g (15½ oz) tins tomatoes, chopped
slivered almonds, to garnish

Remove and discard the chicken skin. Wipe the chicken with paper towels and lightly dust with flour. Spray a large, deep, non-stick frying pan with oil. Cook the chicken for 8 minutes over high heat, turning until golden brown. Remove and set aside.

Add the onion, garlic, cumin, chilli powder, cocoa, 1 teaspoon salt, ½ teaspoon black pepper and 60 ml (2 fl oz/¼ cup) water to the pan and cook for 5 minutes, or until the onion is softened.

Stir in the stock and tomato. Bring to the boil, add the chicken drumsticks, cover and simmer for 45 minutes, or until tender. Uncover and simmer for 5 minutes, until the mixture is thick. Garnish with the almonds.

Note *This Mexican dish is usually flavoured with a special type of dark chocolate rather than cocoa powder.*

Spicy garlic chicken

preparation 30 minutes
cooking 1 hour
serves 6

1.4 kg (3 lb 2 oz) chicken pieces
1 small bunch coriander (cilantro)
1 tablespoon olive oil
4 garlic cloves, crushed
2 red onions, thinly sliced
1 large red capsicum (pepper), cut into squares
1 teaspoon ground ginger
1 teaspoon chilli powder
1 teaspoon caraway seeds, crushed
1 teaspoon ground turmeric
2 teaspoons ground coriander
2 teaspoons ground cumin
60 g (2 oz/½ cup) raisins
90 g (3 oz/½ cup) black olives
1 teaspoon finely grated lemon zest

Remove any fat and sinew from the chicken (if you prefer, remove the skin as well). Finely chop the coriander, including the roots.

Heat the oil in a large heavy-based saucepan. Add the garlic, onion, capsicum, ginger, chilli powder, caraway seeds, turmeric, ground coriander, cumin and chopped coriander. Cook over medium heat for 10 minutes.

Add the chicken pieces and stir until combined. Add 375 ml (13 fl oz/1½ cups) water and bring to the boil. Reduce the heat and simmer for 45 minutes, or until the chicken is tender and cooked through.

Add the raisins, black olives and lemon zest and simmer for a further 5 minutes before serving.

Variation *You can use a whole chicken for this recipe and cut it into 12 pieces yourself.*

Pull the skin off the chicken drumsticks, then wipe the chicken with paper towels.

Wash the coriander and finely chop the whole bunch, including the roots.

Bottom: Spicy garlic chicken. Top: Chicken mole.

Braised pork with prunes

preparation 15 minutes
cooking 35 minutes
serves 4

4 lean pork loin medallions, about 175 g (6 oz) each
500 ml (17 fl oz/2 cups) chicken stock
2 tablespoons oil
1 large onion, cut into wedges
2 garlic cloves, crushed
1 tablespoon thyme leaves
1 large tomato, peeled, seeded and finely chopped
125 ml (4 fl oz/½ cup) pouring (whipping) cream
16 pitted prunes

Shape the meat into rounds by tying a length of string around the medallions. Tie with a bow for easy removal. Bring the stock to the boil in a medium saucepan. Reduce the heat to a simmer and cook for 5 minutes, or until reduced to 185 ml (6 fl oz/¾ cup).

Heat the oil over high heat in a heavy-based frying pan. Cook the meat for 2 minutes each side to seal, turning once. Drain on paper towels.

Add the onion and garlic to the frying pan, and stir for 2 minutes. Return the meat to the pan with the thyme, tomato and stock, then reduce the heat to low. Cover the pan and bring slowly to simmering point. Simmer for 10 minutes, or until the meat is tender, turning once. Add the cream and prunes, and simmer for a further 5 minutes. Remove the string and serve with greens.

Paprika veal with caraway noodles

preparation 10 minutes
cooking 1 hour 35 minutes
serves 4

60 ml (2 fl oz/¼ cup) oil
1 kg (2 lb 4 oz) veal shoulder, diced
1 large onion, thinly sliced
3 garlic cloves, finely chopped
60 g (2 oz/¼ cup) Hungarian paprika
½ teaspoon caraway seeds
2 x 400 g (14 oz) tins chopped tomatoes, one drained
350 g (12 oz) fresh fettuccine
40 g (1½ oz) butter, softened

Heat half the oil in a large saucepan over medium–high heat, then brown the veal in batches for 3 minutes per batch. Remove the veal from the pan and set aside with any pan juices.

Add the remaining oil to the pan and sauté the onion and garlic over medium heat for 5 minutes, or until softened. Add the paprika and ¼ teaspoon of the caraway seeds, and stir for 30 seconds.

Add all the chopped tomatoes and their liquid plus 125 ml (4 fl oz/½ cup) water. Return the veal to the pan with any juices, increase the heat to high and bring to the boil. Reduce the heat to low, then cover and simmer for 1¼ hours, or until the meat is tender and the sauce has reduced and thickened.

About 15 minutes before the veal is ready, cook the pasta in a large saucepan of rapidly boiling salted water according to the packet instructions until al dente. Drain, then return to the pan. Stir in the butter and the remaining caraway seeds. Serve immediately with the paprika veal.

Shape the pork medallions into rounds by securing a length of string around each one.

Cover and simmer until the meat is tender and the sauce has thickened.

Bottom: Paprika veal with caraway noodles. Top: Braised pork with prunes.

Turkey osso bucco

preparation 25 minutes + thawing
cooking 1 hour 30 minutes
serves 4–6

3 red capsicums (peppers)
2 kg (4 lb 8 oz) turkey hindquarters (legs with thighs), chopped (see Note)
seasoned plain (all-purpose) flour
60 ml (2 fl oz/¼ cup) olive oil
60 g (2 oz) butter
185 ml (6 fl oz/¾ cup) chicken stock
¼ teaspoon dried chilli flakes
4 sage leaves, chopped, or ½ teaspoon dried sage
2 garlic cloves, crushed
1 teaspoon finely grated lemon zest
150 g (5½ oz) sliced pancetta, or thinly sliced bacon
1 rosemary sprig
2 tablespoons chopped flat-leaf (Italian) parsley

Cut the capsicums into large flat pieces, removing the seeds and membrane. Place, skin side up, under a hot grill (broiler) until blackened. Leave in a plastic bag until cool, then peel away the skin. Cut the flesh into thick slices.

Pat the turkey pieces with paper towels to remove excess moisture, then coat well in the seasoned flour, dusting off any excess.

Heat the oil and butter in a large saucepan. Brown the turkey pieces in batches over medium–high heat, then drain the pan of oil.

Pour the chicken stock into the pan and stir well, scraping the base and side of the pan to mix in all the pan juices. Add the chilli flakes, sage, garlic and lemon zest, and cook, stirring, for 1 minute.

Return all the turkey pieces to the pan. Cover with the grilled capsicum slices, then layer the pancetta over the top to completely cover. Add the rosemary sprig, cover the pan and cook over low heat for 1 hour, or until the turkey is succulent, yet not falling off the bone.

Discard the rosemary and transfer the pancetta, capsicum slices and turkey pieces to a serving plate. Cover and keep warm. To thicken the sauce, place it over high heat and simmer for 3–4 minutes. Stir in the parsley, spoon the sauce around the turkey to serve.

Note *Ask your butcher or poulterer to saw the turkey into 1.5– 2 cm (¾ inch) pieces for you.*

Place the grilled capsicum halves in a plastic bag, seal and allow to cool.

Coat the turkey pieces in the seasoned flour, dusting off the excess.

Madrid chicken

preparation 10 minutes
cooking 1 hour
serves 4

1 orange
1 tablespoon olive oil
4 boneless, skinless chicken breasts
2 chorizo sausages (about 200 g/7 oz), cut into
1 cm (½ inch) slices
250 ml (9 fl oz/1 cup) chicken stock
250 g (9 oz/1 cup) bottled tomato pasta sauce
12 kalamata olives
kalamata olives, extra, to garnish
flat-leaf (Italian) parsley, to garnish

Using a vegetable peeler, carefully cut 4 thin strips of orange zest (about 1 x 4 cm/½ x 1½ inches). Remove the peel and pith from the orange, and segment the flesh.

Heat the oil in a saucepan and brown the chicken and chorizo slices, in batches if necessary. (Leave the meat side of the chicken browning for 5 minutes.) Add the stock, tomato sauce and orange zest. Bring to the boil, then reduce the heat and simmer, covered, for 25 minutes.

Remove the lid, turn the chicken over and continue to simmer, uncovered, for about 25 minutes, or until the chicken is tender and the sauce reduced. Season with salt and freshly ground black pepper, and stir through the olives and orange segments. Garnish with the extra olives and flat-leaf parsley.

Note *Chorizo sausages can be replaced with any spicy sausages.*

Lamb's liver and bacon stew

preparation 10 minutes
cooking 30 minutes
serves 6

1 lamb's liver, about 750 g (1 lb 10 oz) (see Note)
30 g (1 oz/¼ cup) cornflour (cornstarch)
¼ teaspoon ground black pepper
6 bacon slices, cut into large pieces
2 tablespoons oil
2 onions, thinly sliced
1 beef stock (bouillon) cube, crumbled

Wash the liver and cut it into thin slices, discarding any veins or discoloured spots. Pat the liver dry with paper towels. Combine the cornflour and pepper. Toss the liver slices in the seasoned cornflour, shaking off the excess.

Cook the bacon in a heavy-based saucepan until crisp, then drain on paper towels. Heat the oil in the pan and cook the onion gently until golden, then remove from the pan.

Cook the liver quickly in small batches over medium heat until well browned, then drain on paper towels. Return the liver, bacon and onion to the pan. Dissolve the stock cube in 250 ml (9 fl oz/1 cup) boiling water, then gradually add to the pan. Stir over medium heat for 10 minutes, or until the liquid boils and thickens. Sprinkle with cracked black pepper and serve immediately.

Note *Soaking the liver in milk for 30 minutes before cooking will result in a milder taste.*

Remove the peel and pith from the orange, and cut the flesh into segments.

Toss the liver slices in the seasoned cornflour, shaking off the excess.

Bottom: Lamb's liver and bacon stew. Top: Madrid chicken.

Veal, lemon and caper stew

preparation 30 minutes
cooking 2 hours
serves 6

1 tablespoon olive oil
50 g (2 oz) butter
1 kg (2 lb 4 oz) stewing veal, cut into 4 cm (1½ inch) chunks
300 g (10½ oz) French shallots (eschalots)
3 leeks, white part only, cut into large cubes
2 garlic cloves, crushed
1 tablespoon plain (all-purpose) flour
500 ml (17 fl oz/2 cups) chicken stock
1 teaspoon finely grated lemon zest
80 ml (2½ fl oz/⅓ cup) lemon juice
2 bay leaves
2 tablespoons capers, drained and well rinsed

Preheat the oven to 180°C (350°F/Gas 4). Heat the oil and half the butter in a large, heavy-based saucepan. Brown the veal in batches over medium–high heat and transfer to a large casserole dish.

Blanch the shallots in boiling water for 30 seconds, then peel and add to the saucepan with the leeks. Gently cook for 5 minutes, or until soft and golden. Add the garlic, cook for 1 minute, then transfer to the casserole dish.

Melt the remaining butter in the pan, add the flour and cook for 30 seconds. Remove from the heat, add the stock and stir until well combined. Return to the heat and cook, stirring, until the sauce begins to bubble.

Pour the sauce into the casserole dish and stir in the lemon zest, lemon juice and bay leaves. Cover and bake for 1–1½ hours, or until the veal is tender. During the last 20 minutes of cooking, remove the lid to allow the sauces to reduce a little. Stir in the capers and season with salt and pepper before serving.

Low-fat beef stroganoff

preparation 20 minutes
cooking 25 minutes
serves 4

500 g (1 lb 2 oz) rump steak
cooking oil spray
1 onion, sliced
¼ teaspoon paprika
250 g (9 oz) button mushrooms, halved
2 tablespoons tomato paste (concentrated purée)
125 ml (4 fl oz/½ cup) beef stock
125 ml (4 fl oz/½ cup) low-fat evaporated milk
3 teaspoons cornflour (cornstarch)
1 small handful parsley, chopped

Remove any excess fat from the steak and slice into thin strips. Cook in batches in a large, lightly greased non-stick frying pan over high heat, until just cooked. Remove from the pan.

Lightly spray the pan and cook the onion, paprika and mushrooms over medium heat until the onion has softened. Add the meat, tomato paste, stock and 125 ml (4 fl oz/½ cup) water. Bring to the boil, then reduce the heat and simmer for 10 minutes.

In a small bowl, mix the evaporated milk with the cornflour. Add to the pan and stir until the sauce boils and thickens. Sprinkle with parsley.

Add the leeks and peeled shallots to the pan and gently fry until soft and golden.

Slice the rump steak into thin strips after removing any excess fat.

stews

Bottom: Low-fat beef stroganoff. Top: Veal, lemon and caper stew.

Steak and kidney stew

preparation 35 minutes
cooking 2 hours 30 minutes
serves 4–6

1 kg (2 lb 4 oz) chuck steak, trimmed
8 lamb kidneys
60 ml (2 fl oz/¼ cup) oil
1 bacon slice, rind removed, cut into long, thin strips
40 g (1½ oz) butter
1 large onion, chopped
300 g (10½ oz) button mushrooms, halved
250 ml (9 fl oz/1 cup) Muscat
2–3 garlic cloves, crushed
¼ teaspoon ground allspice
½ teaspoon paprika
2 teaspoons coriander seeds, lightly crushed
1 tablespoon wholegrain mustard
250 ml (9 fl oz/1 cup) beef stock
2–3 tablespoons soft brown sugar
1–2 teaspoons thyme leaves
1–2 teaspoons chopped rosemary

Cut the steak into 2–3 cm (1 inch) cubes. Cut the kidneys in half, remove the core and any fat, then slice them in half again.

Heat 1 teaspoon of the oil in a large heavy-based saucepan. Add the bacon and cook over medium heat until just crisp. Remove and then set aside.

Heat 2 tablespoons of the oil and 30 g (1 oz) of the butter in the pan. Brown the steak cubes in batches, then set aside.

Add the onion to the pan and cook for 3 minutes, or until soft and golden. Add the mushrooms and cook, stirring, for 3 minutes, until starting to brown. Stir in half the Muscat and simmer for 3–4 minutes. Remove and set to the side.

Add the remaining oil and butter to the pan. Stir in the garlic, allspice, paprika and coriander seeds, and cook for 1 minute. Add the kidney and cook until just starting to brown. Stir in the mustard and remaining Muscat, and simmer for 2 minutes.

Stir in the bacon, steak, and onion and mushroom mixture. Stir in the stock, bring to the boil, then reduce the heat, cover and simmer for 1 hour. Add the sugar. Simmer, covered, for 40 minutes, then uncovered for 20 minutes, stirring in the herbs during the last 10 minutes.

Halve the kidneys and remove the cores and fat. Slice in half again.

Add the kidney to the pan-fried spices and cook until just starting to brown.

Osso bucco with gremolata

preparation 30 minutes
cooking 2 hours 40 minutes
serves 4

2 tablespoons olive oil
1 onion, finely chopped
1 garlic clove, crushed
1 kg (2 lb 4 oz) veal shin slices (osso bucco)
2 tablespoons plain (all-purpose) flour
400 g (14 oz) tin chopped tomatoes
250 ml (9 fl oz/1 cup) dry white wine
250 ml (9 fl oz/1 cup) chicken stock

gremolata

2 tablespoons finely chopped parsley
2 teaspoons finely grated lemon zest
1 teaspoon finely chopped garlic

Heat 1 tablespoon oil in a large shallow casserole dish. Add the onion and cook over low heat until soft and golden. Add the garlic. Cook for 1 minute, then remove from the dish.

Heat the remaining oil and brown the veal in batches, then remove. Return the onion to the casserole and stir in the flour. Cook for 30 seconds and remove from the heat. Slowly stir in the tomato, wine and stock, combining well with the flour. Return the veal to the casserole.

Return to the heat and bring to the boil, stirring. Cover and reduce the heat to low so that the casserole is just simmering. Cook for 2½ hours, or until the meat is very tender and almost falling off the bones.

To make the gremolata, combine the parsley, lemon zest and garlic in a bowl. Sprinkle over the osso bucco and serve with risotto or plain rice.

Hint *Try to make this a day in advance to give the flavours time to develop and blend.*

Mediterranean lamb casserole

preparation 15 minutes
cooking 1 hour
serves 4

1 tablespoon olive oil
750 g (1 lb 10 oz) lamb from the bone, diced
1 large onion, sliced
2 garlic cloves, crushed
2 carrots, chopped
2 parsnips, chopped
400 g (14 oz) tin chopped tomatoes
2 tablespoons tomato paste (concentrated purée)
2 teaspoons chopped rosemary
125 ml (4 fl oz/½ cup) dry red wine
250 ml (9 fl oz/1 cup) chicken stock

Heat the oil in a large saucepan and cook the lamb, in batches, for 3–4 minutes, or until browned. Remove from the pan and keep warm. Add the onion and garlic to the pan and cook for 2–3 minutes, or until the onion is soft.

Return the lamb and juices to the pan. Add the carrot, parsnip, tomato, tomato paste, rosemary, wine and stock and bring to the boil. Reduce the heat and cover the pan. Simmer the casserole for 50 minutes, or until the lamb is tender and the sauce has thickened. Serve with soft polenta or couscous.

Add the onion and garlic to the pan and cook until the onion is soft.

Bottom: Mediterranean lamb casserole. Top: Osso bucco with gremolata.

Chicken with tomatoes, olives and capers

preparation 20 minutes
cooking 1 hour
serves 4

2 tablespoons olive oil
1 red onion, cut into thin wedges
1 celery stalk, sliced
150 g (5½ oz) cap mushrooms, sliced
3–4 garlic cloves, thinly sliced
8 boneless, skinless chicken thighs
plain (all-purpose) flour, for dusting
125 ml (4 fl oz/½ cup) dry white wine
300 ml (10½ fl oz) chicken stock
400 g (14 oz) tin chopped tomatoes
1 tablespoon tomato paste (concentrated purée)
60 g (2 oz/⅓ cup) black olives
1 tablespoon capers, drained and well rinsed

Heat half the oil in a large non-stick frying pan. Add the onion, celery, mushrooms and garlic and cook, stirring, for 5 minutes, or until the onion is soft. Remove from the pan.

Coat the chicken lightly in flour, shaking off any excess. Heat the remaining oil in the frying pan and cook the chicken, in batches, turning once, for 5 minutes, or until well browned. Add the wine and stock and cook for a further 2 minutes.

Return the vegetables to the pan and add the tomato and tomato paste. Simmer, partially covered, for 40 minutes, or until thickened. Add the olives and capers and season.

Chicken provençale

preparation 15 minutes
cooking 1 hour 20 minutes
serves 6

1 tablespoon olive oil
1.5 kg (3 lb 5 oz) chicken pieces
1 onion, chopped
1 red capsicum (pepper), chopped
80 ml (2½ fl oz/⅓ cup) dry white wine
80 ml (2½ fl oz/⅓ cup) chicken stock
400 g (14 oz) tin chopped tomatoes
2 tablespoons tomato paste (concentrated purée)
90 g (3 oz/½ cup) black olives
small handful basil, shredded

Heat the oil in a saucepan over high heat, add the chicken, in batches, and cook for 3–4 minutes, or until browned. Return all the chicken to the pan and add the onion and capsicum. Cook for 2–3 minutes, or until the onion is soft.

Add the wine, stock, tomato, tomato paste and olives and bring to the boil. Reduce the heat, cover and simmer for 30 minutes. Remove the lid, turn the chicken pieces over and cook for another 30 minutes, or until the chicken is tender and the sauce thickened. Season to taste, sprinkle with the basil and serve with rice.

Cook the onion, celery, mushrooms and garlic in a frying pan.

Just before serving, season then sprinkle with the shredded basil.

Bottom: Chicken provencale. Top: Chicken with tomatoes, olives and capers.

Corned beef

preparation 5 minutes
cooking 1 hour 40 minutes
serves 6–8

1 tablespoon oil
1.5 kg (3 lb 5 oz) piece corned silverside, trimmed
1 tablespoon white vinegar
1 tablespoon soft brown sugar
4 cloves
4 black peppercorns
2 bay leaves
1 garlic clove, crushed
1 large parsley sprig
4 carrots
4 potatoes
6 small onions

onion sauce
30 g (1 oz) butter
2 white onions, chopped
2 tablespoons plain (all-purpose) flour
330 ml (11 fl oz/1⅓ cups) full-cream (whole) milk

horseradish cream
60 ml (2 fl oz/¼ cup) horseradish relish
1 tablespoon white vinegar
125 ml (4 fl oz/½ cup) thick (double/heavy) cream

Heat the oil in a deep, heavy-based saucepan. Cook the meat over medium–high heat, turning until well browned all over.

Remove the pan from the heat and add the vinegar, sugar, cloves, peppercorns, bay leaves, garlic and parsley sprig.

Pour over enough water to cover. Cover and return to the heat, reduce the heat and bring slowly to a simmering point. Then simmer for a further 30 minutes.

Cut the carrots and potatoes into large pieces and add to the pan with the onions. Simmer, covered, for 1 hour, or until tender. Remove the vegetables and keep warm. Reserve 125 ml (4 fl oz/½ cup) of the cooking liquid.

Meanwhile, to make the onion sauce, heat the butter in a small saucepan. Cook the onion gently for 10 minutes, or until soft but not browned. Transfer to a bowl. Add the flour to the pan and stir over low heat for 2 minutes, or until lightly golden. Gradually add the milk and reserved cooking liquid, and stir until it boils and thickens. Boil for 1 minute, then remove from the heat and stir in the onion. Season.

To make the horseradish cream, combine all of the ingredients in a bowl until smooth.

Drain the meat from the pan, discarding the remaining liquid and spices. Slice the meat, and serve it with the vegetables, onion sauce and horseradish cream.

Add the vinegar, sugar, cloves, peppercorns, bay leaves, garlic and parsley to the meat.

Remove the sauce from the heat and stir in the cooked onion.

Creamy veal with mushrooms

preparation 20 minutes
cooking 25 minutes
serves 4

750 g (1 lb 10 oz) veal steaks, cut into 1 cm (½ inch) strips
30 g (1 oz/¼ cup) plain (all-purpose) flour
30 g (1 oz) butter
1 garlic clove, crushed
1 tablespoon dijon mustard
250 ml (9 fl oz/1 cup) pouring (whipping) cream
125 ml (4 fl oz/½ cup) dry white wine
1 tablespoon chopped thyme
250 ml (9 fl oz/1 cup) chicken stock
375 g (13 oz) button mushrooms, halved

Toss the meat in the flour (inside a plastic bag prevents mess), shaking off the excess. Heat the butter and garlic in a large frying pan. Add the meat and cook quickly in small batches over medium heat until well browned. Drain thoroughly on paper towels.

Brown the mushrooms in the pan and add the mustard, cream, wine, thyme and stock. Bring to the boil, then reduce the heat and simmer, covered, for 10–15 minutes, stirring occasionally, until the sauce thickens.

Add the veal and cook for a further 3–5 minutes, or until the meat is tender and warmed through. Delicious served with pasta and steamed vegetables.

Pork and coriander stew

preparation 15 minutes + overnight marinating
cooking 1 hour 20 minutes
serves 4–6

1½ tablespoons coriander seeds
800 g (1 lb 12 oz) pork fillet, cut into 2 cm (¾ inch) cubes
1 tablespoon plain (all-purpose) flour
60 ml (2 fl oz/¼ cup) olive oil
1 large onion, thinly sliced
375 ml (13 fl oz/1½ cups) red wine
250 ml (9 fl oz/1 cup) chicken stock
1 teaspoon sugar
fresh coriander (cilantro) sprigs, to garnish

Crush the coriander seeds in a mortar with a pestle. Combine the pork, seeds and ½ teaspoon cracked pepper. Cover and marinate overnight in the refrigerator.

Combine the flour and pork, and toss to coat. Heat 2 tablespoons of the oil in a saucepan and cook the pork in batches over high heat. Remove.

Heat the remaining oil, add the onion and cook over medium heat for 2–3 minutes, or until golden. Return the meat to the pan, add the wine, stock and sugar. Season. Bring to the boil, then reduce the heat and simmer, covered, for 1 hour.

Remove the meat. Return the pan to the heat and boil over high heat for 3–5 minutes, or until the liquid reduces and thickens. Pour over the meat and garnish with coriander. Serve with boiled potatoes.

Toss the veal strips in the flour, shaking off any excess flour.

Coat the pork fillet pieces with the ground coriander seeds and cracked pepper.

Bottom: Pork and coriander stew. Top: Creamy veal with mushrooms.

Chilli con pollo

preparation 10 minutes
cooking 45 minutes
serves 4

1 tablespoon olive oil
1 onion, finely chopped
500 g (1 lb 2 oz) minced (ground) chicken
1–2 teaspoons mild chilli powder
400 g (14 oz) tin chopped tomatoes
2 tablespoons tomato paste (concentrated purée)
1–2 teaspoons soft brown sugar
425 g (15 oz) tin red kidney beans, drained and rinsed

Heat the oil in a large saucepan. Add the onion and cook over medium heat for 3 minutes, or until soft. Increase the heat and add the chicken. Cook for 6–8 minutes, or until browned, breaking up any lumps with a wooden spoon.

Add the chilli powder and cook for 1 minute. Add the tomato, tomato paste and 125 ml (4 fl oz/½ cup) water and stir well.

Bring to the boil, then reduce the heat and simmer for 30 minutes. Stir through the sugar to taste and the kidney beans and heat through. Season and serve with baked corn chips and low-fat natural yoghurt.

Chicken stew with white beans and zucchini

preparation 15 minutes
cooking 1 hour
serves 4

1 tablespoon olive oil
8 boneless, skinless chicken thighs
1 onion, halved and thinly sliced
4 garlic cloves, finely chopped
60 ml (2 fl oz/¼ cup) dry white wine
250 ml (9 fl oz/1 cup) chicken stock
1 tablespoon finely chopped rosemary
1 teaspoon finely grated lemon zest
1 bay leaf
2 x 400 g (14 oz) tins cannellini beans, drained and rinsed
3 zucchini (courgettes), halved lengthways, cut on the diagonal

Heat the oil in a large ovenproof casserole dish. Add the chicken in batches, and cook for 4 minutes on each side, or until browned. Remove.

Add the onion to the dish and cook for 5 minutes, or until soft. Add the garlic and cook for 1 minute, or until fragrant, then add the wine and chicken stock and bring to the boil, scraping the bottom of the pan to remove any sediment.

Return the chicken and any juices to the pan along with the rosemary, lemon zest and bay leaf. Reduce the heat and simmer, covered, for 40 minutes, or until the chicken is tender. Stir in the cannellini beans and zucchini and cook for 5 minutes more, or until the zucchini is tender.

Simmer for 30 minutes, then stir in the kidney beans and heat through.

Stir in the drained and rinsed cannellini beans and the zucchini and cook for 5 minutes more.

Bottom: Chicken stew with white beans and zucchini. Top: Chilli con pollo.

Chilli con carne

preparation 25 minutes + overnight soaking
cooking 2 hours 15 minutes
serves 6

185 g (6½ oz) dried black-eyed peas
650 g (1 lb 7 oz) tomatoes
1½ tablespoons oil
900 g (2 lb) trimmed chuck steak, cut into cubes
3 onions, thinly sliced
2 garlic cloves, chopped
2 teaspoons ground cumin
1 tablespoon paprika
½ teaspoon ground allspice
1–2 teaspoons chilli powder
1 tablespoon soft brown sugar
1 tablespoon red wine vinegar

Put the black-eyed peas in a large bowl, cover with cold water and soak overnight.

Drain the peas and rinse under cold water. Score a cross in the base of each tomato. Put the tomatoes in a bowl of boiling water for 30 seconds, then transfer to a bowl of cold water. Drain and peel the skin away from the cross. Halve the tomatoes and remove the seeds with a teaspoon. Chop the flesh finely.

Heat 1 tablespoon of the oil in a large heavy-based saucepan and add half the meat. Cook over medium–high heat for 2 minutes, or until well browned. Remove from the pan and repeat with the remaining meat, then remove from the pan.

Add the rest of the oil to the pan and add the onion. Cook over medium heat for 5 minutes, or until softened. Add the garlic and spices and cook, stirring, for 1 minute, or until aromatic. Add 500 ml (17 fl oz/2 cups) water and stir. Return the meat to the pan with the peas and tomato. Bring to the boil, then reduce the heat to low and simmer, partially covered, for 2 hours, or until the meat is tender and the chilli con carne is thick and dryish, stirring occasionally. Towards the end of the cooking time the mixture may start to catch, so add a little water if necessary. Stir through the sugar and vinegar, and season with salt to taste. Serve with flour tortillas, grated low-fat cheese and lime wedges.

Drain the tomatoes then carefully peel the skin away from the cross.

Remove the tomato seeds with a teaspoon and then finely chop the flesh.

Stuffed squid stew

preparation 50 minutes
cooking 50 minutes
serves 4

100 ml (3½ fl oz) olive oil
1 large onion, finely chopped
2 garlic cloves, crushed
80 g (3 oz/1 cup) fresh breadcrumbs
1 egg, lightly beaten
60 g (2 oz) kefalotyri cheese, grated
60 g (2 oz) haloumi cheese, grated
4 large or 8 small squid (1 kg/2 lb 4 oz), cleaned (see Note)
1 small onion, finely chopped, extra
2 garlic cloves, crushed, extra
500 g (1 lb 2 oz) firm ripe tomatoes, peeled and diced
150 ml (5 fl oz) red wine
1 tablespoon chopped oregano
1 tablespoon chopped flat-leaf (Italian) parsley

Heat 2 tablespoons of the oil in a frying pan, add the onion and cook over medium heat for 3 minutes. Remove. Combine with the garlic, breadcrumbs, egg and cheeses. Season with salt and pepper.

Pat the squid tubes dry with paper towels and, using a teaspoon, fill them three-quarters full with the stuffing. Do not pack them too tightly or the stuffing mixture will swell and burst out during cooking. Secure the ends with wooden toothpicks.

Heat the remaining oil in a large frying pan, add the squid and cook for 1–2 minutes on all sides. Remove. Add the extra onion and cook over medium heat for 3 minutes, or until soft, then add the extra garlic and cook for a further 1 minute. Stir in the tomato and wine, and simmer for 10 minutes, or until thick and pulpy, then stir in the oregano and parsley. Return the squid to the pan and cook, covered, for 20–25 minutes, or until tender. Serve warm with the tomato sauce or cool with a salad.

Note Ask the fishmonger to clean the squid. Or, discard the tentacles and cartilage. Rinse the tubes under running water and pull off the skin.

Chicken with feta and olives

preparation 15 minutes
cooking 1 hour
serves 4

2 tablespoons oil
8 chicken pieces (1.2 kg/2 lb 10 oz)
1 onion, chopped
25 g (1 oz) oregano, leaves picked
2 tablespoons tomato paste (concentrated purée)
2 x 400 g (14 oz) tins chopped tomatoes
150 g (5½ oz) black olives
150 g (5½ oz) feta, crumbled, to serve

Heat half the oil in a saucepan and cook the chicken pieces, in batches, for 3–4 minutes, or until golden. Remove from the pan and set aside.

In the same saucepan, heat the remaining oil and cook the onion and half the oregano leaves for 3 minutes, or until the onion is softened. Add the tomato paste to the onion mixture and stir for 2 minutes, then add the tomato and the chicken pieces.

Simmer, covered, for 40–50 minutes, or until the chicken is cooked through. Add the olives and remaining oregano leaves. To serve, spoon into bowls and top with the crumbled feta.

Fill the squid tubes three-quarter full with the stuffing mixture.

Add the olives and remaining oregano leaves to the chicken pieces.

Bottom: Chicken with feta and olives. Top: Stuffed squid stew.

Italian sausage and chickpea stew

preparation 15 minutes
cooking 45 minutes
serves 4

2 large red capsicums (peppers)
1 tablespoon olive oil
2 large red onions, cut into thick wedges
2 garlic cloves, finely chopped
600 g (1 lb 5 oz) Italian-style thin pork sausages
300 g (10½ oz) tin chickpeas, drained
150 g (5½ oz) flat mushrooms, thickly sliced
125 ml (4 fl oz/½ cup) dry white wine
2 bay leaves
2 teaspoons chopped rosemary
400 g (14 oz) tin chopped tomatoes

Cut the capsicums into large pieces, removing the seeds and membrane. Place skin side up, under a hot grill (broiler) until the skin blackens and blisters. Allow to cool in a sealed plastic bag. Peel away the skin, and slice diagonally into thick strips.

Meanwhile, heat the oil in a large non-stick frying pan. Add the onion and garlic, and stir over medium heat for 6 minutes, or until the onion is soft and browned. Remove the onion from the pan and set aside. Add the sausages to the same pan. Cook over medium heat, turning occasionally, for 8 minutes, or until the sausages are browned. Remove the sausages from the pan, allow to cool and slice diagonally into 3 cm (1¼ inch) pieces.

Combine the capsicum slices, onion, sausage pieces, chickpeas and mushrooms in the frying pan, and cook over medium–high heat.

Add the wine, bay leaves and rosemary to the pan. Bring to the boil, then reduce the heat to low and simmer for 3 minutes. Stir in the tomato and simmer for 20 minutes, or until the sauce has thickened slightly. Remove the bay leaves and season to taste with sugar, salt and cracked black pepper. Delicious served with fettuccine.

Braised beef in red wine

preparation 10 minutes
cooking 2 hours
serves 6

30 g (1 oz/¼ cup) plain (all-purpose) flour
¼ teaspoon ground black pepper
1 kg (2 lb 4 oz) lean round or chuck steak, cut into
3 cm (1¼ inch) cubes
1 tablespoon oil
15 g (½ oz) butter
12 baby onions
250 ml (9 fl oz/1 cup) beef stock
250 ml (9 fl oz/1 cup) red wine
2 tablespoons tomato paste (concentrated purée)
1 tablespoon French mustard
1 bay leaf
¼ teaspoon mixed dried herbs
1 tablespoon chopped flat-leaf (Italian) parsley, to garnish

Combine the flour and pepper. Toss the meat in the seasoned flour, shaking off the excess.

Heat the oil and butter in a heavy-based saucepan. Cook the meat quickly in batches over medium–high heat until well browned. Remove and drain on paper towels.

Add the onions to the saucepan and cook over medium heat until softened. Return the meat to the pan, add the stock, wine, tomato paste, mustard and herbs. Bring to the boil, reduce the heat and cook, covered, for 1½ hours, or until the meat is tender, stirring occasionally.

Remove the skin from the cooked capsicums and slice them into thin strips.

Toss the meat in the seasoned flour, shaking off the excess flour.

Bottom: Braised beef in red wine. Top: Italian sausage and chickpea stew.

Catalan fish stew

preparation 30 minutes
cooking 40 minutes
serves 6–8

300 g (10½ oz) red mullet fillets
400 g (14 oz) firm white fish fillets
300 g (10½ oz) cleaned squid
1.5 litres (52 fl oz/6 cups) fish stock
80 ml (2½ fl oz/⅓ cup) olive oil
1 onion, chopped
6 garlic cloves, chopped
1 small red chilli, chopped
1 teaspoon paprika
pinch of saffron threads
150 ml (5 fl oz) white wine
400 g (14 oz) tin chopped tomatoes
16 raw prawns (shrimp), peeled and deveined, leaving the tails intact
2 tablespoons brandy
24 black mussels, scrubbed and hairy beards removed
1 tablespoon chopped flat-leaf (Italian) parsley

picada
2 tablespoons olive oil
2 slices day-old bread, cubed
2 garlic cloves
5 blanched almonds, toasted
2 tablespoons chopped flat-leaf (Italian) parsley

Cut the fish and squid into 4 cm (1½ inch) pieces and set aside. Place the stock in a large saucepan, bring to the boil and boil for 15 minutes, or until reduced by half.

To make the picada, heat the oil in a frying pan, add the bread and cook, stirring, for 2–3 minutes, or until golden, adding the garlic at the last minute. Place the almonds, bread, garlic and parsley in a food processor and process, adding a little of the stock to make a smooth paste.

Heat 2 tablespoons of the oil in a large saucepan, add the onion, garlic, chilli and paprika, and cook, stirring, for 1 minute. Add the saffron, wine, tomato and stock. Bring to the boil, then reduce the heat and simmer.

Heat the remaining oil in a frying pan and quickly fry the fish and squid for 3–5 minutes. Remove from the pan. Add the prawns, cook for 1 minute and then pour in the brandy. Carefully ignite the brandy with a match and let the flames burn down. Remove from the pan.

Add the mussels to the stock and simmer, covered, for 2–3 minutes, or until opened. Discard any that do not open. Add all the seafood and the picada to the pan, stirring until the sauce has thickened and the seafood has cooked through. Season to taste with salt and pepper, sprinkle with the parsley, and serve.

Lamb tagine

preparation 15 minutes + 1 hour marinating
cooking 1 hour 45 minutes
serves 6–8

1.5 kg (3 lb 5 oz) leg or shoulder of lamb, cut into
2.5 cm (1 inch) pieces
3 garlic cloves, chopped
80 ml (2½ fl oz/⅓ cup) olive oil
2 teaspoons ground cumin
1 teaspoon ground ginger
1 teaspoon ground turmeric
1 teaspoon paprika
½ teaspoon ground cinnamon
2 onions, thinly sliced
600 ml (21 fl oz) beef stock
¼ preserved lemon, pulp discarded, zest rinsed and
cut into thin strips
425 g (15 oz) tin chickpeas, drained
35 g (1 oz) cracked green olives (see Note)
1 large handful chopped coriander (cilantro) leaves, plus
extra, to garnish

Place the lamb pieces in a non-metallic bowl, add the garlic,
2 tablespoons of the oil and the ground cumin, ginger,
turmeric, paprika, cinnamon, and ½ teaspoon ground black
pepper and 1 teaspoon salt. Mix well to coat, then leave to
marinate for 1 hour.

Heat the remaining oil in a large saucepan, add the lamb in
batches and cook over high heat for 2–3 minutes, or until
browned. Remove from the pan. Add the onion and cook
for 2 minutes, then return the meat to the pan and add
the beef stock. Reduce the heat and simmer, covered,
for 1 hour.

Add the preserved lemon strips, drained chickpeas and
olives, and cook, uncovered, for a further 30 minutes, or
until the lamb is tender and the sauce has reduced and
thickened. Stir in the coriander. Serve in bowls and garnish
with extra coriander.

Note *Cracked green olives are marinated in herbs and are
available from specialty shops.*

Add the lemon strips, drained chickpeas and olives
and cook, uncovered.

Veal goulash

preparation 25 minutes
cooking 2 hours
serves 4

500 g (1 lb 2 oz) veal, cut into 2.5 cm (1 inch) pieces
2 tablespoons plain (all-purpose) flour
2 tablespoons olive oil
2 onions, thinly sliced
2 garlic cloves, finely chopped
1 tablespoon sweet paprika
1 teaspoon ground cumin
400 g (14 oz) tin chopped tomatoes
2 carrots, sliced
½ red capsicum (pepper), chopped
½ green capsicum (pepper), chopped
250 ml (9 fl oz/1 cup) beef stock
125 ml (4 fl oz/½ cup) red wine
125 g (4½ oz/½ cup) sour cream
chopped flat-leaf (Italian) parsley, to garnish

Put the veal and flour in a plastic bag and shake to coat the
veal with the flour. Shake off any excess. Heat 1 tablespoon
of the oil in a large, deep heavy-based saucepan over
medium heat. Brown the meat well in batches, then remove
the meat and set aside.

Add the remaining oil to the pan. Cook the onion, garlic,
paprika and cumin for 5 minutes, stirring frequently. Return
the meat and any juices to the pan with the tomato, carrot
and capsicum. Cover and cook for 10 minutes.

Add the stock and wine, and season with salt and pepper.
Stir well, then cover and simmer over very low heat for
1½ hours. Stir in half the sour cream, season with more salt
and pepper if needed and serve garnished with parsley and
the remaining sour cream, if desired. Delicious served with
buttered boiled small potatoes or noodles.

Note *If you prefer your sauce to be a little thicker, cook,
uncovered, for 5 minutes over high heat before adding
the sour cream.*

Put the veal and flour in a plastic bag and shake to
coat well.

Beef bourguignonne

preparation 10 minutes
cooking 2 hours
serves 4

1 kg (2 lb 4 oz) stewing beef, cubed
30 g (1 oz/¼ cup) seasoned plain (all-purpose) flour
1 tablespoon oil
150 g (5½ oz) bacon slices, diced
8 bulb spring onions (scallions), greens trimmed to
2 cm (¾ inch)
200 g (7 oz) button mushrooms
500 ml (17 fl oz/2 cups) red wine
2 tablespoons tomato paste (concentrated purée)
500 ml (17 fl oz/2 cups) beef stock
1 bouquet garni (see Note)

Toss the beef in the seasoned flour until evenly coated, shaking off any excess. Heat the oil in a large saucepan over high heat. Cook the beef in three batches for about 3 minutes, or until well browned all over, adding a little extra oil as needed. Remove from the pan.

Add the bacon to the pan and cook for 2 minutes, or until browned. Remove with a slotted spoon and add to the beef. Add the spring onions and mushrooms, and cook for 5 minutes, or until the onions are browned. Remove.

Slowly pour the red wine into the pan, scraping up any sediment from the bottom with a wooden spoon. Stir in the tomato paste and stock. Add the bouquet garni and return the beef, bacon and any juices. Bring to the boil, then reduce the heat and simmer for 45 minutes. Return the spring onions and mushrooms to the pan. Cook for 1 hour, or until the meat is very tender and the sauce is glossy. Serve with steamed new potatoes or mash.

Note *To make a bouquet garni, wrap the green part of a leek around a bay leaf, a sprig of thyme, a sprig of parsley and celery leaves, and tie with string. The combination of herbs can be varied according to taste.*

French-style octopus

preparation 25 minutes
cooking 1 hour 30 minutes
serves 6

1 kg (2 lb/4 oz) baby octopus
60 ml (2 fl oz/¼ cup) olive oil
1 large brown onion, chopped
2 garlic cloves
500 g (1 lb 2 oz) ripe tomatoes, peeled, seeded and chopped
330 ml (11 fl oz/1⅓ cups) dry white wine
¼ teaspoon saffron threads
2 thyme sprigs
2 tablespoons roughly chopped flat-leaf (Italian) parsley

To clean the octopus, use a small sharp knife and cut each head from the tentacles. Remove the eyes by cutting a round of flesh from the base of each head. To clean the heads, carefully slit them open and remove the gut, avoiding the ink sac. Rinse thoroughly. Cut the heads in half. Push out the beaks from the centre of the tentacles from the cut side. Cut the tentacles into sets of four or two, depending on the size of the octopus. Rinse thoroughly under running water.

Blanch all the octopus in boiling water for 2 minutes, then drain and allow to cool slightly. Pat dry with paper towels.

Heat the olive oil in a heavy-based frying pan and cook the onion for 7–8 minutes over medium heat until lightly golden. Add the octopus and garlic to the pan, and cook for another 2–3 minutes. Add the tomato, wine, saffron and thyme. Add just enough water to cover the octopus.

Simmer, covered, for 1 hour. Uncover and cook for another 15 minutes, or until the octopus is tender and the sauce has thickened a little. The cooking time will vary depending upon the size of the octopus. Season to taste. Serve hot or at room temperature, sprinkled with parsley.

Slowly pour the red wine into the pan, scraping up any sediment with a wooden spoon.

Carefully cut between the head and the tentacles of the octopus, just below the eyes.

Bottom: French-style octopus. Top: Beef bourguignonne.

Beef stroganoff

preparation 25 minutes
cooking 30 minutes
serves 6

1 kg (2 lb 4 oz) piece rump steak, trimmed
40 g (1½ oz/⅓ cup) plain (all-purpose) flour
¼ teaspoon ground black pepper
60 ml (2 fl oz/¼ cup) olive oil
1 large onion, chopped
500 g (1 lb 2 oz) baby mushrooms
1 tablespoon sweet paprika
1 tablespoon tomato paste
2 teaspoons French mustard
125 ml (4 fl oz/½ cup) dry white wine
60 ml (2 fl oz/¼ cup) chicken stock
185 g (6½ oz/¾ cup) sour cream
1 tablespoon finely chopped flat-leaf (Italian) parsley

Slice the meat across the grain into short, thin pieces. Combine the flour and pepper. Toss the meat in the seasoned flour, shaking off the excess.

Heat 2 tablespoons of the oil in a heavy-based saucepan. Cook the meat quickly in small batches over medium–high heat until well browned. Drain on paper towels.

Heat the remaining oil in the pan. Cook the onion over medium heat for 3 minutes, or until softened. Add the mushrooms and stir for 5 minutes.

Add the paprika, tomato paste, mustard, wine and stock to the pan, and bring to the boil. Reduce the heat and simmer for 5 minutes, uncovered, stirring occasionally. Return the meat to the pan with the sour cream, and stir until combined and just heated through. Sprinkle with the parsley just before serving.

Toss the meat in the seasoned flour, shaking off any of the excess.

Add the mushrooms to the cooked onion and stir for 5 minutes.

Ham, leek and potato ragu

preparation 25 minutes
cooking 45 minutes
serves 4–6

50 g (2 oz) butter
2 tablespoons olive oil
250 g (9 oz) piece double-smoked ham, cut into cubes
(see Note)
3 garlic cloves, finely chopped
3 leeks, white part only, sliced
1.5 kg (3 lb 5 oz) potatoes, peeled and cut into large chunks
500 ml (17 fl oz/2 cups) chicken stock
2 tablespoons brandy
125 ml (4 fl oz/½ cup) pouring (whipping) cream
1 tablespoon each of chopped oregano and parsley

Heat the butter and oil in a large heavy-based saucepan.
Cook the ham, garlic and leek over low heat for 10 minutes,
stirring regularly.

Add the potato and cook for 10 minutes, stirring regularly.

Slowly stir in the stock and brandy. Cover and gently
simmer. Cook for another 15–20 minutes until the potato is
tender but still chunky, and sauce has thickened. Add cream
and herbs, and season. Simmer for another 5 minutes.

Note You can use any type of ham for this recipe. A double-
smoked ham will give a good, hearty flavour.

Seafood and fennel stew

preparation 10 minutes
cooking 30 minutes
serves 6

2 tablespoons olive oil
1 large fennel bulb, thinly sliced
2 leeks, white part only, thinly sliced
2 garlic cloves, crushed
½ teaspoon paprika
2 tablespoons Pernod or Ricard
200 ml (7 fl oz) dry white wine
18 mussels, scrubbed and hairy beards removed
¼ teaspoon saffron threads
¼ teaspoon thyme leaves
6 baby octopus
16 raw prawns (shrimp), peeled and deveined,
leaving the tails intact
500 g (1 lb 2 oz) swordfish steaks, cut into large chunks
400 g (14 oz) baby new potatoes
fennel greens, to garnish

Heat the oil in a large saucepan over medium heat. Add
the fennel, leek and garlic. Stir in the paprika, season
lightly with salt and pepper and cook for 8 minutes, or until
softened. Add the Pernod and wine, and stir for 1 minute,
or until reduced by one-third.

Add the mussels, firstly discarding any open or cracked
ones. Cover and cook for 1 minute, or until opened,
discarding any that do not open. Remove from the pan to
cool; remove from the shells and set aside.

Add the saffron and thyme to the pan, and cook for
1–2 minutes, stirring. Adjust the seasoning and transfer to a
large, flameproof casserole dish.

Use a small sharp knife to remove the octopus heads.
Grasp the bodies and push the beaks out with your index
finger; remove and discard. Slit the heads and remove the
gut. Mix the octopus, prawns, fish and potatoes into the
stew. Cover and cook gently for 10 minutes, or until tender.
Add the mussels, cover and heat through. Garnish with
fennel greens and serve.

Heat the butter and oil in a pan, then cook the ham,
garlic and leek.

Cut off the octopus heads. Grasp the body firmly
and push out the beak.

Bottom: Seafood and fennel stew. Top: Ham, leek and potato ragu.

Moroccan chicken

preparation 10 minutes + 5 minutes standing
cooking 35 minutes
serves 4

1 tablespoon Moroccan spice blend
800 g (1 lb 12 oz) boneless, skinless chicken thighs, halved
1 tablespoon oil
60 g (2¼ oz) butter
1 large onion, cut into wedges
1 cinnamon stick
2 garlic cloves, crushed
2 tablespoons lemon juice
250 ml (9 fl oz/1 cup) chicken stock
75 g (2½ oz/⅓ cup) pitted prunes, halved
280 g (10 oz/1½ cups) couscous
lemon wedges, to serve

Sprinkle half the spice blend over the chicken. Heat the oil and 20 g (¾ oz) of the butter in a large deep-sided frying pan over medium heat. Cook the chicken in batches for 5 minutes, or until evenly browned. Remove from the pan, then add the onion and cinnamon stick, and cook for 2–3 minutes before adding the garlic. Return the chicken to the pan and add the lemon juice and the remaining spice blend. Season to taste with salt and pepper, then cook, covered, for 5 minutes.

Add the stock and prunes to the pan, and bring to the boil. Reduce the heat to low–medium and cook, uncovered, for 15 minutes, or until the chicken is cooked and the liquid has reduced. Before serving, stir 20 g (¾ oz) of the butter into the sauce.

About 10 minutes before the chicken is ready, place the couscous in a heatproof bowl, add 375 ml (13 fl oz/1½ cups) boiling water and stand for 3–5 minutes. Stir in the remaining butter and fluff with a fork until the butter has melted and the grains have separated. Serve with the chicken and lemon wedges.

Note Depending on the quality and freshness of the Moroccan spice blend you buy, you may need to use a little more than specified in the recipe.

Lamb meatballs

preparation 30 minutes
cooking 1 hour
serves 4

1 kg (2 lb 4 oz) minced (ground) lamb
1 onion, finely chopped
2 garlic cloves, finely chopped
2 tablespoons finely chopped flat-leaf (Italian) parsley
2 tablespoons finely chopped coriander (cilantro) leaves
½ teaspoon cayenne pepper
½ teaspoon ground allspice
½ teaspoon ground ginger
½ teaspoon ground cardamom
1 teaspoon ground cumin
1 teaspoon paprika

sauce
2 tablespoons olive oil
1 onion, finely chopped
2 garlic cloves, finely chopped
2 teaspoons ground cumin
½ teaspoon ground cinnamon
1 teaspoon paprika
2 x 400 g (14 oz) tins chopped tomatoes
2 teaspoons harissa
1 bunch coriander (cilantro) leaves, chopped

Preheat the oven to 180°C (350°F/Gas 4). Lightly grease two baking trays. Place the lamb, onion, garlic, herbs and spices in a bowl, and mix together well and then season. Roll tablespoons of the mixture into balls and place on trays. Bake for 18–20 minutes, or until browned.

Meanwhile, to make the sauce, heat the oil in a large saucepan, add the onion and cook over medium heat for 5 minutes, or until soft. Add the garlic, cumin, cinnamon and paprika, and cook for 1 minute, or until fragrant.

Stir in the tomato and harissa, and bring to the boil. Reduce heat and simmer for 20 minutes, then add the meatballs and simmer for another 10 minutes, or until cooked. Stir in the coriander, and serve.

Bottom: Lamb meatballs. Top: Moroccan chicken.

Chicken with balsamic vinegar

preparation 5 minutes
cooking 50 minutes
serves 4

2 tablespoons olive oil
8 chicken pieces
125 ml (4 fl oz/½ cup) chicken stock
125 ml (4 fl oz/½ cup) dry white wine
125 ml (4 fl oz/½ cup) good-quality balsamic vinegar
40 g (1½ oz) chilled butter

Heat the oil in a large flameproof casserole dish over medium heat and cook the chicken, in batches, for 7–8 minutes, or until browned. Pour off any excess fat.

Add the stock, bring to the boil, then reduce the heat and simmer, covered, for 30 minutes, or until the chicken is cooked through.

Add the white wine and vinegar and increase the heat to high. Boil for 1 minute, or until the liquid has thickened. Remove from the heat, stir in the butter until melted, and season. Spoon the sauce over the chicken to serve.

Lamb and mustard stew

preparation 15 minutes
cooking 1 hour 40 minutes
serves 4

750 g (1 lb 10 oz) lean lamb fillets, cut into
2.5 cm (1 inch) cubes
60 g (2 oz/½ cup) plain (all-purpose) flour
1 tablespoon oil
16 baby onions
250 ml (9 fl oz/1 cup) dry white wine
250 ml (9 fl oz/1 cup) chicken stock
125 g (4½ oz/½ cup) dijon mustard
2 tablespoons chopped thyme

Toss the lamb cubes in the flour, shaking off any excess. Heat the oil in a heavy-based saucepan over high heat. Add the lamb in small batches and cook for 3 minutes, or until well browned, turning occasionally. Drain the meat on paper towels.

Return the lamb to the pan. Add the onions, wine, stock, mustard and thyme. Bring to the boil, then reduce the heat to low and simmer, covered, for 1 hour, stirring occasionally. Remove the lid and simmer for another 30 minutes, or until the lamb is tender. Serve with pasta.

Braised chicken and leek in wine

preparation 15 minutes
cooking 1 hour
serves 4

2 tablespoons oil
1.2 kg (2 lb 10 oz) chicken pieces
1 leek, white part only, thinly sliced
5 spring onions (scallions), thinly sliced on the diagonal
2 tablespoons marjoram
150 ml (5 fl oz) dry white wine
400 ml (14 fl oz) chicken stock
100 ml (3½ fl oz) pouring (whipping) cream

With a sharp knife, score the thickest part of the chicken drumsticks. Heat 1 tablespoon of the oil in a frying pan and cook the chicken pieces in batches for 3–4 minutes, or until browned.

Heat the remaining oil in a large flameproof casserole dish and cook the leek, spring onion and marjoram for 4 minutes, or until soft. Add the chicken and wine, and cook for 2 minutes. Add the stock, cover and bring to the boil. Reduce the heat and simmer for 30 minutes. Stir in the cream and simmer, uncovered, for 15 minutes, or until the chicken is tender. Season to taste. Serve with steamed rice.

Chinese braised chicken

preparation 10 minutes
cooking 1 hour
serves 4–6

250 ml (9 fl oz/1 cup) soy sauce
1 cinnamon stick
90 g (3 oz/⅓ cup) sugar
80 ml (2½ fl oz/⅓ cup) balsamic vinegar
2.5 cm (1 inch) piece fresh ginger, thinly sliced
4 garlic cloves
¼ teaspoon dried chilli flakes
1.5 kg (3 lb 5 oz) chicken pieces (skin removed)
1 tablespoon sesame seeds, toasted

Combine 1 litre (35 fl oz/4 cups) water with the soy sauce, cinnamon stick, sugar, balsamic vinegar, ginger, garlic and chilli flakes in a saucepan. Bring to the boil, then reduce the heat and simmer for 5 minutes.

Add the chicken pieces and simmer, covered, for 50 minutes, or until cooked through. Serve the chicken on a bed of steamed vegetables, drizzled with the poaching liquid and sprinkled with toasted sesame seeds.

Top left: Chicken with balsamic vinegar. Top right: Braised chicken and leek in wine. Bottom right: Chinese braised chicken. Bottom left: Lamb and mustard stew.

Pork sausage and white bean stew

preparation 25 minutes + overnight soaking
cooking 1 hour 40 minutes
serves 4

350 g (12 oz) dried white haricot beans
150 g (5½ oz) tocino, speck or pancetta, unsliced
½ leek, white part only, thinly sliced
2 garlic cloves
1 bay leaf
1 small red chilli, halved and seeded
1 small onion
2 cloves
1 rosemary sprig
3 thyme sprigs
1 parsley sprig
60 ml (2 fl oz/¼ cup) olive oil
8 pork sausages
½ onion, finely chopped
1 green capsicum (pepper), finely chopped
½ teaspoon paprika
125 g (4½ oz/½ cup) tomato paste (concentrated purée)
1 teaspoon cider vinegar

Soak the beans overnight in cold water. Drain and rinse the beans under cold water. Put them in a large saucepan with the tocino, leek, garlic, bay leaf and chilli. Stud the onion with the cloves and add to the saucepan. Tie the rosemary, thyme and parsley together, and add to the saucepan. Pour in 750 ml (26 fl oz/ 3 cups) cold water and bring to the boil. Add 1 tablespoon of the oil, reduce the heat and simmer, covered, for about 1 hour, or until the beans are tender. When necessary, add a little more boiling water to keep the beans covered.

Prick each sausage five or six times and twist tightly in opposite directions in the middle to give two short fat sausages joined in the middle. Put in a single layer in a large frying pan and add enough cold water to reach halfway up their sides. Bring to the boil and simmer, turning two or three times, until all the water has evaporated and the sausages brown lightly in the little fat that is left in the pan. Remove from the pan and cut the short sausages apart. Add the remaining oil, the chopped onion and capsicum to the pan, and fry over medium heat for 5–6 minutes. Stir in the paprika, cook for 30 seconds, then add the tomato paste. Season to taste. Cook, stirring, for 1 minute.

Remove the tocino, herb sprigs and any loose large pieces of onion from the bean mixture. Leave in any loose leaves from the herbs and any small pieces of onion. Add the sausages and sauce to the pan, and stir the vinegar through. Bring to the boil. Adjust the seasoning and serve.

Stud the onion with the cloves by pushing the cloves firmly into the onion.

Twist each sausage tightly in the opposite directions so that it forms two short fat sausages.

Mexican beef stew

preparation 30 minutes
cooking 1 hour 40 minutes
serves 6

500 g (1 lb 2 oz) roma (plum) tomatoes, halved
6 flour tortillas
1–2 red chillies, finely chopped
1 tablespoon olive oil
1 kg (2 lb 4 oz) stewing beef, cubed
½ teaspoon black pepper
2 onions, thinly sliced
375 ml (13 fl oz/1½ cups) beef stock
60 g (2 oz/¼ cup) tomato paste (concentrated purée)
375 g (13 oz) tin kidney beans, drained
1 teaspoon chilli powder
125 g (4½ oz/½ cup) sour cream
flat-leaf (Italian) parsley to garnish

Preheat the oven to 180°C (350°F/Gas 4). Grill (broil) the tomatoes, skin side up, under a hot grill (broiler) for 6–8 minutes, or until the skin is black and blistered. Place in a plastic bag and seal. Cool, remove the skin and roughly chop the flesh.

Bake two of the tortillas for 4 minutes, or until crisp. Break into pieces and put in a food processor with the tomato and chopped chilli. Process for 30 seconds, or until almost smooth.

Heat the oil in a large heavy-based saucepan. Brown the beef in batches, season with pepper, then remove. Add the onion to the pan and cook for 5 minutes. Return the meat to the pan. Stir in the processed mixture, stock and tomato paste, and bring to the boil. Reduce the heat, cover and simmer for 1¼ hours. Add the beans and chilli powder, and heat through.

Grill the remaining tortillas for 2–3 minutes on each side, then cool and cut into wedges. Serve the stew with the sour cream, and toasted tortilla wedges on the side.

Hint *If this stew becomes too thick during cooking, thin it with a little extra stock.*

Once the tortillas are crisp, break into pieces and put in the food processor.

Chinese beef in soy

preparation 20 minutes + overnight marinating
cooking 1 hour 45 minutes
serves 4

700 g (1 lb 9 oz) chuck steak, trimmed and cut into
2 cm (¾ inch) cubes
80 ml (2½ fl oz/⅓ cup) dark soy sauce
2 tablespoons honey
1 tablespoon wine vinegar
60 ml (2 fl oz/¼ cup) oil
4 garlic cloves, chopped
8 spring onions (scallions), thinly sliced
1 tablespoon finely grated fresh ginger
2 star anise
½ teaspoon ground cloves
375 ml (13 fl oz/1½ cups) beef stock
125 ml (4 fl oz/½ cup) red wine
sliced spring onions (scallions), extra, to garnish

Place the meat in a non-metallic dish. Combine the soy sauce, honey and vinegar in a small bowl, then pour over the meat. Cover with plastic wrap and marinate for at least 2 hours, or preferably overnight. Drain, reserving the marinade, and pat the cubes dry.

Place 1 tablespoon of the oil in a saucepan and brown the meat in 3 batches, for 3–4 minutes per batch—add another tablespoon of oil, if necessary. Remove the meat. Add the remaining oil and fry the garlic, spring onion, ginger, star anise and cloves for 1–2 minutes, or until fragrant.

Return all the meat to the pan, and add the reserved marinade, stock and wine. Bring to the boil, then reduce the heat and simmer, covered, for 1¼ hours. Cook, uncovered, for a further 15 minutes, or until the sauce is syrupy and the meat is tender.

Garnish with the extra sliced spring onion and serve immediately with steamed rice.

Finely grate a piece of fresh ginger on a wooden ginger grater.

Bottom: Chinese beef in soy. Top: Mexican beef stew.

Beef and peppercorn stew

preparation 15 minutes
cooking 2 hours
serves 4

1 kg (2 lb 4 oz) chuck steak, cut into 3 cm (1¼ inch) cubes
2 teaspoons cracked black peppercorns
40 g (1½ oz) butter
2 tablespoons oil
1 large onion, thinly sliced
2 garlic cloves, sliced
1½ tablespoons plain (all-purpose) flour
2 tablespoons brandy
750 ml (26 fl oz/3 cups) beef stock
1 tablespoon worcestershire sauce
2 teaspoons dijon mustard
500 g (1 lb 2 oz) baby new potatoes
60 ml (2 fl oz/¼ cup) pouring (whipping) cream
2 tablespoons chopped parsley

Toss the steak in the peppercorns. Heat half the butter and half the oil in a large heavy-based saucepan. Brown half the steak over high heat, then remove and set aside. Heat the remaining butter and oil, and brown the remaining steak. Remove from the pan and set aside.

Add the onion and garlic to the pan and cook, stirring, until the onion is golden. Add the flour and stir until browned. Remove from the heat.

Combine the brandy, beef stock, worcestershire sauce and mustard, and gradually stir into the onion mixture. Return to the heat, add the steak and any juices, then simmer, covered, for 1¼ hours.

Add the potatoes and simmer, uncovered, for a further 30 minutes, or until the meat and potatoes are tender. Stir in the cream and parsley, and season to taste with salt and freshly ground black pepper. This is delicious served with a green salad.

Beef and red wine stew

preparation 15 minutes
cooking 2 hours
serves 6

30 g (1 oz) butter
2 tablespoons oil
1 kg (2 lb 4 oz) topside steak, trimmed and cut into 3 cm (1¼ inch) cubes
100 g (3½ oz) bacon pieces, cut into 1.5 cm (⅝ inch) cubes
18 baby onions
2 garlic cloves, crushed
30 g (1 oz/¼ cup) plain (all-purpose) flour
500 ml (17 fl oz/2 cups) red wine
750 ml (26 fl oz/3 cups) beef stock
300 g (10½ oz) small mushrooms, halved

Heat the butter and oil in a heavy-based saucepan. Cook the meat quickly in small batches over medium–high heat until browned, then drain on paper towels.

Add the bacon, onions and garlic to the pan, and cook, stirring, for 2 minutes, or until browned. Add the flour and stir over low heat until lightly golden. Gradually pour in the wine and stock, and stir until smooth. Stir continuously over medium heat for 2 minutes, or until the mixture boils and thickens.

Return the meat to the pan and reduce the heat to a simmer. Cook, covered, for 1½ hours, or until the meat is tender, stirring occasionally. Add the mushrooms and cook for 15 minutes. Delicious served with mashed potato.

212

Cook the meat in small batches until browned, then drain on paper towels.

Bottom: Beef and red wine stew. Top: Beef and peppercorn stew.

Creamy garlic seafood stew

preparation 20 minutes
cooking 20 minutes
serves 6

12 scallops, with roe
500 g (1 lb 2 oz) skinless firm white fish fillets (see Note)
6 raw Moreton Bay bugs/flat-head lobster or crabs
500 g (1 lb 2 oz) raw prawns (shrimp), peeled and deveined, leaving the tails intact
50 g (2 oz) butter
1 onion, finely chopped
5–6 large garlic cloves, finely chopped
125 ml (4 fl oz/½ cup) dry white wine
500 ml (17 fl oz/2 cups) pouring (whipping) cream
1½ tablespoons dijon mustard
2 teaspoons lemon juice
2 tablespoons chopped flat-leaf (Italian) parsley
lemon wedges, to serve

Slice or pull off any membrane or hard muscle from the scallops. Cut the fish into 2 cm (¾ inch) cubes. Cut the heads off the bugs, then use kitchen scissors to cut down around the sides of the tail so you can flap open the shell. Remove the flesh in one piece, then slice each piece in half. Refrigerate all the seafood, covered, until ready to use.

Melt the butter in a frying pan and cook the onion and garlic over medium heat for 2 minutes, or until the onion is softened (be careful not to burn the garlic— it may become a little bitter).

Add the wine to the pan and cook for 4 minutes, or until reduced by half. Stir in the cream, mustard and lemon juice, and simmer for 5–6 minutes, or until reduced to almost half.

Add the prawns to the pan and cook for 1 minute, then add the bug meat and cook for another minute, or until white. Add the fish and cook for 2 minutes, or until cooked through (the flesh will flake easily when tested with a fork). Finally, add the scallops and cook for 1 minute. If any of the seafood is still not cooked, cook for another minute or so, but be careful not to overcook as this will result in tough flesh. Remove the frying pan from the heat and toss the parsley through. Season to taste. Serve with lemon wedges and bread, if desired.

Note *Try using perch, ling, bream, tuna or blue-eye.*

Use strong kitchen scissors to cut through the sides of each bug tail.

Pull back the shell of the bug and remove the flesh in one piece.

Beef in beer with capers

preparation 25 minutes
cooking 3 hours 20 minutes
serves 4–6

1 kg (2 lb 4 oz) gravy beef
seasoned plain (all-purpose) flour
olive oil, for cooking
4 garlic cloves, finely chopped
500 ml (17 fl oz/2 cups) beef stock
375 ml (13 fl oz/1½ cups) beer
2 onions, chopped
3 bay leaves
55 g (2 oz/⅓ cup) stuffed or pitted green olives, sliced
6 anchovies
2 tablespoons capers, drained

Cut the beef into 4 cm (1½ inch) chunks. Lightly coat the beef in the flour. Heat 60 ml (2 fl oz/¼ cup) of oil in a deep heavy-based saucepan, add the garlic, then brown the beef over a high heat.

Add the stock, beer, onion and bay leaves, season well and bring to the boil. Reduce the heat and gently simmer, covered, for 2½ hours, stirring about three times during cooking. Remove the lid and simmer for 30 minutes more. Stir, then mix in the olives.

Heat 2 teaspoons of oil in a small saucepan. Add the anchovies and capers, gently breaking up the anchovies. Cook over medium heat for 4 minutes, or until brown and crisp. To serve, place the meat on serving plates, drizzle with the sauce, sprinkle with anchovies and capers, and season with salt and freshly cracked black pepper.

Note *The capers should be squeezed very dry before being added to the pan, or they will spit in the hot oil.*

Lemon and rosemary chicken stew

preparation 10 minutes
cooking 30 minutes
serves 4

8 large chicken drumsticks
60 g (2¼ oz) butter
2 garlic cloves, crushed
2 teaspoons finely grated lemon zest
2 tablespoons chopped rosemary
1 tablespoon plain (all-purpose) flour
375 ml (13 fl oz/1½ cups) chicken stock
2 tablespoons lemon juice

Using a sharp knife, make two deep cuts in the thickest part of each chicken drumstick.

Melt the butter in a large frying pan. Add the drumsticks and cook over medium heat for 2 minutes on each side, or until brown. Add the garlic, lemon zest and rosemary.

Blend the flour, stock and lemon juice until smooth. Add to the pan and bring to the boil. Reduce the heat and simmer, covered, for 25 minutes, or until the drumsticks are tender, stirring occasionally. Season, and serve, ladling the sauce over the chicken. Delicious with green beans.

Hint *To check whether chicken is cooked, insert a skewer into the thickest part. If the juice runs clear, the chicken is cooked.*

Using a sharp knife, cut the gravy beef into large even-sized chunks.

Make two deep cuts in the thickest part of the chicken drumsticks.

Bottom: Lemon and rosemary chicken stew. Top: Beef in beer with capers.

Moroccan seafood with coriander

preparation 50 minutes
cooking 50 minutes
serves 6

2 tablespoons olive oil
2 red onions, roughly chopped
1 red capsicum (pepper), chopped
4 garlic cloves, crushed
2 teaspoons ground cumin
1 teaspoon ground coriander
2 teaspoons sweet paprika
½ teaspoon dried chilli flakes
250 ml (9 fl oz/1 cup) chicken or fish stock
400 g (14 oz) tin chopped tomatoes
80 ml (2½ fl oz/⅓ cup) orange juice
1 tablespoon sugar
40 g (1½ oz/⅓ cup) raisins
375 g (13 oz) baby new potatoes
500 g (1 lb 2 oz) baby octopus, cleaned
12 raw king prawns (shrimp), peeled and deveined, leaving the tails intact
1 kg (2 lb 4 oz) thick white fish fillets, cut into chunks

coriander purée
2 very large handfuls coriander (cilantro) leaves
2 tablespoons ground almonds
80 ml (2½ fl oz/⅓ cup) extra virgin olive oil
½ teaspoon ground cumin
1 teaspoon honey

Heat the olive oil in a large saucepan and then cook the onion over medium heat for about 5 minutes, or until soft. Add the capsicum and garlic, and cook for another minute. Add the cumin, coriander, paprika and chilli flakes, and cook until fragrant.

Pour in the stock, tomato, orange juice, sugar and raisins, and bring to the boil. Add the potatoes, reduce the heat to low and gently simmer for 20–30 minutes, or until the potatoes are just tender. Season to taste.

Use a small sharp knife to remove the octopus heads; slit the heads open and remove the gut. Grasp the body firmly and push the beak out with your index finger; remove and discard. Add the octopus, prawns and fish to the pan and cook, covered, for 10 minutes, or until the fish flakes when tested with a fork.

To make the coriander purée, place the coriander leaves and ground almonds in a food processor. With the motor running, drizzle in the oil and process until smooth, then add the cumin, honey and salt to taste. Process until well combined.

To serve, dish the stew onto serving plates and drizzle a spoonful of purée on top. Serve with couscous and a green leaf salad.

Peel and devein the prawns, and cut the cleaned octopus into bite-sized pieces.

Process the coriander leaves and ground almonds, gradually drizzling in the oil.

curries

Burmese chicken curry

preparation 45 minutes
cooking 1 hour
serves 6

1 kg (2 lb 4 oz) chicken drumsticks or thighs
2 large onions, roughly chopped
3 large garlic cloves, peeled
5 cm (2 inch) piece fresh ginger, peeled
2 tablespoons peanut oil
½ teaspoon shrimp paste or 60 ml (2 fl oz/¼ cup) fish sauce
500 ml (17 fl oz/2 cups) coconut milk
1 teaspoon chilli powder (optional)

traditional accompaniments
200 g (7 oz) bean starch noodles
6 spring onions (scallions), diagonally sliced
4 tablespoons chopped coriander (cilantro) leaves
2 tablespoons garlic flakes, lightly fried
2 tablespoons onion flakes, lightly fried
3 lemons, cut into wedges
4 dried chillies, fried in oil to crisp
60 ml (2 fl oz/¼ cup) fish sauce

Pat the chicken with paper towels. Place the onion, garlic and ginger in a food processor, and process until smooth. Add a little water to help blend the mixture, if necessary.

Heat the oil in a pan and add the onion mixture. Add the shrimp paste and cook, stirring, over high heat for 5 minutes. Add the chicken and cook over medium heat, turning until browned. Add some salt, coconut milk and chilli powder and bring to the boil. Reduce the heat to a simmer and cook, covered, for 30 minutes, stirring occasionally. Uncover, cook for 15 minutes, or until the chicken is tender.

Meanwhile, place the noodles in a bowl and cover with boiling water. Set aside for 20 minutes. Drain, then place in a serving bowl. Place the traditional accompaniments in separate, small bowls. Each person helps them self to a portion of noodles, chicken and a selection, or all, of the accompaniments.

Saffron chicken

preparation 25 minutes
cooking 1 hour 20 minutes
serves 6

1 teaspoon saffron threads
2 tablespoons hot water
2 tablespoons oil
2 onions, chopped
3 garlic cloves, crushed
3 cm (1¼ inch) piece fresh ginger, chopped
2 red chillies, seeded and sliced
1 teaspoon ground cardamom
1 teaspoon ground cumin
½ teaspoon ground turmeric
2 kg (4 lb 8 oz) chicken pieces (thighs, wings, drumsticks)
500 ml (17 fl oz/2 cups) chicken stock

Dry-fry the saffron threads in a frying pan over low heat for 1–2 minutes. Transfer to a small bowl, add the hot water and set aside.

Heat the oil in a saucepan over medium heat. Add the onion, garlic, ginger and chilli. Cover and cook for 10 minutes, or until very soft.

Add the cardamom, cumin and turmeric, and cook over medium heat for 2 minutes. Add the chicken pieces and cook over high heat for 3 minutes, or until the meat is well coated. Add the saffron liquid and the chicken stock. Bring to the boil, then reduce the heat and cook, covered, stirring occasionally, for 30 minutes.

Uncover, and cook for a further 20 minutes. Remove the chicken and keep warm. Reduce the stock to about 375 ml (13 fl oz/1½ cups) over very high heat. Pour over the chicken. Season to taste with salt and freshly ground black pepper. Serve with steamed rice.

Bottom: Saffron chicken. Top: Burmese chicken curry.

Vietnamese chicken curry

preparation 30 minutes
cooking 1 hour
serves 4

1.5 kg (3 lb 5 oz) chicken pieces, such as thighs, drumsticks and wings
2 tablespoons oil
4 garlic cloves, finely chopped
5 cm (2 inch) piece fresh ginger, finely chopped
2 lemongrass stems, white part only, finely chopped
2 teaspoons dried chilli flakes
2 tablespoons Asian curry powder (see Note)
2 brown onions, chopped
2 teaspoons sugar
375 ml (13 fl oz/1½ cups) coconut milk
garlic chives, cut into long strips, to serve
coriander leaves (cilantro), to serve
roasted peanuts, to serve

Using a large heavy knife or cleaver, chop each piece of chicken into two, chopping straight through the bone. Pat the chicken pieces dry with paper towels.

Heat the oil in a large deep frying pan. Add the garlic, ginger, lemongrass, chilli and curry powder and stir constantly over medium heat for 3 minutes, or until fragrant. Add the chicken, onion, sugar and 1 teaspoon of salt; toss gently. Cover, cook for 8 minutes, or until the onion has softened and then toss well to coat the chicken evenly with the curry mixture. Cover again and cook for 15 minutes over low heat.

Add the coconut milk and water to the pan. Bring to the boil, stirring occasionally. Reduce the heat and simmer, uncovered, for 30 minutes, or until the chicken is very tender. Serve the curry garnished with the chives, coriander and peanuts.

Note *Asian curry powders are available from speciality shops. There are different mixtures available for meat, chicken or fish.*

Chop each piece of chicken into two pieces, or ask your butcher to do it.

Toss the chicken pieces through the curry mixture, using two wooden spoons.

Nonya chicken curry

preparation 20 minutes
cooking 35 minutes
serves 4

curry paste
2 red onions, chopped
4 small red chillies, seeded and sliced
4 garlic cloves, sliced
2 lemongrass stems, white part only, sliced
3 cm x 2 cm (1¼ inch x ¾ inch) piece fresh galangal, sliced
8 makrut (kaffir lime) leaves, roughly chopped
1 teaspoon ground turmeric
½ teaspoon shrimp paste, roasted (see Note)

2 tablespoons oil
750 g (1 lb 10 oz) chicken thigh fillets, cut into bite-sized pieces
400 ml (14 fl oz) tin coconut milk
60 g (2 oz/¼ cup) tamarind purée
1 tablespoon fish sauce
3 makrut (kaffir lime) leaves, finely shredded, to garnish

To make the curry paste, place all the ingredients in a food processor or blender and process to a thick paste.

Heat a wok or large saucepan over high heat, add the oil and swirl to coat the side. Add the curry paste and cook, stirring occasionally, over low heat for 8–10 minutes, or until fragrant. Add the chicken and stir-fry with the paste for 2–3 minutes.

Add the coconut milk, tamarind purée and fish sauce to the wok, and simmer, stirring occasionally, for 15–20 minutes, or until the chicken is tender. Garnish with the makrut leaves. Serve with rice and steamed bok choy (pak choy).

Note *To dry-roast the shrimp paste, wrap it in foil and place it under a hot grill (broiler) for 1 minute.*

Beef and lentil curry

preparation 45 minutes + 10 minutes soaking
cooking 1 hour 50 minutes
serves 6

3–4 small dried red chillies
60 ml (2 fl oz/¼ cup) oil
2 red onions, cut into thin wedges
4 garlic cloves, finely chopped
1 tablespoon grated fresh ginger
1 tablespoon garam masala
3 cardamom pods, lightly crushed
1 cinnamon stick
2 teaspoons ground turmeric
750 g (1 lb 10 oz) chuck steak, cut into cubes
400 g (14 oz) tin chopped tomatoes
95 g (3 oz/½ cup) brown or green lentils
125 g (4½ oz/½ cup) red lentils
200 g (7 oz) pumpkin (winter squash), diced
150 g (5½ oz) eggplant (aubergine), diced
125 g (4½ oz) baby English spinach
1 tablespoon tamarind purée
2 tablespoons grated palm sugar (jaggery) or soft brown sugar

Soak the chillies in boiling water for 10 minutes, then drain and finely chop.

Heat the oil in a large saucepan. Add the onion and cook, stirring, over medium heat for 5 minutes, or until soft. Add the garlic and ginger, and cook for a further 2 minutes.

Add the chilli, garam masala, cardamom pods, cinnamon, turmeric and ½ teaspoon black pepper. Cook, stirring, for 2 minutes, or until fragrant. Add beef and stir constantly for 3–4 minutes, or until meat is coated in spices.

Add the tomato, lentils, 1 teaspoon salt and 750 ml (26 fl oz/ 3 cups) water. Simmer, covered, for 1 hour until tender. Stir often to prevent burning. Add extra water, if needed.

Add the pumpkin and eggplant to pan, and cook, covered, for 20 minutes, or until tender. Stir in the spinach, tamarind and palm sugar, and cook for a further 10 minutes.

Bottom: Beef and lentil curry. Top: Nonya chicken curry.

Lamb kofta curry

preparation 25 minutes
cooking 35 minutes
serves 4

500 g (1 lb 2 oz) minced (ground) lean lamb
1 onion, finely chopped
1 garlic clove, finely chopped
1 teaspoon grated fresh ginger
1 small fresh chilli, finely chopped
1 teaspoon garam masala
1 teaspoon ground coriander
25 g (1 oz/¼ cup) ground almonds
2 tablespoons coriander (cilantro) leaves
plain yoghurt, to serve

sauce
2 teaspoons oil
1 onion, finely chopped
60 g (2 oz/¼ cup) korma curry paste
400 g (14 oz) tin chopped tomatoes
125 g (4½ oz/½ cup) low-fat yoghurt
1 teaspoon lemon juice

Combine the lamb, onion, garlic, ginger, chilli, garam masala, ground coriander, ground almonds and 1 teaspoon salt in a bowl. Roll into walnut-sized balls.

Heat a large non-stick frying pan and cook the koftas in batches until brown on both sides—they don't have to be cooked all the way through.

To make the sauce, heat the oil in a frying pan over low heat. Add the onion and cook for 6–8 minutes, or until soft and golden. Add the curry paste and cook until fragrant. Add the tomatoes and simmer for 5 minutes. Stir in the yoghurt, a tablespoon at a time, and then the lemon juice.

Put the koftas in the tomato sauce. Cook, covered, over low heat for 20 minutes. Garnish with the coriander leaves and serve with the yoghurt.

Malaysian fish curry

preparation 25 minutes
cooking 25 minutes
serves 4

5 cm (2 inch) piece fresh ginger
3–6 medium red chillies
1 onion, chopped
4 garlic cloves, chopped
3 lemongrass stems, white part only, sliced
2 teaspoons shrimp paste
60 ml (2 fl oz/¼ cup) oil
1 tablespoon fish curry powder (see Note)
250 ml (9 fl oz/1 cup) coconut milk
1 tablespoon tamarind concentrate
1 tablespoon kecap manis
500 g (1 lb 2 oz) firm white skinless fish fillets, cut into cubes
2 ripe tomatoes, chopped
1 tablespoon lemon juice

Slice the ginger and mix in a small food processor with the chillies, onion, garlic, lemongrass and shrimp paste until roughly chopped. Add 2 tablespoons of the oil and process until a paste forms, regularly scraping the side of the bowl with a spatula.

Heat the remaining oil in a wok or deep, heavy-based frying pan and add the paste. Cook for 3–4 minutes over low heat, stirring constantly, until fragrant. Add the curry powder and stir for 2 minutes. Add the coconut milk, tamarind, kecap manis and 250 ml (9 fl oz/1 cup) water. Bring to the boil, stirring occasionally, then reduce the heat and simmer for 10 minutes.

Add the fish, tomato and lemon juice. Season to taste, then simmer for 5 minutes, or until the fish is just cooked (it will flake easily).

Note Fish curry powder blend is available from speciality Asian grocery stores.

Roll the lamb mixture into walnut-sized balls with your hands.

Add the curry powder to the wok and stir for 2 minutes.

Bottom: Malaysian fish curry. Top: Lamb kofta curry.

Curried chicken in spicy tomato sauce

preparation 35 minutes
cooking 1 hour 40 minutes
serves 10

1 tablespoon olive oil
2 x 1.5 kg (3 lb 5 oz) chickens, jointed
1 onion, sliced
½ teaspoon ground cloves
1 teaspoon ground turmeric
2 teaspoons garam masala
3 teaspoons chilli powder
3 garlic cloves
1 tablespoon finely chopped fresh ginger
1 tablespoon poppy seeds
2 teaspoons fennel seeds
3 cardamom pods, seeds removed (see Note)
250 ml (9 fl oz/1 cup) light coconut milk
1 star anise
1 cinnamon stick
4 large tomatoes, roughly chopped
2 tablespoons lime juice

Heat the olive oil in a large frying pan, add the chicken in batches and cook for 5–10 minutes, or until browned, then transfer to a large saucepan.

Add the onion to the frying pan and cook, stirring, for 10–12minutes, or until golden. Stir in the ground cloves, turmeric, garam masala and chilli powder, and cook, stirring, for 1 minute, then add to the chicken.

Put the garlic, ginger, poppy seeds, fennel seeds, cardamom seeds and 2 tablespoons of the coconut milk in a food processor or blender, and process until smooth. Add the spice mixture, remaining coconut milk, star anise, cinnamon, tomato and 60 ml (2 fl oz/¼ cup) water to the chicken.

Simmer, covered, for 45 minutes, or until the chicken is tender. Remove the chicken, cover and keep warm. Bring the cooking liquid to the boil and boil for 20–25 minutes, or until reduced by half. Mix the lime juice with the cooking liquid and pour over the chicken. Serve with low-fat yoghurt.

Note *To remove the cardamom seeds from the cardamom pods, crush the pods with the flat side of a heavy knife, then peel away the pod with your fingers, scraping out the seeds.*

Crush the cardamom pods with the back of a knife and then remove the seeds.

Process the garlic, spices and coconut milk until the mixture is smooth.

Thai duck and pineapple curry

preparation 10 minutes
cooking 15 minutes
serves 4–6

1 tablespoon peanut oil
8 spring onions (scallions), sliced on the diagonal
into 3 cm (1¼ inch) lengths
2 garlic cloves, crushed
2–4 tablespoons Thai red curry paste
750 g (1 lb 10 oz) Chinese roast duck, chopped
400 ml (14 fl oz) tin coconut milk
450 g (1 lb) tin pineapple pieces in syrup, drained
3 makrut (kaffir lime) leaves
1 large handful coriander (cilantro) leaves, chopped, plus extra
leaves, to garnish
2 tablespoons chopped mint, plus extra leaves, to garnish

Heat a wok until very hot, add the peanut oil and swirl to coat the side. Add the spring onion, garlic and red curry paste, and stir-fry for 1 minute, or until fragrant.

Add the roast duck, coconut milk, pineapple pieces, makrut leaves, and half each of the coriander and mint. Bring to the boil, then reduce the heat and simmer for 10 minutes, or until the duck is heated through and the sauce has thickened slightly. Stir in the remaining fresh herbs. Garnish with extra coriander and mint leaves and serve with steamed jasmine rice.

Crab curry

preparation 25 minutes
cooking 20 minutes
serves 6

4 raw large blue swimmer or mud crabs
1 tablespoon oil
1 large onion, finely chopped
2 garlic cloves, crushed
1 lemongrass stem, white part only, finely chopped
1 teaspoon sambal oelek (Southeast Asian chilli paste)
1 teaspoon ground cumin
1 teaspoon ground turmeric
1 teaspoon ground coriander
270 ml (9½ fl oz) coconut cream
500 ml (17 fl oz/2 cups) chicken stock
1 large handful basil leaves

Pull back the apron and remove the top shell from the crabs. Remove the intestines and grey feathery gills. Cut each crab into four pieces. Use a cracker to crack the claws open; this will make it easier to eat later and will also allow the flavours to get into the crabmeat.

Heat the oil in a large saucepan or wok. Add the onion, garlic, lemongrass and sambal oelek, and cook for 2–3 minutes, or until softened.

Add the cumin, turmeric, coriander and ½ teaspoon salt, and cook for a further 2 minutes, or until fragrant.

Stir in the coconut cream and stock. Bring to the boil, then reduce the heat, add the crab pieces and cook, stirring occasionally, for 10 minutes, or until the liquid has reduced and thickened slightly and the crabs are cooked. Scatter the basil leaves over the crab and serve with rice.

Simmer until the duck is heated through and the sauce has thickened slightly.

Remove the intestines and grey feathery gills from the crabs.

Bottom: Crab curry. Top: Thai duck and pineapple curry.

Goan-style chicken with sultanas and almonds

preparation 20 minutes
cooking 20 minutes
serves 3–4

2 teaspoons ground cumin
2 teaspoons ground coriander
1 teaspoon ground cinnamon
½ teaspoon cayenne pepper
½ teaspoon ground cardamom
oil, for cooking
1 large onion, cut into thin wedges
2 garlic cloves, finely chopped
500 g (1 lb 2 oz) boneless, skinless chicken breasts,
cut into cubes
2 teaspoons finely grated orange zest
2 tablespoons orange juice
2 tablespoons sultanas (golden raisins)
1 teaspoon soft brown sugar
60 g (2 oz/¼ cup) thick plain yoghurt
40 g (1½ oz/⅓ cup) slivered almonds, toasted

Dry-fry the spices in a wok over low heat for about
1 minute, or until fragrant, shaking the wok regularly.

Add 1 tablespoon oil to the wok and stir-fry the onion
wedges and garlic over high heat for 3 minutes. Remove
from the wok.

Reheat the wok, add 1 tablespoon of the oil and stir-fry the
chicken in two batches until it is golden and just cooked.
Return all the chicken to the wok with the onion mixture,
orange zest, juice, sultanas and sugar. Cook for 1 minute,
tossing until most of the juice evaporates.

Stir in the yoghurt and reheat gently, without boiling or the
yoghurt will separate. Season well with salt and pepper.
Serve garnished with the toasted almonds.

Note *Yoghurt separates easily when heated due to its acid
balance. Yoghurt also separates when shaken, whipped or
stirred too much.*

Toast the almonds by dry-frying them in the wok
until golden brown.

Spiced liver curry

preparation 25 minutes + 2 hours marinating
cooking 20 minutes
serves 4

60 ml (2 fl oz/¼ cup) dark soy sauce
3 garlic cloves, crushed
1 tablespoon sesame seeds, toasted
1 teaspoon sesame oil
500 g (1 lb 2 oz) chicken livers, trimmed and sliced
2 tablespoons olive oil
1 onion, sliced
1 red capsicum (pepper), sliced
1 teaspoon ground coriander
1 teaspoon ground cumin
2 tablespoons peanut oil
125 ml (4½ fl oz/½ cup) chicken stock
100 g (3½ oz) snow peas (mangetouts), trimmed
sesame seeds, toasted, to garnish

Combine the soy sauce, garlic, sesame seeds and sesame
oil with 2 tablespoons water. Place the liver in a dish and
pour over the marinade. Cover and refrigerate for 2 hours.

Heat half the olive oil in a large, heavy-based saucepan and
cook the onion and capsicum over medium–low heat for
5–10 minutes, or until softened. Remove from the pan and
set aside.

Sprinkle the liver with coriander and cumin and season
well with pepper. Remove from the dish, reserving the
marinade.

Heat the remaining olive oil and the peanut oil in a
saucepan and add the liver. Cook over high heat, turning
often, for about 3–5 minutes, or until firm but still slightly
pink inside. Return the onion, capsicum and reserved
marinade to the pan. Add the stock and snow peas, and
simmer gently for 2–3 minutes. Serve immediately, with
rice, if desired. Garnish with toasted sesame seeds.

Mix together the marinade ingredients and then
pour over the liver to coat.

Bottom: Spiced liver curry. Top: Goan-style chicken with sultanas and almonds.

Pork and tamarind curry

preparation 20 minutes
cooking 1 hour 50 minutes
serves 6

80 ml (2½ fl oz/⅓ cup) oil
2 onions, thickly sliced
4 large garlic cloves, crushed
60 g (2 oz/¼ cup) Sri Lankan curry powder
1 tablespoon grated fresh ginger
10 dried curry leaves or 5 fresh curry leaves
2 teaspoons chilli powder
¼ teaspoon fenugreek seeds
1.25 kg (2 lb 12 oz) lean pork shoulder, cubed
1 lemongrass stem, white part only, finely chopped
2 tablespoons tamarind purée
4 cardamom pods, crushed
400 ml (14 fl oz) tin coconut cream

cucumber sambal
1–2 large cucumbers, halved, seeded and finely chopped
500 g (1 lb 2 oz/2 cups) plain yoghurt
2 tablespoons coriander (cilantro) leaves, finely chopped
1 tablespoon lemon juice
2 garlic cloves, crushed

Heat the oil in a heavy-based Dutch oven or deep, lidded frying pan. Add the onion, garlic, curry powder, ginger, curry leaves, chilli powder, fenugreek seeds and 1 teaspoon salt, and cook, stirring, over medium heat for 5 minutes.

Add the pork, lemongrass, tamarind purée, cardamom and 375 ml (13 fl oz/1½ cups) hot water, then reduce the heat and simmer, covered, for 1 hour.

Stir in the coconut cream and simmer on a low heat, uncovered, for 40–45 minutes, or until the sauce has reduced and become thick and creamy.

To make the cucumber sambal, place the cucumber in a bowl and stir in the yoghurt, coriander, lemon juice and garlic. Season to taste with salt and pepper.

Serve the curry with the cucumber sambal, steamed basmati rice and chapattis.

Halve the cucumber, remove the seeds and finely chop the flesh.

Cook the onion, garlic and spices in a heavy-based frying pan.

curries

Burmese pork curry

preparation 30 minutes
cooking 1 hour
serves 6

2 lemongrass stems, white part only, sliced
1 red onion, chopped
1 garlic clove
1 teaspoon grated fresh ginger
2 large red dried chillies
1 teaspoon fenugreek seeds, roasted and ground
1 teaspoon yellow mustard seeds, roasted and ground
2 teaspoons paprika
2 tablespoons worcestershire sauce
750 g (1 lb 10 oz) lean boneless shoulder of pork, cut into cubes
2 tablespoons fish sauce
6 new potatoes, peeled and sliced
2 small red onions, diced
1 tablespoon olive oil
2 tablespoons mango chutney

Put the lemongrass, onion, garlic, ginger, chillies, seeds, paprika and sauce in a processor or blender and mix to a thick paste.

Place the pork in a bowl, sprinkle with the fish sauce and ¼ teaspoon ground black pepper.

Place the potato and onion in another bowl, add 60 g (2 oz/¼ cup) of the paste and toss to coat. Add the remaining paste to the pork. Mix well.

Heat the oil in a frying pan or wok over medium heat. Add the pork and cook in batches, stirring, for 8 minutes, or until the meat begins to brown. Remove from the pan. Add the potato and onion and cook, stirring, for 5 minutes, or until soft and starting to brown.

Return the meat to the pan and stir in 750 ml (26 fl oz/ 3 cups) water, adding 250 ml (9 fl oz/1 cup) at a time. Stir in the mango chutney, then reduce the heat and simmer for 30 minutes.

Rogan josh

preparation 25 minutes
cooking 1 hour 40 minutes
serves 6

1 kg (2 lb 4 oz) boned leg of lamb
1 tablespoon oil
2 onions, chopped
125 g (4½ oz/½ cup) low-fat plain yoghurt
1 teaspoon chilli powder
1 tablespoon ground coriander
2 teaspoons ground cumin
1 teaspoon ground cardamom
½ teaspoon ground cloves
1 teaspoon ground turmeric
3 garlic cloves, crushed
1 tablespoon grated fresh ginger
400 g (14 oz) tin chopped tomatoes
30 g (1 oz/¼ cup) slivered almonds
1 teaspoon garam masala
chopped coriander (cilantro) leaves, to serve

Trim the lamb of any fat or sinew and cut into small cubes.

Heat the oil in a large saucepan, add the onion and cook, stirring, for 5 minutes, or until soft. Stir in the yoghurt, chilli powder, coriander, cumin, cardamom, cloves, turmeric, garlic and ginger. Add the tomato and 1 teaspoon salt and simmer for 5 minutes.

Add the lamb and stir until coated. Cover and cook over low heat, stirring occasionally, for 1–1½ hours, or until the lamb is tender. Uncover and simmer until the liquid thickens.

Meanwhile, toast the almonds in a dry frying pan over medium heat for 3–4 minutes, shaking the pan gently, until the nuts are golden. Remove from the pan at once to prevent them burning.

Add the garam masala to the curry and mix through well. Sprinkle the slivered almonds and coriander leaves over the top and serve.

Bottom: Rogan josh. Top: Burmese pork curry.

Prawn curry

preparation 25 minutes
cooking 15 minutes
serves 6

1 tablespoon butter
1 onion, finely chopped
1 garlic clove, crushed
1½ tablespoons curry powder
2 tablespoons plain (all-purpose) flour
500 ml (17 fl oz/2 cups) skim milk
1 kg (2 lb 4 oz) raw prawns (shrimp), peeled and deveined
1½ tablespoons lemon juice
2 teaspoons sherry
1 tablespoon finely chopped parsley

Heat the butter in a large saucepan. Add the onion and garlic, and cook for 5 minutes, or until softened. Add the curry powder and cook for 1 minute, then stir in the flour and cook for a further 1 minute.

Remove from the heat and stir in the milk until smooth. Return to the heat and stir constantly until the sauce has thickened. Simmer for 2 minutes and then stir in the prawns. Continue to simmer for 5 minutes, or until the prawns are just cooked.

Stir in the lemon juice, sherry and parsley and serve immediately with rice.

Bombay curry

preparation 20 minutes
cooking 2 hours
serves 6

1 kg (2 lb 4 oz) chuck steak
1 tablespoon olive oil
2 onions, chopped
2 garlic cloves, crushed
2 green chillies, chopped
1 tablespoon grated fresh ginger
1½ teaspoons ground turmeric
1 teaspoon ground cumin
1 tablespoon ground coriander
½–1 teaspoon chilli powder
400 g (14 oz) tin tomatoes
250 ml (9 fl oz/1 cup) light coconut milk

Cut the beef into cubes. Heat the oil in a large saucepan and cook the onion until just soft.

Add the garlic, chilli, ginger, turmeric, cumin, coriander and chilli powder. Stir until heated; add the beef and cook, stirring, over high heat until coated with the spice mixture.

Add 1 teaspoon salt and tomatoes. Simmer, covered, for 1–1½ hours, or until the beef is tender. Stir in the coconut milk and simmer, uncovered, for a further 5–10 minutes, or until slightly thickened.

Note *Bombay curry is best made 1–2 days in advance to give the flavours time to develop. Store, covered, in the refrigerator.*

Add the prawns and continue to simmer until they are just cooked.

Add the garlic, chilli, ginger, turmeric, cumin, coriander and chilli powder.

Bottom: Bombay curry. Top: Prawn curry.

Thai beef and peanut curry

preparation 30 minutes + 5 minutes soaking
cooking 1 hour 30 minutes
serves 4–6

curry paste
8–10 large dried red chillies
6 red Asian shallots (eschalots), chopped
6 garlic cloves, chopped
1 teaspoon ground coriander
1 tablespoon ground cumin
1 teaspoon ground white pepper
2 lemongrass stems, white part only, bruised and sliced
1 tablespoon chopped fresh galangal
6 coriander (cilantro) roots
2 teaspoons shrimp paste
2 tablespoons roasted peanuts
peanut oil, if needed

1 tablespoon peanut oil
400 ml (14 fl oz) tin coconut cream (do not shake the tin—see Note)
1 kg (2 lb 4 oz) round or blade steak, thinly sliced
400 ml (14 fl oz) tin coconut milk
4 makrut (kaffir lime) leaves, whole
90 g (3 oz/⅓ cup) crunchy peanut butter
60 ml (2 fl oz/¼ cup) lime juice
2½ tablespoons fish sauce
60–80 g (2–3 oz/¼–⅓ cup) grated palm sugar (jaggery) or soft brown sugar
Thai basil leaves, to garnish
1 tablespoon chopped peanuts, extra, to garnish (optional)

To make the curry paste, soak the chillies in boiling water for 5 minutes, or until soft. Remove the stem and seeds, then chop. Place all the curry paste ingredients in a food processor and process to a smooth paste. Add a little peanut oil if it is too thick.

Place the oil and the thick cream from the top of the coconut cream (reserving the rest) in a large saucepan over high heat. Add 6–8 tablespoons of the curry paste and cook, stirring, for 5 minutes, or until fragrant. Cook for 5–10 minutes, or until the cream splits and becomes oily.

Add the beef, the reserved coconut cream, the coconut milk, makrut leaves and peanut butter, and cook for 8 minutes, or until the beef just starts to change colour. Reduce the heat and simmer for 1 hour, or until the beef is tender.

Stir in the lime juice, fish sauce and palm sugar, and transfer to a serving dish. Garnish with the Thai basil leaves, and extra peanuts, if desired, and serve immediately.

Note *Good-quality coconut cream has a layer of very thick cream at the top which splits more readily than the rest of the cream.*

Place all the curry paste ingredients in a food processor and process until smooth.

Cook the coconut cream and curry paste until it splits and becomes oily.

Thai beef and pumpkin curry

preparation 20 minutes
cooking 1 hour 30 minutes
serves 6

2 tablespoons oil
750 g (1 lb 10 oz) blade steak, thinly sliced
80 g (3 oz/⅓ cup) ready-made Massaman curry paste
2 garlic cloves, finely chopped
1 onion, sliced lengthways
6 curry leaves, torn
750 ml (26 fl oz/3 cups) coconut milk
450 g (1 lb) butternut pumpkin (squash), roughly diced
2 tablespoons chopped unsalted peanuts
1 tablespoon grated palm sugar (jaggery) or soft brown sugar
2 tablespoons tamarind purée
2 tablespoons fish sauce
curry leaves, extra, to garnish

Heat a wok or frying pan over high heat. Add the oil and swirl to coat the side. Add the meat in batches and cook for 5 minutes, or until browned. Remove from the wok.

Add the curry paste, garlic, onion and curry leaves to the wok, and stir to coat. Return the meat to the wok and cook, stirring, over medium heat for 2 minutes.

Add the coconut milk to the wok, then reduce the heat to low and gently simmer for 45 minutes. Add the pumpkin and simmer for 25–30 minutes, or until the meat and the pumpkin are tender and the sauce has thickened.

Stir in the peanuts, palm sugar, tamarind purée and fish sauce, and simmer for 1 minute. Garnish with curry leaves and season with black pepper. Serve with steamed rice.

Lamb neck curry

preparation 30 minutes
cooking 1 hour 40 minutes
serves 4–6

1 tablespoon oil
8 best lamb neck chops (see Note)
2 onions, sliced
3 garlic cloves, finely chopped
2 teaspoons finely chopped fresh ginger
1 small green chilli, seeded and finely chopped
½ teaspoon ground cumin
1 teaspoon ground fennel
1½ teaspoons ground turmeric
1½ teaspoons chilli powder
2 teaspoons garam masala
1 star anise
1 cinnamon stick
5 curry leaves
2 bay leaves
500 ml (17 fl oz/2 cups) beef stock
8 tomatoes, peeled and quartered
coriander (cilantro) leaves, to garnish

Heat the oil in a large frying pan and cook the lamb in batches for 5–8 minutes, or until browned. Place the chops in a large saucepan.

Add the onion to the frying pan and cook, stirring frequently, for 5 minutes, or until soft and browned. Stir in the garlic, ginger and chilli, and cook for 1 minute. Then stir in the cumin, fennel, turmeric, chilli powder, garam masala, star anise, cinnamon stick, curry leaves and bay leaves, and cook, stirring to prevent sticking, for a further 1 minute.

Add 2 tablespoons cold water to the frying pan, mix well, and then add the beef stock. Bring to the boil, then pour over the lamb. Stir in the tomato, reduce the heat and simmer, covered, for 1¼ hours. Garnish with coriander and serve with jasmine rice.

Note *Best lamb neck chops come from the meat just under the shoulder and are sweeter, leaner and meatier than lamb neck.*

Add the meat to the wok and cook in small batches until browned.

Stir the spices to prevent them from sticking to the base of the pan.

Bottom: Lamb neck curry. Top: Thai beef and pumpkn curry.

Chicken kapitan

preparation 35 minutes
cooking 1 hour 20 minutes
serves 4–6

1 teaspoon small dried shrimp
80 ml (2½ fl oz/⅓ cup) oil
6–8 red chillies, seeded and finely chopped
4 garlic cloves, finely chopped
3 lemongrass stems, white part only, finely chopped
2 teaspoons ground turmeric
10 macadamia nuts
2 large onions, chopped
250 ml (9 fl oz/1 cup) coconut milk
1.5 kg (3 lb 5 oz) whole chicken, cut into 8 pieces
125 ml (4 fl oz/½ cup) coconut cream
2 tablespoons lime juice
lime wedges, to serve

Put the shrimp in a frying pan and dry-fry (no oil) over a low heat, shaking the pan regularly, for 3 minutes, or until the shrimp are dark orange and are giving off a strong aroma. Transfer to a mortar and pound with a pestle until finely ground. Alternatively, you may process in a food processor.

Place half of the oil, the chilli, garlic, lemongrass, turmeric and nuts in a food processor, and process in short bursts until very finely chopped, regularly scraping down the side of the bowl.

Heat the remaining oil in a wok or frying pan, add the onion and ¼ teaspoon salt, and cook, stirring regularly, over low heat for 8 minutes, or until golden.

Add the spice mixture and shrimp, and stir for 5 minutes. If the mixture begins to stick, add 2 tablespoons of the coconut milk. It is important to cook the mixture thoroughly to develop the flavours.

Add the chicken to the wok and cook, stirring, for 5 minutes, or until beginning to brown. Stir in the remaining coconut milk and 250 ml (9 fl oz/1 cup) water, and bring to the boil. Reduce the heat and simmer for 50 minutes, or until the chicken is cooked and the sauce has thickened slightly. Add the coconut cream and bring the mixture back to the boil, stirring constantly. Add the lime juice and serve immediately with rice and lime wedges.

Dry-fry the shrimp over low heat until they turn dark orange and fragrant.

Place the shrimp in a mortar and pound with a pestle until finely ground.

Lamb korma

preparation 30 minutes + 1 hour marinating
cooking 1 hour 10 minutes
serves 4–6

2 kg (4 lb 8 oz) leg of lamb, boned
1 onion, chopped
2 teaspoons grated fresh ginger
3 garlic cloves
2 teaspoons ground coriander
2 teaspoons ground cumin
1 teaspoon cardamom seeds
large pinch cayenne pepper
2 tablespoons ghee or oil
1 onion, extra, sliced
2½ tablespoons tomato paste (concentrated purée)
125 g (4½ oz/½ cup) plain yoghurt
125 ml (4 fl oz/½ cup) coconut cream
55 g (2 oz/½ cup) ground almonds
toasted slivered almonds, to serve

Trim any excess fat or sinew from the lamb, cut it into 3 cm (1¼ inch) cubes and place in a large bowl.

Place the chopped onion, ginger, garlic, coriander, cumin, cardamom seeds, cayenne pepper and ½ teaspoon salt in a food processor. Process the ingredients until they form a smooth paste. Add the spice mixture to the cubed lamb and mix well to coat the lamb in the spices. Leave to marinate for 1 hour.

Heat the ghee in a large saucepan, add the sliced onion and cook, stirring, over low heat for 7 minutes, or until the onion is soft. Add the lamb and spice mixture, and cook, stirring constantly, for 8–10 minutes, or until the lamb changes colour. Stir in the tomato paste, yoghurt, coconut cream and ground almonds.

Reduce the heat and simmer the curry, covered, stirring occasionally, for 50 minutes, or until the meat is tender. Add a little water if the mixture becomes too dry. Season the curry with salt and pepper, and garnish with the toasted slivered almonds. Serve with steamed rice.

Coconut seafood and tofu curry

preparation 30 minutes
cooking 30 minutes
serves 4

2 tablespoons soya bean oil, or cooking oil
500 g (1 lb 2 oz) firm white fish (ling, perch),
cut into 2 cm (¾ inch) cubes
250 g (9 oz) raw prawns (shrimp), peeled and deveined, leaving the tails intact
2 x 400 ml (14 fl oz) tins coconut milk
1 tablespoon Thai red curry paste
4 fresh or 8 dried makrut (kaffir lime) leaves
2 tablespoons fish sauce
2 tablespoons finely chopped lemongrass, white part only
2 garlic cloves, crushed
1 tablespoon finely chopped fresh galangal
1 tablespoon shaved palm sugar (jaggery) or soft brown sugar
300 g (10½ oz) silken firm tofu, cut into 1.5 cm (⅝ inch) cubes
125 g (4½ oz/½ cup) bamboo shoots, trimmed and cut into matchsticks
1 large red chilli, thinly sliced
2 teaspoons lime juice
spring onions (scallions), chopped, to garnish
coriander (cilantro) leaves, to garnish

Heat the oil in a large frying pan or wok over medium heat. Sear fish and prawns for 1 minute on each side. Remove the seafood from the pan.

Place 60 ml (2 fl oz/¼ cup) of the coconut milk and the curry paste in the frying pan, and cook over medium heat for 2 minutes, or until fragrant and the oil separates. Add the remaining coconut milk, makrut leaves, fish sauce, lemongrass, garlic, galangal, palm sugar and 1 teaspoon salt. Cook over low heat for 15 minutes.

Add the tofu, bamboo shoots and chilli. Simmer for a further 3–5 minutes. Return to medium heat, add the seafood and lime juice, and cook for a further 3 minutes, or until the seafood is just cooked. Serve with steamed rice and garnish with the spring onion and coriander.

Bottom: Coconut seafood and tofu curry. Top: Lamb korma.

Beef rendang

preparation 20 minutes
cooking 2 hours 30 minutes
serves 6

2 onions, roughly chopped
2 garlic cloves, crushed
400 ml (14 fl oz) tin coconut milk
2 teaspoons ground coriander seeds
½ teaspoon ground fennel seeds
2 teaspoons ground cumin seeds
¼ teaspoon ground cloves
1.5 kg (3 lb 5 oz) chuck steak, cut into 3 cm (1¼ inch) cubes
4–6 small fresh red chillies, chopped
1 tablespoon lemon juice
1 lemongrass stem, white part only, bruised, cut lengthways
2 teaspoons grated palm sugar (jaggery) or soft brown sugar
coriander (cilantro) sprigs, to garnish

Place the onion and garlic in a food processor, and process until smooth, adding water, if necessary.

Place the coconut milk in a large saucepan and bring to the boil, then reduce the heat to medium and cook, stirring occasionally, for 15 minutes, or until the milk has reduced by half and the oil has separated. Do not allow the milk to brown.

Add the coriander seeds, fennel, cumin and cloves to the pan, and stir for 1 minute. Add the meat and cook for 2 minutes, or until it changes colour. Add the onion mixture, chilli, lemon juice, lemongrass and palm sugar. Cook, covered, over medium heat for 2 hours, or until the liquid has reduced and the mixture has thickened. Stir frequently to prevent it sticking to the bottom of the pan.

Uncover and continue cooking until the oil from the coconut milk begins to emerge again, letting the curry develop. Be careful that it does not burn. The curry is cooked when it is brown and dry. Serve with rice and coriander sprigs.

Goan fish curry

preparation 20 minutes
cooking 35 minutes
serves 6

60 ml (2 fl oz/¼ cup) oil
1 large onion, finely chopped
4–5 garlic cloves, chopped
2 teaspoons grated fresh ginger
4–6 small dried red chillies
1 tablespoon coriander seeds
2 teaspoons cumin seeds
1 teaspoon ground turmeric
¼ teaspoon chilli powder
30 g (1 oz/⅓ cup) desiccated coconut
270 ml (9½ fl oz) coconut milk
2 tomatoes, peeled and chopped
2 tablespoons tamarind purée
1 tablespoon white vinegar
6 curry leaves
1 kg (2 lb 4 oz) boneless, skinless firm fish fillets, such as flake or ling, cut into 8 cm (3 inch) pieces
coriander (cilantro) leaves, to garnish

Heat the oil in a large saucepan. Add the onion and cook, stirring, over low heat for 10 minutes, or until softened. Add the garlic and ginger, and cook for a further 2 minutes.

Place the chillies, coriander seeds, cumin seeds, turmeric, chilli powder and desiccated coconut in a frying pan, and dry-fry, stirring constantly, over medium heat for 2 minutes, or until aromatic. Place in a food processor and finely grind.

Add the spice mixture, coconut milk, tomato, tamarind purée, vinegar and curry leaves to the onion mixture. Stir to mix thoroughly, add 250 ml (9 fl oz/1 cup) water and simmer for 10 minutes, or until mixture has softened and just thickened. Stir frequently to prevent sticking.

Add the fish and cook, covered, over low heat for 10 minutes, or until cooked through. Stir gently once or twice and add water if needed. Garnish with coriander and serve with rice and poppadoms.

Process the onion and garlic in a food processor until the mixture is smooth.

Simmer until the tomato has softened and the mixture has thickened slightly.

Bottom: Goan fish curry. Top: Beef rendang.

Lamb and spinach curry

preparation 30 minutes
cooking 2 hours 20 minutes
serves 6

1 kg (2 lb 4 oz) English spinach
125 ml (4 fl oz/½ cup) oil
1.5 kg (3 lb 5 oz) boned leg of lamb, cut into 3 cm (1¼ inch) cubes (see Note)
2 red onions, finely chopped
6 garlic cloves, crushed
1½ tablespoons grated fresh ginger
2 bay leaves
2 tablespoons ground coriander
1 tablespoon ground cumin
1 teaspoon ground turmeric
2 large vine-ripened tomatoes, peeled, seeded and chopped
2–3 small green chillies, seeded and finely chopped
100 g (3½ oz) Greek-style yoghurt
1 cinnamon stick
2 teaspoons garam masala
coriander (cilantro) leaves, to garnish

Preheat the oven to 170°C (325°F/Gas 3). Trim the spinach and quickly blanch in simmering water. Drain, cool slightly and squeeze to remove any excess moisture, then process in a food processor until smooth.

Heat half the oil in a large saucepan. Add the lamb pieces in batches and cook over high heat for 4–5 minutes, or until browned. Remove the lamb from the pan.

Heat the remaining oil in the saucepan. Add the onion and cook, stirring frequently, for 10 minutes, or until golden brown but not burnt. Add the garlic, ginger and bay leaves, and cook, stirring, for 3 more minutes.

Add the spices and cook, stirring, for 2 minutes, or until fragrant. Add the tomato and chilli, and stir over low heat for 5 minutes, or until the tomato is thick and pulpy. Remove from the heat and cool for 5 minutes. Transfer to a 4 litre (140 fl oz/16 cup) casserole dish and stir in the yoghurt.

Add the meat to the dish and add the cinnamon stick and 1 teaspoon salt. Bake, covered, for 1 hour and then uncovered for a further 15 minutes. Stir in the spinach and garam masala, and cook, stirring occasionally, for 15 minutes, or until the meat is tender. Remove the bay leaves and cinnamon stick, garnish with coriander and serve with rice.

Note Ask your butcher to bone and cut the lamb for you. A 2.2 kg (4 lb 15 oz) leg will yield about 1.5 kg (3 lb 5 oz) meat.

Squeeze the blanched, cooled spinach to remove any excess moisture.

Process the cooked spinach in a food processor until it becomes smooth.

Beef and pineapple curry

preparation 10 minutes
cooking 12 minutes
serves 4

2 tablespoons peanut oil
500 g (1 lb 2 oz) rump steak, thinly sliced across the grain
2 tablespoons penang curry paste
2 onions, cut into thin wedges
2 garlic cloves, crushed
500 ml (17 fl oz/2 cups) coconut milk
8 makrut (kaffir lime) leaves
320 g (11 oz/2 cups) chopped fresh pineapple
2 teaspoons soft brown sugar
2 tablespoons lime juice
1 tablespoon fish sauce
3 tablespoons chopped coriander (cilantro) leaves

Heat a wok over high heat, add half the oil and swirl to coat the sides. Add the beef in batches and stir-fry for 2 minutes, or until browned. Remove.

Heat the remaining oil in the wok over high heat, add the curry paste and cook for 1 minute, or until fragrant. Add the onion and garlic and cook for 1–2 minutes, or until the onion is soft.

Return the beef to the wok, add the coconut milk, makrut leaves and pineapple and bring to the boil, then reduce the heat and simmer for 5 minutes, or until the beef is just cooked. Stir in the sugar, lime juice, fish sauce and coriander just before serving.

Kashmir lamb with spinach

preparation 20 minutes
cooking 1 hour 30 minutes
serves 4

2 tablespoons oil
750 g (1 lb 10 oz) diced leg of lamb
2 large onions, chopped
3 garlic cloves, crushed
5 cm (2 inch) piece fresh ginger, grated
2 teaspoons ground cumin
2 teaspoons ground coriander
2 teaspoons ground turmeric
¼ teaspoon ground cardamom
¼ teaspoon ground cloves
3 bay leaves
375 ml (13 fl oz/1½ cups) chicken stock
125 ml (4 fl oz/½ cup) pouring (whipping) cream
2 bunches English spinach leaves, washed and chopped

Heat the oil in a heavy-based pan and brown the lamb in batches. Remove from the pan. Add the onion, garlic and ginger and cook for 3 minutes, stirring regularly. Add the cumin, coriander, turmeric, cardamom and cloves and cook, stirring, for 1–2 minutes, or until fragrant. Return the lamb to the pan with any juices. Add the bay leaves and stock.

Bring to the boil and then reduce the heat, stir well, cover and simmer for 35 minutes. Add the cream and cook, covered, for a further 20 minutes or until the lamb is tender.

Add the spinach and cook until it has softened. Season to taste before serving.

Add the onion and garlic to the wok and cook until the onion is soft.

Stir in the cream and simmer, covered, until the lamb is very tender.

Bottom: Kashmir lamb with spinach. Top: Beef and pineapple curry.

Thai green chicken curry

preparation 40 minutes
cooking 30 minutes
serves 4–6

500 ml (17 fl oz/2 cups) coconut cream (do not shake
the tin—see Note)
80 g (3 oz/⅓ cup) Thai green curry paste
2 tablespoons grated palm sugar (jaggery)
2 tablespoons fish sauce
4 makrut (kaffir lime) leaves, finely shredded
1 kg (2 lb 4 oz) boneless, skinless chicken thighs or breasts,
cut into thick strips
200 g (7 oz) tinned bamboo shoots, cut into thick strips
100 g (3½ oz) snake (yard-long) beans, cut into short lengths
1 handful Thai basil leaves, plus extra, to garnish

Open the tin of coconut cream and lift off the thick cream
from the top; you should have about 125 ml (4 fl oz/½ cup)
thick cream. Put this in a wok or saucepan and bring to
the boil. Add the curry paste, then reduce the heat and
simmer for 15 minutes, or until fragrant and the oil starts
to separate from the cream. Add the palm sugar, fish sauce
and makrut leaves.

Stir in the remaining coconut cream and the chicken,
bamboo shoots and beans and simmer for 15 minutes, or
until the chicken is tender. Stir in the Thai basil just before
serving. Garnish with the extra leaves.

Note *Do not shake the tin, because good-quality coconut
cream has a layer of very thick cream at the top. This has a
higher fat content, which causes it to split or separate more
readily than the rest of the coconut cream or milk.*

Thai prawn curry

preparation 30 minutes
cooking 10 minutes
serves 4

5 cm (2 inch) piece fresh galangal
1 small onion, roughly chopped
3 garlic cloves
4 dried long red chillies
4 whole black peppercorns
2 tablespoons chopped lemongrass, white part only
1 tablespoon chopped coriander (cilantro) root
2 teaspoons finely grated lime zest
2 teaspoons cumin seeds
1 teaspoon sweet paprika
1 teaspoon ground coriander
60 ml (2 fl oz/¼ cup) oil
1–2 tablespoons fish sauce
2 makrut (kaffir lime) leaves
500 ml (17 fl oz/2 cups) coconut cream
1 kg (2 lb 4 oz) raw prawns (shrimp), peeled and deveined

Peel the galangal and thinly slice. Mix the onion, garlic,
chillies, peppercorns, lemongrass, coriander root, lime zest,
cumin seeds, paprika, ground coriander, 2 tablespoons oil
and ½ teaspoon salt in a food processor until a smooth
paste forms.

Heat the remaining oil in a frying pan. Add half the curry
paste and stir over medium heat for 2 minutes. Stir in the
fish sauce, galangal, makrut leaves and coconut cream.

Add the prawns to the pan and simmer for 5 minutes, or
until the prawns are cooked through and the sauce has
thickened slightly.

Note *Leftover curry paste can be kept in the refrigerator for up
to 2 weeks. It can also be frozen for up to 2 months.*

Lift off the thick cream from the top of the tin of
coconut cream.

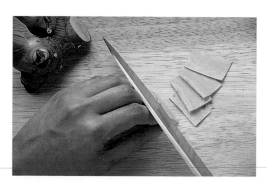

Peel the galangal and use a sharp knife to cut it into
very thin slices.

Bottom: Thai prawn curry. Top: Thai green chicken curry.

Spicy prawns

preparation 30 minutes + 15 minutes standing
cooking 1 hour 20 minutes
serves 4–6

1 kg (2 lb 4 oz) raw prawns (shrimp), peeled and deveined,
leaving the tails intact (reserve shells and heads)
1 teaspoon ground turmeric
60 ml (2 fl oz/¼ cup) oil
2 onions, finely chopped
4–6 garlic cloves, finely chopped
1–2 small green chillies, seeded and chopped
2 teaspoons ground cumin
2 teaspoons ground coriander
1 teaspoon paprika
90 g (3 oz/⅓ cup) plain yoghurt
80 ml (2½ fl oz/⅓ cup) thick (double/heavy) cream
2 large handfuls coriander (cilantro) leaves, chopped

Bring 1 litre (35 fl oz/4 cups) water to the boil in a large saucepan. Add the reserved prawn shells and heads, reduce the heat and simmer for 25–30 minutes. Skim any scum that forms on the surface during cooking with a skimmer or slotted spoon. Drain, discard the shells and heads, and return the liquid to the pan. You will need 750 ml (26 fl oz/3 cups) liquid. Make up with water, if necessary. Add the turmeric and peeled prawns, and cook for 1 minute, or until the prawns just turn pink. Remove the prawns and set the stock aside.

Heat the oil in a large saucepan. Cook the onion on low–medium heat, stirring, for 8 minutes, or until light golden brown. Take care not to burn the onion. Add the garlic and chilli, cook for 2 minutes, then add the cumin, coriander and paprika, and cook, stirring, for 2–3 minutes, or until it becomes fragrant.

Gradually add the reserved prawn stock, bring to the boil and cook, stirring occasionally, for 35 minutes, or until the mixture has reduced by half and thickened.

Remove from the heat and stir in the yoghurt. Add the prawns and stir over low heat for 2–3 minutes, or until the prawns are warmed through, but do now allow the mixture to boil. Stir in the cream and coriander leaves. Cover and leave to stand for 15 minutes to allow the flavours to infuse. Reheat gently and serve with rice.

Note You can also remove the prawn tails, if you prefer.

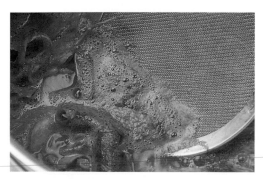

Skim any scum on the surface with a skimmer or a slotted spoon.

Boil the mixture, stirring occasionally, until it has been reduced by half and thickened.

Chicken dumplings in green curry

preparation 25 minutes + 2–3 hours refrigeration
cooking 35 minutes
serves 4

500 g (1 lb 2 oz) minced (ground) chicken
3 spring onions (scallions), finely chopped
2 tablespoons small coriander (cilantro) leaves
1 lemongrass stem, white part only, thinly sliced
60 ml (2 fl oz/¼ cup) fish sauce
1 teaspoon chicken stock (bouillon) powder
280 g (10 oz/1½ cups) cooked jasmine rice
1 egg, plus 1 egg white
2 teaspoons oil
2 tablespoons Thai green curry paste
2 x 400 ml (14 fl oz) tins coconut milk
4 fresh makrut (kaffir lime) leaves
2 very large handfuls basil leaves
1 tablespoon lemon juice

Mix together the chicken, spring onion, coriander leaves, lemongrass, 2 tablespoons of the fish sauce, stock powder and some pepper. Add the rice and mix well.

In a separate bowl, beat the egg and egg white with electric beaters until thick and creamy and then fold into the chicken mixture. With lightly floured hands, roll tablespoons of the mixture into balls. Place on a tray, cover and refrigerate for 2–3 hours, or until firm.

Heat the oil in a large frying pan, add the curry paste and stir over medium heat for 1 minute. Gradually stir in the coconut milk, then reduce the heat to a simmer. Add the makrut leaves and chicken dumplings to the sauce, cover and simmer for 25–30 minutes, stirring occasionally. Stir in the basil leaves, remaining fish sauce and lemon juice.

Prawn and coconut curry

preparation 30 minutes
cooking 20 minutes
serves 4

1 onion, chopped
2 garlic cloves, crushed
1 lemongrass stem, white part only, finely chopped
½ teaspoon sambal oelek (Southeast Asian chilli paste)
2 teaspoons garam masala
4 makrut (kaffir lime) leaves, finely shredded
3 tablespoons chopped coriander (cilantro) stems
1 tablespoon peanut oil
250 ml (9 fl oz/1 cup) chicken stock
400 ml (14 fl oz) tin coconut milk
1 kg (2 lb 4 oz) raw prawns (shrimp), peeled and deveined
1 tablespoon fish sauce

For the curry paste, mix the onion, garlic, lemongrass, sambal oelek, garam masala, makrut leaves, coriander stems and 2 tablespoons water in a food processor until you have a smooth paste.

Heat the oil in a saucepan, add the curry paste and cook for 2–3 minutes, or until fragrant. Stir in the stock and coconut milk, bring to the boil, then reduce the heat and simmer for 10 minutes, or until slightly thickened.

Add the prawns and cook for 3–5 minutes, or until cooked through. Stir in the fish sauce.

Variation *Instead of prawns, you can use bite-sized pieces of boneless ling or gemfish fillets. Cook for 3–5 minutes, or until cooked through.*

Flour your hands and roll tablespoons of the mixture into balls.

Process the curry paste ingredients in a processor or blender until smooth.

Bottom: Prawn and coconut curry. Top: Chicken dumplings in green curry.

Pork vindaloo

preparation 20 minutes
cooking 2 hours
serves 4

60 ml (2 fl oz/¼ cup) oil
1 kg (2 lb 4 oz) pork fillets, cut into bite-sized pieces
2 onions, finely chopped
4 garlic cloves, finely chopped
1 tablespoon finely chopped fresh ginger
1 tablespoon garam masala
2 teaspoons brown mustard seeds
80 g (3 oz/⅓ cup) vindaloo paste
plain yoghurt, to serve

Heat the oil in a saucepan, add the pork in small batches and cook over medium heat for 5–7 minutes, or until browned. Remove meat from the pan.

Add the onion, garlic, ginger, garam masala and mustard seeds to the saucepan, and cook, stirring, for 5 minutes, or until the onion is soft.

Return all the meat to the pan, add the paste and cook, stirring, for 2 minutes. Add 625 ml (21½ fl oz/2½ cups) water and bring to the boil. Reduce the heat and simmer, covered, for 1½ hours, or until the meat is tender. Serve with a dollop of yoghurt, rice and naan bread, if desired.

Madras beef curry

preparation 20 minutes
cooking 1 hour 45 minutes
serves 4

1 tablespoon oil or ghee
1 onion, chopped
60–80 g (2–3 oz/¼–⅓ cup) Madras curry paste
1 kg (2 lb 4 oz) skirt or chuck steak, trimmed of fat and cut into 2.5 cm (1 inch) cubes
60 g (2 oz/¼ cup) tomato paste (concentrated purée)
250 ml (9 fl oz/1 cup) beef stock
coriander (cilantro) sprigs, to garnish

Heat the oil in a large frying pan, add the onion and cook over medium heat for 10 minutes, or until browned. Add the curry paste and stir for 1 minute, or until fragrant. Then add the meat and cook, stirring, until coated with the paste.

Stir in the tomato paste and stock. Reduce the heat and simmer, covered, for 1¼ hours, Add more stock or water if necessary. Simmer uncovered for 15 minutes, or until the meat is tender. Garnish with coriander and serve with steamed rice.

Chu chee seafood

preparation 30 minutes
cooking 20 minutes
serves 4

2 x 270 ml (9½ fl oz) tins coconut cream (do not shake the tins)
60 g (2 oz/¼ cup) chu chee curry paste
500 g (1 lb 2 oz) scallops, roe removed
500 g (1 lb 2 oz) raw prawns, peeled and deveined, tails intact
2–3 tablespoons fish sauce
2 tablespoons grated palm sugar (jaggery) or soft brown sugar
8 makrut (kaffir lime) leaves, finely shredded
2 red chillies, thinly sliced
2 large handfuls Thai basil leaves

Place 250 ml (9 fl oz/1 cup) of the thick coconut cream from the top of the tins in a wok. Heat until just boiling, then stir in the paste, reduce the heat and simmer for 10 minutes, or until fragrant and the oil just begins to separate.

Stir in the remaining coconut cream and seafood, and cook for 5 minutes, or until tender. Add the fish sauce, sugar, makrut leaves and chilli, and cook for 1 minute. Stir in half the basil and garnish with the rest before serving.

Chicken curry with apricots

preparation 40 minutes + 1 hour soaking
cooking 1 hour 15 minutes
serves 6–8

1 tablespoon ghee or oil
2 x 1.5 kg (3 lb 5 oz) chickens, cut into pieces
3 onions, thinly sliced
3 garlic cloves, crushed
3 large green chillies, seeded and finely chopped
1 teaspoon cumin seeds
1 teaspoon chilli powder
½ teaspoon ground turmeric
4 cardamom pods, bruised
4 large tomatoes, peeled and cut into eighths
18 dried apricots, soaked in 250 ml (9 fl oz/1 cup) hot water

Melt the ghee in a large saucepan, add the chicken in batches and cook over high heat for 5 minutes. Remove from the pan. Add the onion and cook, stirring, for 10 minutes, or until soft and golden. Add the garlic and chilli and cook for 2 minutes. Add the rest of the spices and cook for a minute. Return the chicken to the pan, add the tomato and apricots (and liquid) and mix. Simmer, covered, for 35 minutes. Remove the chicken, cover and keep warm.

Bring the liquid to the boil and boil for 5 minutes, or until thickened. Spoon over the chicken. Serve with spiced rice.

Top left: Pork vindaloo. Top right: Chu chee seafood. Bottom right: Chicken curry with apricots. Bottom left: Mad'as beef curry.

Balti chicken

preparation time 25 minutes
total cooking time 1 hour
serves 6

1 kg (2 lb 4 oz) boneless, skinless
chicken thighs
80 ml (2½ fl oz/⅓ cup) oil
1 large red onion, finely chopped
4–5 garlic cloves, finely chopped
1 tablespoon grated fresh ginger
2 teaspoons ground cumin
2 teaspoons ground coriander
1 teaspoon ground turmeric
½ teaspoon chilli powder
425 g (15 oz) tin chopped tomatoes
1 green capsicum (pepper), seeded and diced
1–2 small green chillies, seeded and
finely chopped
4 tablespoons chopped coriander (cilantro)
2 spring onions (scallions), chopped,
to garnish

Remove any excess fat or sinew from the chicken thighs
and cut into four or five even-sized pieces.

Heat a large wok over high heat, add the oil and swirl to
coat the side. Add the onion and stir-fry over medium heat
for 5 minutes, or until softened but not browned. Add the
garlic and ginger and stir-fry for 3 more minutes.

Add the spices, 1 teaspoon salt and 60 ml (2 fl oz/¼ cup)
water. Increase the heat to high and stir-fry for 2 minutes, or
until the mixture has thickened. Take care not to burn.

Add the tomato and 250 ml (9 fl oz/1 cup) water and cook,
stirring often, for a further 10 minutes, or until the mixture
is thick and pulpy and the oil comes to the surface.

Add the chicken to the pan, reduce the heat and simmer,
stirring often, for 15 minutes. Add the capsicum and chilli
and simmer for a further 25 minutes, or until the chicken is
tender. Add a little water if the mixture is too thick. Stir in
the coriander and garnish with the spring onion.

Note *This curry is traditionally cooked in a Karahi pan—a wok is
a good substitute.*

Massaman beef curry

preparation 30 minutes
cooking 1 hour 45 minutes
serves 4

1 tablespoon tamarind pulp
2 tablespoons oil
750 g (1 lb 10 oz) lean stewing beef, cubed
500 ml (17 fl oz/2 cups) coconut milk
4 cardamom pods, bruised
500 ml (17 fl oz/2 cups) coconut cream
2–3 tablespoons Massaman curry paste
8 baby onions, peeled (see Note)
8 baby potatoes, peeled and quartered (see Note)
2 tablespoons fish sauce
2 tablespoons grated palm sugar (jaggery) or soft brown sugar
80 g (3 oz/½ cup) unsalted peanuts, roasted and ground
coriander (cilantro) leaves, to garnish

Place the tamarind pulp and ½ cup (125 ml/4 fl oz) boiling
water in a bowl and set aside to cool. When cool, mash the
pulp to dissolve in the water, then strain and reserve the
liquid. Discard the pulp.

Heat the oil in a wok or a large saucepan and cook the beef
in batches over high heat for 5 minutes, or until browned.
Reduce the heat, add the coconut milk and cardamom,
and simmer for 1 hour, or until the beef is tender. Remove
the beef, strain and reserve the meat and also the cooking
liquid separately.

Heat the coconut cream in the wok and stir in the curry
paste. Cook for 5 minutes, or until the oil starts to separate
from the cream.

Add the onions, potatoes, fish sauce, palm sugar, peanuts,
beef mixture, reserved cooking liquid and tamarind water,
and simmer for 25–30 minutes. Serve with coriander and
steamed rice.

Note *Use small onions and potatoes, about 20–30 g (¾–1 oz)
each. Baby onions are also called pickling onions.*

Bottom: Massaman beef curry. Top: Balti chicken.

Fish koftas in tomato curry sauce

preparation 40 minutes
cooking 30 minutes
serves 6

750 g (1 lb 10 oz) firm fish fillets, such as
snapper or ling, roughly chopped
1 onion, chopped
2–3 garlic cloves, chopped
1 tablespoon grated fresh ginger
2 large handfuls coriander (cilantro) leaves
1 teaspoon garam masala
¼ teaspoon chilli powder
1 egg, lightly beaten

tomato curry sauce
2 tablespoons oil
1 large onion, finely chopped
3–4 garlic cloves, finely chopped
1 tablespoon grated fresh ginger
1 teaspoon ground turmeric
1 teaspoon ground cumin
1 teaspoon ground coriander
½ teaspoon garam masala
¼ teaspoon chilli powder
2 x 400 g (14 oz) tins chopped tomatoes
2 large handfuls coriander (cilantro) leaves, chopped, plus extra, to garnish

oil, for shallow-frying

Place the fish in a food processor and process until smooth. Add the onion, garlic, ginger, coriander leaves, garam masala, chilli powder and egg, and process using the pulse button until well combined. Using wetted hands, form 1 tablespoon of the mixture into a ball. Repeat with the remaining mixture.

To make the tomato curry sauce, heat the oil in a large saucepan, add the onion, garlic and ginger, and cook, stirring frequently, over medium heat for 8 minutes, or until lightly golden. Add the spices and cook, stirring, for 2 minutes, or until aromatic. Add the tomato and 250 ml (9 fl oz/1 cup) water, then reduce the heat and simmer, stirring frequently, for 15 minutes, or until the sauce has reduced and thickened.

Meanwhile, heat 2 cm (¾ inch) of the oil in a large frying pan. Add the fish koftas in three to four batches and cook for 3 minutes, or until browned all over. Drain on paper towels.

Add the koftas to the sauce and simmer over low heat for 5 minutes, or until cooked through. Gently fold in the coriander, season with salt. Serve with steamed rice and warm naan bread. Garnish with coriander.

Note *The fish mixture is quite moist. Wetting your hands will stop the mixture from sticking to them.*

Gingered duck curry

preparation 30 minutes + 30 minutes refrigeration + soaking
cooking 1 hour 30 minutes
serves 4

1.8 kg (4 lb) duck
1 garlic clove, crushed
1 teaspoon grated fresh ginger
1 tablespoon dark soy sauce
½ teaspoon sesame oil
8 dried Chinese mushrooms
5 cm (2 inch) piece fresh ginger, extra, thinly sliced
2 tablespoons Thai yellow curry paste
2 tablespoons chopped lemongrass, white part only
400 ml (14 fl oz) tin coconut milk
4 makrut (kaffir lime) leaves, shredded
100 g (3½ oz) Thai pea eggplants (aubergines)
2 teaspoons soft brown sugar
2 teaspoons fish sauce
1 tablespoon lime juice

Cut the duck in half by cutting down both sides of the backbone, and through the breastbone. Discard the backbone. Cut each duck half into four portions, removing any fat. Rub the duck with the combined garlic, ginger, soy sauce and oil. Refrigerate for 30 minutes.

Soak the mushrooms in boiling water for 20 minutes. Drain. Remove and discard the stalks and cut the caps in half.

Heat a lightly oiled pan. Brown the duck over medium heat. Leaving only 1 tablespoon of fat in the pan, stir-fry the extra ginger, curry paste and lemongrass for 3 minutes. Stir in the coconut milk, makrut leaves and 125 ml (4 fl oz/½ cup) water. Add the duck, cover and simmer for 45 minutes. Skim well.

Remove the eggplant stems; add the eggplants to the pan with the sugar, fish sauce and mushrooms. Simmer, partly covered, for 30 minutes, or until tender. Stir in juice to taste.

Beef and spinach curry

preparation 30 minutes
cooking 1 hour 15 minutes
serves 4

2 tablespoons oil
1 onion, finely chopped
2 garlic cloves, finely chopped
2 teaspoons ground cumin
2 teaspoons ground coriander
2 teaspoons paprika
1 teaspoon garam masala
1 teaspoon ground turmeric
½ teaspoon finely chopped red chilli
1 teaspoon finely chopped green chilli
2 teaspoons grated fresh ginger
500 g (1 lb 2 oz) lean minced (ground) beef or lamb
1 tomato, chopped
250 ml (9 fl oz/1 cup) beef stock or water
500 g (1 lb 2 oz) English spinach, chopped
200 g (7 oz) plain yoghurt

Heat 1 tablespoon of the oil in a large saucepan and cook the onion over medium heat until golden brown. Add the garlic, cumin, coriander, paprika, garam masala, turmeric, red and green chilli and the grated ginger and stir for 1 minute. Remove and set aside.

Heat the remaining oil in the pan and brown the meat over high heat, breaking up any lumps with a fork or wooden spoon. Return the onion mixture to the pan and add the tomato and stock or water.

Bring the mixture to the boil and then reduce the heat and simmer for about 1 hour. Season with salt, to taste. Meanwhile, cook the spinach briefly. Just before serving, add the spinach to the mixture and stir in the yoghurt.

Note If possible, make the meat mixture in advance and refrigerate overnight for the flavours to develop.

Remove the stems from the pea eggplants and add the eggplants to the pan.

Add the garlic, spices, red and green chilli and ginger to the pan and stir.

Bottom: Beef and spinach curry. Top: Gingered duck curry.

Butter chicken

preparation 10 minutes
cooking 35 minutes
serves 4–6

2 tablespoons peanut oil
1 kg (2 lb 4 oz) boneless, skinless chicken thighs, quartered
60 g (2 oz) butter or ghee
2 teaspoons garam masala
2 teaspoons sweet paprika
2 teaspoons ground coriander
1 tablespoon finely chopped fresh ginger
¼ teaspoon chilli powder
1 cinnamon stick
6 cardamom pods, bruised
350 g (12 oz) tomato passata (puréed tomatoes)
1 tablespoon sugar
60 g (2 oz/¼ cup) plain yoghurt
125 ml (4 fl oz/½ cup) pouring (whipping) cream
1 tablespoon lemon juice
coriander (cilantro) leaves, to garnish

Heat a wok until very hot, add 1 tablespoon oil and swirl to coat. Add half the chicken thighs and stir-fry for 4 minutes, or until browned. Remove. Add extra oil, as needed, and cook the remaining chicken. Remove.

Reduce the heat, add the butter or ghee to the wok and melt. Add the garam masala, sweet paprika, ground coriander, ginger, chilli powder, cinnamon stick and cardamom pods and stir-fry for 1 minute, or until fragrant. Return the chicken to the wok and mix to coat in the spices.

Add the tomato passata and sugar, and simmer, stirring, for 15 minutes, or until the chicken is tender and the sauce has thickened.

Add the yoghurt, cream and juice and simmer for 5 minutes, or until the sauce has thickened slightly. Serve with rice or poppadoms and garnish with coriander leaves.

Thai green fish curry

preparation 15 minutes
cooking 15 minutes
serves 4

1 tablespoon peanut oil
1 onion, chopped
1½ tablespoons Thai green curry paste
375 ml (13 fl oz/1½ cups) coconut milk
750 g (1 lb 10 oz) boneless firm white fish fillets, cut into bite-sized pieces
3 makrut (kaffir lime) leaves
1 tablespoon fish sauce
2 teaspoons grated palm sugar (jaggery)
2 tablespoons lime juice
1 long green chilli, thinly sliced

Heat a wok until very hot, add the oil and swirl to coat. Add the onion and stir-fry for 2 minutes, or until soft. Add the curry paste and stir-fry for 1–2 minutes, or until fragrant. Stir in the coconut milk and bring to the boil.

Add the fish and makrut leaves to the wok, reduce the heat and simmer, stirring occasionally, for 8–10 minutes, or until the fish is cooked through.

Stir in the fish sauce, palm sugar and lime juice. Scatter the chilli slices over the curry before serving.

Simmer until the chicken is tender and the sauce has thickened.

To prevent skin irritation, wear rubber gloves when slicing the chilli.

Bottom: Thai green fish curry. Top: Butter chicken.

Japanese pork schnitzel curry

preparation 25 minutes
cooking 40 minutes
serves 4

1 tablespoon oil
1 onion, cut into thin wedges
2 large carrots, diced
1 large potato, diced
60 g (2 oz) Japanese curry paste block, broken into small pieces (see Note)
plain (all-purpose) flour, for coating
4 x 120 g (4¼ oz) pork schnitzels, pounded until thin
2 eggs, lightly beaten
150 g (5½ oz/2½ cups) Japanese breadcrumbs (panko)
oil, for deep-frying
pickled ginger, pickled daikon, umeboshi (pickled baby plums)
and crisp-fried onion, to garnish

Heat the oil in a saucepan, add the onion, carrot and potato and cook over medium heat for 10 minutes, or until starting to brown. Add 500 ml (17 fl oz/2 cups) water and the curry paste and stir until the curry paste dissolves and the sauce has a smooth consistency. Reduce the heat and simmer for 10 minutes, or until the vegetables are cooked through.

Season the flour well with salt and pepper. Dip each schnitzel into the flour, shake off any excess and dip into the beaten egg, allowing any excess to drip off. Coat with the Japanese breadcrumbs by pressing each side of the schnitzel firmly into the crumbs on a plate.

Fill a deep heavy-based saucepan one-third full of oil and heat to 180°C (350°F), or until a cube of bread browns in 15 seconds. Cook the schnitzels, one at a time, turning once or twice, for 5 minutes, or until golden brown all over and cooked through. Drain on crumpled paper towels.

Slice each schnitzel and then arrange in the original shape over rice. Ladle the curry sauce over the schnitzels. Garnish with fried onions and serve with the pickles on the side.

Note *Japanese curry comes in a solid block or in powder form and is available in Asian supermarkets. It varies in heat from mild to very hot.*

Cook the onion, carrot and potato until they are starting to brown.

Coat the schnitzels in flour, egg and then the Japanese breadcrumbs.

Red beef and eggplant curry

preparation 40 minutes
cooking 1 hour 30 minutes
serves 4

250 ml (9 fl oz) tin coconut cream (do not shake
the tin—see Notes)
2 tablespoons Thai red curry paste
500 g (1 lb 2 oz) round or topside steak, cut into strips
(see Notes)
2 tablespoons fish sauce
1 tablespoon grated palm sugar (jaggery) or soft brown sugar
5 makrut (kaffir lime) leaves, halved
500 ml (17 fl oz/2 cups) coconut milk
8 Thai eggplants (aubergines), halved
2 tablespoons finely shredded Thai basil leaves

Place the thick coconut cream from the top of the tin in a
wok and bring to the boil. Boil for 10 minutes, or until the
oil starts to separate. Add the curry paste and simmer,
stirring to prevent it sticking to the bottom, for 5 minutes,
or until fragrant.

Add the meat and cook, stirring, for 3–5 minutes, or until
it changes colour. Add the fish sauce, palm sugar, makrut
leaves, coconut milk and remaining coconut cream, and
simmer for 1 hour, or until the meat is tender and the sauce
has slightly thickened.

Add the eggplant and cook for 10 minutes, or until tender.
If the sauce is too thick, add a little water. Stir in half the
shredded basil leaves. Garnish with the remaining basil
leaves and serve with steamed rice.

Notes *Do not shake the tin of coconut cream because good-
quality coconut cream has a layer of very thick cream at the top
that has separated from the rest of the cream. This has a higher
fat content, which causes it to split or separate more readily
than the rest of the coconut cream.*

*Cut the meat into 5 x 5 x 2 cm (2 x 2 x ¾ inch) pieces, then cut
across the grain at a 45° angle into 5 mm (¼ inch) thick slices.*

Jungle curry prawns

preparation 30 minutes + 10 minutes soaking
cooking 15 minutes
serves 6

curry paste
10–12 dried red chillies
4 red Asian shallots (eschalots), chopped
4 garlic cloves, sliced
1 lemongrass stem (white part only), sliced
1 tablespoon finely chopped fresh galangal
2 small coriander (cilantro) roots, chopped
1 tablespoon finely chopped fresh ginger
1 tablespoon shrimp paste, dry-roasted
60 ml (2 fl oz/¼ cup) oil

1 tablespoon oil
1 garlic clove, crushed
40 g (1½ oz/¼ cup) ground candlenuts
1 tablespoon fish sauce
300 ml (10½ fl oz) fish stock
1 tablespoon whisky
600 g (1 lb 5 oz) raw prawns (shrimp), peeled and deveined,
leaving the tails intact
1 small carrot, slivered
200 g (7 oz) snake (yard-long) beans, trimmed and cut into
2 cm (¾ inch) lengths
50 g (2 oz) bamboo shoots
3 makrut (kaffir lime) leaves, crushed
basil leaves, to garnish

To make the paste, soak the chillies in 250 ml (9 fl oz/1 cup)
boiling water for 10 minutes, then drain and place in a
food processor with the remaining curry paste ingredients.
Season with salt and white pepper, and process to a paste.

Heat a wok over medium heat, add the oil and stir to coat
the side. Add 60 g (2 oz/¼ cup) of the curry paste and the
garlic, and cook, stirring constantly, for 5 minutes, or until
fragrant. Stir in the candlenuts, fish sauce, stock, whisky,
prawns, vegetables and makrut leaves, and bring to the
boil. Reduce the heat and simmer for 5 minutes, or until
cooked through. Garnish with the basil and serve with rice.

Boil the thick coconut cream until the oil separates
from the cream.

Cook the curry paste and crushed garlic in a wok
until fragrant.

Bottom: Jungle curry prawns. Top: Red beef and eggplant curry.

Duck and coconut curry

preparation 20 minutes
cooking 1 hour 15 minutes
serves 6

curry paste
1 red onion, chopped
2 garlic cloves
2 coriander (cilantro) roots, chopped
2 teaspoons chopped fresh ginger
1½ teaspoons coriander seeds, dry-roasted and ground
1 teaspoon cardamom seeds, dry-roasted and ground
1 teaspoon fenugreek seeds, dry-roasted and ground
1 teaspoon brown mustard seeds, dry-roasted and ground
10 black peppercorns, ground
2 teaspoons garam masala
¼ teaspoon ground turmeric
2 teaspoons tamarind purée

6–8 boneless, skinless duck breasts
1 red onion, sliced
125 ml (4 fl oz/½ cup) white vinegar
500 ml (17 fl oz/2 cups) coconut milk
2 tablespoons coriander (cilantro) leaves

To make the curry paste, place all the ingredients in a food processor and process to a thick paste. Put aside.

Trim any excess fat from the duck breasts, then place, skin side down, in a large saucepan and cook over medium heat for 10 minutes, or until the skin is brown and any remaining fat has melted. Turn the fillets over and cook for 5 minutes, or until tender. Remove and drain on paper towels.

Reserve 1 tablespoon duck fat, discarding the remaining fat. Add the onion and cook for 5 minutes, then add the curry paste and stir over low heat for 10 minutes, or until fragrant.

Return the duck to the pan and stir to coat with the paste. Stir in the vinegar, coconut milk, 1 teaspoon salt and 125 ml (4 fl oz/½ cup) water. Simmer, covered, for 45 minutes, or until the duck breasts are tender. Stir in the coriander just prior to serving. Serve with steamed rice and naan bread.

Use a sharp knife to trim any excess fat from the duck breasts.

Cook the duck, skin side down, until the skin is brown and the fat has melted.

Thai chicken and potato curry

preparation 20 minutes
cooking 30 minutes
serves 4–6

2 tablespoons oil
1 onion, chopped
1–2 tablespoons Thai yellow curry paste (see Notes)
¼ teaspoon ground turmeric
420 ml (14½ fl oz/1⅔ cups) coconut milk
300 g (10½ oz) potatoes, peeled and cubed
250 g (9 oz) orange sweet potatoes, peeled and cubed
250 g (9 oz) boneless, skinless chicken thighs, diced
2 makrut (kaffir lime) leaves (see Notes)
2 teaspoons fish sauce
2 teaspoons soft brown sugar
1 tablespoon lime juice
1 teaspoon finely grated lime zest
1 large handful coriander (cilantro) leaves
60 g (2 oz/⅓ cup) roasted peanuts, roughly chopped, to garnish

Heat the oil in a large heavy-based saucepan or wok and cook the onion until softened. Add the curry paste and turmeric and stir for 1 minute, or until aromatic.

Stir in the coconut milk and 250 ml (9 fl oz/1 cup) water and bring to the boil. Reduce the heat and add the potato, sweet potato, chicken and makrut leaves. Simmer for 15–20 minutes, or until the vegetables are tender and the chicken is cooked through.

Stir in the fish sauce, sugar, lime juice and zest and coriander leaves. Garnish with the peanuts to serve.

Notes *Thai yellow curry paste is not as common as the red or green but is available from most Asian food stores. Makrut leaves are now available in most supermarkets.*

Lemongrass and coriander fish

preparation 15 minutes
cooking 40 minutes
serves 4

4 x 200 g (7 oz) fish cutlets
plain (all-purpose) flour, seasoned with salt and pepper
2–3 tablespoons peanut oil
2 onions, sliced
2 lemongrass stems, white part only, finely chopped
4 makrut (kaffir lime) leaves, finely shredded
1 teaspoon ground cumin
1 teaspoon ground coriander
1 teaspoon finely chopped red chilli
185 ml (6 fl oz/¾ cup) chicken stock
375 ml (13 fl oz/1½ cups) coconut milk
1 very large handful fresh coriander (cilantro), chopped
2 teaspoons fish sauce

Preheat the oven to 180°C (350°F/Gas 4). Toss the fish lightly in the flour. Heat half the oil in a large heavy-based frying pan and cook the fish over medium heat until lightly browned on both sides. Transfer the cutlets to a shallow ovenproof dish.

Heat the remaining oil in the pan. Add the onion and lemongrass and cook, stirring, for 5 minutes, or until the onion softens. Add the makrut leaves, ground spices and chilli and stir for about 2 minutes, or until fragrant.

Add the stock and coconut milk and bring to the boil. Pour over the fish, then cover and bake for 30 minutes, or until tender. Transfer to a plate.

Stir the coriander and fish sauce into the remaining sauce and season to taste. Pour over the fish to serve.

Note *Makrut leaves are glossy, dark green double leaves with a floral citrus smell. They are tough and need to be finely shredded before use.*

When the onion has softened, stir in the curry paste and turmeric.

Finely chop the white part of the lemongrass stems and shred the makrut leaves.

Bottom: Lemongrass and coriander fish. Top: Thai chicken and potato curry.

one-pots

Caramel pork with Shanghai noodles

preparation 15 minutes
cooking 2 hours 30 minutes
serves 4

500 g (1 lb 2 oz) Shanghai noodles
700 g (1 lb 9 oz) boneless pork belly
2 teaspoons peanut oil
150 g (5½ oz) caster (superfine) sugar
5 garlic cloves, crushed
5 thin slices fresh ginger
2 lemongrass stems, white part only, bruised
1 teaspoon ground white pepper
500 ml (17 fl oz/2 cups) chicken stock
70 ml (2 fl oz) fish sauce
100 g (3½ oz) tinned bamboo shoots, drained well
4 spring onions (scallions), cut into 3 cm (1¼ inch) pieces
1 tablespoon lime juice
1 tablespoon chopped coriander (cilantro) leaves (optional)
1 bunch bok choy (pak choy) (optional)

Cook the Shanghai noodles in a large saucepan of boiling water for 4–5 minutes, or until tender. Rinse, drain and cut the noodles into 10 cm (4 inch) lengths.

Preheat the oven to 180°C (350°F/Gas 4). Cut the pork belly across the grain into 1 cm (½ inch) thick slices, then cut each slice into 2 cm (¾ inch) pieces. Heat the oil in a 4 litre (140 fl oz/16 cup) flameproof casserole dish over medium–high heat. Cook the pork in two batches for 5 minutes, or until it starts to brown all over. Remove the pork and drain off the fat.

Add the sugar and 2 tablespoons water to the casserole dish, stirring until the sugar has dissolved and scraping up any sediment that may have stuck to the bottom. Increase heat to high and cook for 2–3 minutes without stirring until dark golden, being careful not to burn—you should just be able to smell the caramel.

Return the pork to the casserole dish, then stir in the garlic, ginger, lemongrass, white pepper, stock, 2 tablespoons of the fish sauce and 375 ml (12 fl oz/1½ cups) water. Place the dish in the oven and bake, covered, for 1 hour, then remove the lid and cook for a further 1 hour, or until the pork is very tender. Carefully remove the slices of ginger and the lemongrass stems.

Add the noodles to the casserole dish with the bamboo shoots, spring onion, lime juice and remaining fish sauce, and stir to combine. Return the dish to the oven for a further 10 minutes to heat through. Stir in the coriander, if desired, and serve with steamed bok choy and steamed Asian greens, if desired.

Return all the browned pork belly pieces to the casserole dish.

Carefully remove the ginger slices and lemongrass from the casserole.

Prawns with jasmine rice

preparation 15 minutes
cooking 30 minutes
serves 4

1 tablespoon peanut oil
8 spring onions (scallions), sliced
1 tablespoon finely chopped fresh ginger
1 tablespoon thinly sliced lemongrass, white part only
2 teaspoons crushed coriander seeds (see Note)
400 g (14 oz/2 cups) jasmine rice
1 litre (35 fl oz/4 cups) vegetable stock
1 tablespoon shredded lime zest
1 kg (2 lb 4 oz) raw prawns (shrimp), peeled,
deveined and chopped
2 tablespoons lime juice
2 very large handfuls coriander (cilantro) leaves
fish sauce, to serve

Heat the oil in a saucepan, add the spring onion and cook over low heat for 4 minutes, or until soft. Add the ginger, lemongrass, coriander seeds and rice, and stir for 1 minute.

Add the stock and lime zest and bring to the boil while stirring. Reduce the heat to very low and cook, covered, for 15–20 minutes, or until the rice is tender.

Remove the pan from the heat and stir in the prawns. Cover and leave for 4–5 minutes, or until the prawns are cooked. Add the lime juice and coriander leaves and fluff the rice with a fork. Sprinkle with a few drops of fish sauce to serve.

Note *To crush coriander seeds, place in a small plastic bag and, using a rolling pin, crush until fine.*

Add the ginger, lemongrass, coriander seeds and rice to the saucepan.

Mussels in chunky tomato sauce

preparation 15 minutes
cooking 30 minutes
serves 6

1.5 kg (3 lb 5 oz) black mussels
1 tablespoon olive oil
1 large onion, diced
4 garlic cloves, finely chopped
2 x 400 g (14 oz) tins chopped tomatoes
60 g (2 oz/¼ cup) tomato paste (concentrated purée)
30 g (1 oz/¼ cup) pitted black olives
1 tablespoon capers, drained and well rinsed
125 ml (4 fl oz/½ cup) fish stock
3 tablespoons chopped parsley

Scrub the mussels with a stiff brush and pull out the hairy beards. Discard any broken mussels, or open ones that don't close when tapped on the work surface. Rinse well.

In a large saucepan, heat the olive oil and cook the onion and garlic over medium heat for 1–2 minutes, until softened. Add the tomato, tomato paste, olives, capers and fish stock. Bring to the boil, then reduce the heat and simmer, stirring occasionally, for 20 minutes, or until the sauce is thick.

Stir in the mussels and cover the saucepan. Shake or toss the mussels occasionally and cook for 4–5 minutes, or until the mussels begin to open. Remove the pan from the heat and discard any mussels that haven't opened in the cooking time. Just before serving, toss the parsley through.

Cook the mussels until they open. Discard any that don't open in the cooking time.

Bottom: Mussels in chunky tomato sauce. Top: Prawns with jasmine rice.

Paella

preparation 25 minutes
cooking 45 minutes
serves 6

500 g (1 lb 2 oz) raw prawns (shrimp)
300 g (10½ oz) skinless firm white fish fillets
250 g (9 oz) black mussels
200 g (7 oz) squid rings
2 tablespoons olive oil
1 large onion, diced
3 garlic cloves, finely chopped
1 small red capsicum (pepper), thinly sliced
1 small red chilli, seeded and chopped
2 teaspoons paprika
1 teaspoon ground turmeric
2 tomatoes, peeled and diced
1 tablespoon tomato paste (concentrated purée)
400 g (14 oz/2 cups) long-grain rice
125 ml (4 fl oz/½ cup) dry white wine
1.25 litres (44 fl oz/5 cups) fish stock
3 tablespoons chopped parsley, to serve
lemon wedges, to serve

Peel the prawns, leaving the tails intact. Gently pull out the dark vein from each prawn back. Cut the fish into cubes. Scrub the mussels and pull out the hairy beards. Discard any broken mussels, or open ones that don't close when tapped on the work surface. Refrigerate the seafood, covered, until ready to use.

Heat the oil in a paella pan or a large deep frying pan with a lid. Add the onion, garlic, capsicum and chilli and cook over medium heat for about 2 minutes. Add the paprika, turmeric and 1 teaspoon salt and stir-fry for 1–2 minutes, or until aromatic. Add the tomato and cook for 5 minutes, or until softened. Add the tomato paste. Stir in the rice until it is well coated. Pour in the wine and simmer until almost absorbed. Add the fish stock and bring to the boil. Reduce the heat and simmer for 20 minutes, or until almost all the liquid is absorbed. There is no need to stir the rice. You may occasionally wish to fluff it up with a fork.

Add the mussels to the pan, poking the shells into the rice, cover and cook for 2–3 minutes over low heat. Add the prawns and cook for 2–3 minutes. Add the fish, cover and cook for 3 minutes. Finally, add the squid rings and cook for 1–2 minutes. By this time, the mussels should have opened—discard any unopened ones. The prawns should be pink and the fish should flake easily when tested with a fork. The squid should be moist and tender. Cook for another 2–3 minutes if the seafood is not quite cooked. Serve with parsley and lemon wedges and a green salad.

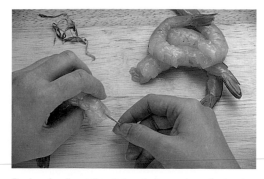

Peel and pull out the dark vein from along the back of each prawn.

Cook the squid rings for 1–2 minutes. Don't overcook or they will be tough.

Mongolian lamb hotpot

preparation 15 minutes + 10 minutes soaking
cooking 5 minutes
serves 6

250 g (9 oz) dried rice vermicelli
600 g (1 lb 5 oz) lamb backstraps, thinly sliced across the grain
4 spring onions (scallions), sliced

sauce
80 ml (2½ fl oz/⅓ cup) light soy sauce
2 tablespoons Chinese sesame paste
1 tablespoon Chinese rice wine
1 teaspoon chilli and garlic paste
1.5 litres (52 fl oz/6 cups) light chicken stock
3 cm x 6 cm (1¼ inch x 2½ inch) piece fresh ginger,
cut into 6 slices
2 tablespoons Chinese rice wine
300 g (10½ oz) silken firm tofu, cut into 1.5 cm (⅝ inch) cubes
300 g (10½ oz) Chinese broccoli (gai larn), cut into
4 cm (1½ inch) lengths
90 g (3 oz/2 cups) shredded Chinese cabbage (wong bok)

Place the vermicelli in a large heatproof bowl, cover with boiling water and soak for 6–7 minutes. Drain well and divide among six serving bowls. Top with the lamb slices and spring onion.

To make the sauce, combine the soy sauce, sesame paste, rice wine and the chilli and garlic paste in a small bowl.

Place the stock, ginger and rice wine in a 2.5 litre (87 fl oz/ 10 cup) flameproof hotpot or large saucepan. Cover and bring to the boil over high heat. Add the tofu, Chinese broccoli and Chinese cabbage and simmer, uncovered, for 1 minute, or until the cabbage has wilted. Divide the tofu, broccoli and cabbage among the serving bowls, then ladle on the hot stock. Drizzle a little of the sauce on top and serve the rest on the side.

Pork and eggplant hotpot

preparation 20 minutes
cooking 1 hour 30 minutes
serves 4

olive oil, for cooking
375 g (13 oz) slender eggplants (aubergines), cut into
3 cm (1¼ inch) slices
8 bulb spring onions (scallions)
400 g (14 oz) tin chopped tomatoes
2 garlic cloves, crushed
2 teaspoons ground cumin
500 g (1 lb 2 oz) pork fillet, cut into 3 cm (1¼ inch) thick slices
seasoned plain (all-purpose) flour
170 ml (5½ fl oz/⅔ cup) cider
1 rosemary sprig
2 tablespoons chopped toasted almonds

Heat 60 ml (2 fl oz/¼ cup) of oil in a large heavy-based frying pan. Brown the eggplant in batches over high heat, adding oil as needed. Remove and set aside.

Quarter the spring onions along their length. Add some oil to the pan and fry the spring onion over medium heat for 5 minutes. Add the tomato, garlic and cumin, and cook for 2 minutes. Remove and set aside.

Coat the pork in the seasoned flour, shaking off any excess. Brown in batches over medium–high heat until golden, adding oil as needed. Remove and set aside.

Add the cider to the pan and stir well, scraping down the side and base. Allow to boil for 1–2 minutes, then add 125 ml (4 fl oz/½ cup) water. Reduce the heat and stir in the spring onion and tomato mixture. Add the pork, season, and poke the rosemary sprig into the stew. Partially cover and simmer gently for 20 minutes.

Layer the eggplant on top, partially cover and cook for 25 minutes, or until the pork is tender. Just before serving, gently toss the almonds through.

Cover the vermicelli with boiling water in a heatproof bowl and leave to soak.

Bottom: Pork and eggplant hotpot. Top: Mongolian lamb hotpot.

Japanese beef hotpot

preparation 20 minutes + 40 minutes freezing
cooking 10 minutes
serves 4

300 g (10½ oz) beef fillet, trimmed
1.5 litres (52 fl oz/6 cups) chicken stock
2 cm x 6 cm (¾ inch x 2½ inch) piece fresh ginger, thinly sliced
80 ml (2½ fl oz/⅓ cup) light soy sauce
2 tablespoons mirin (sweet rice wine)
1 teaspoon sesame oil
200 g (7 oz) fresh udon noodles
150 g (5½ oz) English spinach, stems removed, thinly sliced
400 g (14 oz) cabbage, finely shredded
100 g (3½ oz) fresh shiitake mushrooms, stems removed and caps thinly sliced
200 g (7 oz) firm tofu, cut into 2 cm (¾ inch) cubes
80 ml (2½ fl oz/⅓ cup) ponzu sauce (see Notes), or 60 ml
(2 fl oz/¼ cup) soy sauce combined with 1 tablespoon lemon juice

Wrap the beef fillet in plastic wrap and freeze for 40 minutes, or until it begins to harden. Remove and slice as thinly as possible across the grain.

Place the stock, ginger, soy sauce, mirin and sesame oil in a 2.5 litre (87 fl oz/10 cup) flameproof casserole dish or hotpot over medium heat, and simmer for 3 minutes. Separate the noodles gently, add them to the stock and cook for 1–2 minutes. Add the spinach, cabbage, mushrooms and tofu, and simmer for 1 minute, or until the cabbage leaves have wilted.

Divide the noodles among four serving bowls using tongs, and top with the beef slices, vegetables and tofu. Ladle the hot stock on top and serve the ponzu sauce on the side.

Notes To make your own ponzu sauce, combine 1 tablespoon each of lemon juice, lime juice, rice vinegar and tamari and 1½ tablespoons mirin (sweet rice wine), 2½ tablespoons Japanese soy sauce, a 5 cm (2 inch) piece of kombu (kelp), wiped with a damp cloth, and 1 tablespoon bonito flakes in a non-metallic bowl. Cover with plastic wrap and refrigerate overnight, then strain through a sieve. Discard any sediment.

Traditionally, raw beef slices are arranged on a plate with the tofu, mushrooms, vegetables and noodles. The stock and seasoning are heated on a portable gas flame at the table. Guests dip the meat and vegetables in the hot stock and eat as they go, dipping into the sauce. The noodles are added at the end and served with the broth.

Shred the cabbage as finely as possible. This will ensure it wilts quickly in the broth.

Using a sharp knife, cut the partially frozen beef fillet as thinly as possible.

Sichuan chicken

preparation 10 minutes
cooking 30 minutes
serves 4

¼ teaspoon Chinese five-spice
750 g (1 lb 10 oz) boneless, skinless chicken thighs, halved
2 tablespoons peanut oil
1 tablespoon fresh ginger, cut into matchsticks
1 teaspoon sichuan peppercorns, crushed
1 teaspoon chilli bean paste (toban djan)
2 tablespoons light soy sauce
1 tablespoon Chinese rice wine
250 g (9 oz/1¼ cups) jasmine rice
600 g (1 lb 5 oz) baby bok choy (pak choy), leaves separated

Sprinkle the five-spice powder over the halved chicken fillets. Heat a wok until very hot, add half the oil and swirl to coat the side. Add the chicken pieces and cook for 2 minutes each side, or until browned. Remove from the wok and set aside.

Reduce the heat to medium. Add the ginger to the wok and cook for 30 seconds. Add the crushed sichuan peppercorns and chilli bean paste. Return the chicken pieces to the wok, add the soy sauce, wine and 125 ml (4 fl oz/½ cup) water, then simmer for 15–20 minutes, or until the chicken is cooked through.

Meanwhile, bring a saucepan of water to the boil. Add the rice and cook for 12 minutes, stirring occasionally. Drain.

Heat the remaining peanut oil in a saucepan. Add the bok choy and toss gently for 1 minute, or until the leaves wilt and the stems are tender. Serve with the chicken and rice.

Sprinkle the Chinese five-spice powder over the chicken pieces.

Japanese-style sukiyaki

preparation 10 minutes
cooking 10 minutes
serves 4

sauce
½–1 teaspoon dashi granules
80 ml (2½ fl oz/⅓ cup) soy sauce
2 tablespoons sake (dry rice wine)
2 tablespoons mirin (sweet rice wine)
1 tablespoon caster (superfine) sugar

300 g (10½ oz) shirataki noodles
50 g (2 oz) lard
5 large spring onions (scallions), cut into 1 cm (½ inch) slices on the diagonal
16 fresh shiitake mushrooms, cut into smaller pieces if large
800 g (1 lb 12 oz) rump steak, thinly sliced across the grain
100 g (3½ oz) watercress, trimmed
4 eggs (optional)

To make the sauce, dissolve the dashi granules in 125 ml (4 fl oz/½ cup) water. Add the soy sauce, sake, mirin and sugar, and stir until combined.

Drain the noodles, then soak them in boiling water for 2 minutes. Rinse in cold water and drain well.

Melt the lard in a large frying pan over medium heat. Cook the spring onion, mushrooms and beef in batches, stirring, for 1–2 minutes each batch, or until just brown. Return the meat, spring onion and mushrooms to the pan, then add the sauce and watercress. Cook for 1 minute, or until heated through and the watercress has wilted—the sauce needs to just cover the ingredients but not drown them.

To serve, divide the noodles among four serving bowls and spoon the sauce evenly over the top. If desired, crack an egg into each bowl and break up through the sauce using chopsticks until it partially cooks.

Bottom: Japanese-style sukiyaki. Top: Sichuan chicken.

Easy seafood paella

preparation 25 minutes
cooking 45 minutes
serves 6

250 g (9 oz) black mussels
300 g (10½ oz) skinless firm white fish fillets, cut into 2.5 cm (1 inch) cubes (see Note)
500 g (1 lb 2 oz) raw prawns (shrimp), peeled and deveined, leaving the tails intact
200 g (7 oz) squid rings
60 ml (2 fl oz/¼ cup) olive oil
1 large onion, diced
3 garlic cloves, finely chopped
1 small red capsicum (pepper), thinly sliced
1 small red chilli, seeded and chopped (optional)
2 teaspoons paprika
1 teaspoon ground turmeric
2 tomatoes, peeled and diced
1 tablespoon tomato paste (concentrated purée)
400 g (14 oz/2 cups) long-grain rice
125 ml (4 fl oz/½ cup) dry white wine
1.25 litres (44 fl oz/5 cups) fish stock
2 tablespoons chopped flat-leaf (Italian) parsley, to serve
lemon wedges, to serve

Scrub the mussels with a stiff brush and pull out the hairy beards. Discard any broken mussels, or open ones that don't close when tapped on the bench. Rinse well. Refrigerate all the seafood, covered, until ready to use.

Heat the oil in a paella pan or a large deep frying pan with a lid. Add the onion, garlic, capsicum and chilli to the pan, and cook over medium heat for 2 minutes, or until the onion and capsicum are soft. Add the paprika, turmeric and 1 teaspoon salt, and stir-fry for 1–2 minutes, or until aromatic. Add the tomato and cook for 5 minutes, or until softened. Add the tomato paste. Stir in the rice until it is well coated.

Pour in the wine and simmer until almost absorbed. Add all the fish stock and bring to the boil. Reduce heat to low–medium and simmer for 20 minutes, or until almost all of the liquid is absorbed into the rice. There is no need to stir the rice, but you may wish to fluff it up with a fork.

Add the mussels to the pan, cover and cook for 2–3 minutes over low heat. Add the prawns and cook for 2–3 minutes. Add the fish, cover and cook for 3 minutes. Finally, add the squid rings and cook for 1–2 minutes. By this time, the mussels should have opened—discard any unopened ones. The prawns should be pink and the fish should flake easily when tested with a fork. The squid should be white, moist and tender. Cook for another 2–3 minutes if the seafood is not quite cooked, but avoid overcooking as the seafood will toughen and dry out.

Serve with parsley and lemon wedges. Delicious with a tossed salad.

Note *You can use just fish, or other seafood such as scampi, octopus and crabs. If using just fish, choose one with few bones and chunky flesh, such as ling, blue-eye or warehou.*

Pull out the dark vein from along the back of each prawn, leaving the tail intact.

Protect your hands with rubber gloves when seeding the chilli.

Baked chicken and leek risotto

preparation 10 minutes
cooking 40 minutes
serves 6

1 tablespoon oil
1 leek, white part only, thinly sliced
2 boneless, skinless chicken breasts, cubed
440 g (15½ oz/2 cups) arborio rice
60 ml (2 fl oz/¼ cup) dry white wine
1.25 litres (44 fl oz/5 cups) chicken stock
35 g (1 oz/⅓ cup) grated parmesan cheese
2 tablespoons thyme leaves
thyme leaves and parmesan cheese, to serve

Preheat the oven to 150°C (300°F/Gas 2) and place a 5 litre (175 fl oz/20 cup) ovenproof dish with a lid in the oven to warm. Heat the oil in a saucepan over medium heat, add the leek and cook for 2 minutes, or until soft.

Add the chicken and cook, stirring, for 2–3 minutes, or until it colours. Add the rice and stir so that it is well coated. Cook for 1 minute.

Add the wine and stock and bring to the boil. Pour the mixture into the warm ovenproof dish and cover. Place in the oven and cook for 30 minutes, stirring halfway through. Remove from the oven and stir through the parmesan and thyme leaves. Season to taste. Sprinkle with extra thyme leaves and a little parmesan and serve.

Pork and apple braise

preparation 20 minutes
cooking 40 minutes
serves 4

1 tablespoon oil
1 large onion, thinly sliced
1 garlic clove, chopped
2 teaspoons soft brown sugar
2 green apples, cut into wedges
4 pork loin steaks or medallions
2 tablespoons brandy
2 tablespoons seeded mustard
250 ml (90 fl oz/1 cup) chicken stock
140 g (5 oz/⅔ cup) pitted prunes
125 ml (4 fl oz/½ cup) light pouring (whipping) cream

Heat the oil in a large heavy-based saucepan. Cook the onion and garlic for 10 minutes over low heat, stirring often, until softened and golden brown. Add the sugar and apple and cook, stirring regularly, until the apple begins to brown. Remove the apple and onion from the pan.

Reheat the pan and lightly brown the pork steaks, two at a time, then return them all to the pan. Add the brandy and stir until it has nearly all evaporated. Add the mustard and stock. Simmer over low heat, covered, for 15 minutes.

Return the apple to the pan with the prunes and cream and simmer for 10 minutes, or until the pork is tender. Season to taste before serving.

Hint *Take care not to overcook the pork or it can become tough and dry.*

Add the arborio rice to the pan and stir until it is well coated.

Stir the apple regularly over the heat until it begins to brown.

Bottom: Pork and apple braise. Top: Baked chicken and leek risotto.

Seafood and herb risotto

preparation 40 minutes
cooking 50 minutes
serves 4

150 g (5½ oz) white boneless fish fillet, such as sea perch
8 black mussels, about 200 g (7 oz)
8 raw prawns (shrimp), about 250 g (9 oz)
1.75 litres (61 fl oz/7 cups) chicken stock
cooking oil spray
2 onions, finely chopped
2 garlic cloves, finely chopped
1 celery stalk, finely chopped
440 g (15½ oz/2 cups) arborio rice
2 tablespoons chopped parsley
1 tablespoon chopped oregano
1 tablespoon chopped thyme leaves
2 tablespoons grated parmesan cheese

Cut the fish into small cubes. Scrub the mussels with a stiff brush and pull out the hairy beards. Discard any broken mussels, or open ones that don't close when tapped on the bench. Rinse well. Peel the prawns, leaving the tail intact, and gently pull out the dark vein from each prawn back, starting at the head end. Put the seafood in a bowl and refrigerate until required.

Put the stock in a saucepan and bring to the boil. Reduce the heat until just simmering.

Spray a large saucepan with oil and heat over medium heat. Add the onion, garlic and celery and cook for 2–3 minutes. Add 2 tablespoons water, cover and cook for 5 minutes. Add the arborio rice and 2 tablespoons water and stir over medium heat for 3–4 minutes. Gradually add 125 ml (4 fl oz/½ cup) of the stock to the rice, stirring constantly over low heat, until all the stock has been absorbed. Repeat, adding 125 ml of stock each time until all but a small amount of stock is left and the rice is just tender.

Meanwhile, bring a small amount of water to the boil in a saucepan. Add the mussels, cover and cook for about 3 minutes, shaking the pan occasionally, until the mussels have opened. Drain, and discard any that did not open.

Add the fish and prawns and the remaining stock to the rice. Stir well and continue to cook for about 5–10 minutes, or until the seafood is just cooked. Remove from the heat, add the cooked mussels, cover and set aside for 5 minutes. Stir the herbs and parmesan through the risotto, then season well. Serve immediately.

Scrub the mussels thoroughly and pull off the beards. Discard any open mussels.

Add the arborio rice to the pan and stir over the heat until the rice is well coated.

Lemon chilli chicken

preparation 20 minutes
cooking 35 minutes
serves 4

2 garlic cloves, chopped
1 tablespoon grated fresh ginger
2 tablespoons olive oil
600 g (1 lb 5 oz) boneless, skinless chicken thighs
1 teaspoon ground coriander
2 teaspoons ground cumin
½ teaspoon ground turmeric
1 red chilli, chopped
125 ml (4 fl oz/½ cup) lemon juice
185 ml (6 fl oz/¾ cup) dry white wine
3 large handfuls coriander (cilantro) leaves

Blend the garlic, ginger and 1 tablespoon water into a paste in a small food processor or with a mortar and pestle. Heat the olive oil in a heavy-based frying pan and brown the chicken in batches. Remove and set aside.

Add the garlic paste to the pan and cook, stirring, for 1 minute. Add the coriander, cumin, turmeric and chilli and stir-fry for 1 minute more. Stir in the lemon juice and wine.

Add the chicken pieces to the pan. Bring to the boil, reduce the heat, cover and cook for 20–25 minutes, stirring occasionally, until the chicken is tender. Uncover and cook the sauce over high heat for 5 minutes to reduce it by half. Stir in the fresh coriander leaves and season to taste with salt and pepper. Serve with rice.

Add the coriander, cumin, turmeric and chilli and stir-fry for 1 minute.

Fish, ginger and tomato hotpot

preparation 20 minutes + 20 minutes soaking
cooking 1 hour
serves 4

1 tablespoon peanut oil
1 onion, cut into thin wedges
1 small red chilli, sliced
3 garlic cloves, finely chopped
2 cm x 2 cm (¾ inch x ¾ inch) piece fresh ginger,
cut into matchsticks
½ teaspoon ground turmeric
400 g (14 oz) tin chopped tomatoes
1 litre (35 fl oz/4 cups) chicken stock
1 tablespoon tamarind purée
80 g (3 oz) dried rice stick noodles
600 g (1 lb 5 oz) snapper fillets, skin removed, cut into
3 cm (1¼ inch) cubes
coriander (cilantro) leaves, to garnish

Preheat the oven to 220°C (425°F/Gas 7). Heat the oil in a frying pan over medium–high heat, and cook the onion for 1–2 minutes, or until softened. Add the chilli, garlic and ginger, and cook for a further 30 seconds. Add the turmeric, tomato, stock and tamarind purée, and bring to the boil over high heat. Transfer to a 2.5 litre (87 fl oz/10 cup) heatproof hotpot or casserole dish and bake, covered, for 40 minutes.

Place the rice stick noodles in a large heatproof bowl and cover with warm water. Soak the noodles for 15–20 minutes, or until tender. Drain, rinse and drain again.

Remove the hotpot from the oven and stir in the drained noodles. Add the fish cubes, then cover and return to the oven for a further 10 minutes, or until the fish is cooked through. Serve garnished with coriander leaves.

Using tongs, gently add the fish cubes to the hotpot mixture.

Bottom: Fish, ginger and tomato hotpot. Top: Lemon chilli chicken.

Beef pot roast

preparation 15 minutes
cooking 3 hours 15 minutes
serves 6

300 g (10½ oz) small baby onions
2 carrots
3 parsnips, peeled
30 g (1 oz) butter
1–1.5 kg (2 lb 4 oz–3 lb 5 oz) piece of silverside,
trimmed of fat (see Note)
60 ml (2 fl oz/¼ cup) red wine
1 large tomato, finely chopped
250 ml (9 fl oz/1 cup) beef stock

Put the onions in a heatproof bowl and cover with boiling water. Leave for 1 minute, then drain well. Allow to cool and then peel off the skins.

Cut the carrots and parsnips in half lengthways then into even-sized pieces. Heat half the butter in a large heavy-based saucepan that will tightly fit the meat (it will shrink during cooking), add the onions, carrot and parsnip and cook, stirring, over medium–high heat until browned. Remove from the pan.

Add the remaining butter to the pan and add the meat, browning well all over. Increase the heat to high and pour in the wine. Bring to the boil, then add the tomato and stock. Return to the boil, then reduce the heat to low, cover and simmer for 2 hours, turning once. Add the vegetables and simmer, covered, for 1 hour.

Remove the meat from the pan and put it on a board ready for carving. Cover with foil and leave it to stand while you finish the sauce.

Increase the heat to high and boil the pan juices with the vegetables for 10 minutes to reduce and thicken slightly. Skim off any fat and taste before seasoning. Serve the meat and vegetables with the pan juices. Serve with mustard.

Note Eye of silverside is a tender, long-shaped cut of silverside, which carves easily into serving-sized pieces. A regular piece of silverside or topside may be substituted.

Put the pickling onions in a bowl and cover with boiling water.

Add the piece of meat to the pan and brown well on all sides.

French-style beef pot roast

preparation 15 minutes
cooking 2 hours 20 minutes
serves 6

2 tablespoons oil
2 kg (4 lb 8 oz) rolled beef brisket, trimmed
750 ml (26 fl oz/3 cups) beef stock
250 ml (9 fl oz/1 cup) red wine
60 ml (2 fl oz/¼ cup) brandy
2 onions, quartered
3 garlic cloves, crushed
3 tomatoes, peeled, seeded and chopped
2 bay leaves
1 large handful chopped parsley
2 tablespoons thyme leaves
12 pitted black olives
6 small carrots, thickly sliced
2 tablespoons plain (all-purpose) flour

Heat the oil in a deep heavy-based saucepan. Cook the meat over medium–high heat until browned all over, then remove from the heat.

Add the stock to the pan with the wine, brandy, onion, garlic, tomato, bay leaves, parsley and thyme. Cover and bring to simmering point over low heat. Simmer for 1½ hours.

Add the olives and carrot, and cook for 30 minutes. Remove the meat and leave it in a warm place, and covered with foil, for 10 minutes before slicing.

Combine the flour and 60 ml (2 fl oz/¼ cup) water to make a smooth paste. Add to the sauce, stir over medium heat until the sauce thickens, and cook for 3 minutes. Pour over the sliced meat to serve.

Turkey pot roast

preparation 20 minutes
cooking 1 hour 15 minutes
serves 6

1 kg (2 lb 4 oz) frozen turkey breast roll
2 tablespoons oil
20 g (¾ oz) butter
1 onion, cut into wedges
125 ml (4 fl oz/½ cup) chicken stock
125 ml (4 fl oz/½ cup) dry white wine
300 g (10½ oz) orange sweet potato,
cut into 3 cm (1¼ inch) pieces
2 zucchini (courgettes), cut into 2 cm (¾ inch) slices
160 g (5½ oz/½ cup) redcurrant jelly
1 tablespoon cornflour (cornstarch)

Preheat the oven to 180°C (350°F/Gas 4). Thaw the turkey according to the instructions on the label. Remove the elasticised string from the turkey and tie up securely with kitchen string, at regular intervals, to retain its shape.

Heat the oil and butter in a frying pan over high heat, and brown the turkey all over. Transfer the turkey to a 2 litre (70 fl oz/8 cup) casserole dish. Place the onion wedges around the turkey, and pour over the stock and wine. Cover and bake for 40 minutes. Add the sweet potato and bake for 10 minutes. Add the zucchini and bake for a further 20 minutes.

Transfer the turkey and vegetables to a plate and keep warm. Strain the remaining liquid into a small saucepan. Stir in the redcurrant jelly. Combine the cornflour and 1 tablespoon water, and stir until smooth. Add gradually to the pan, stirring until the mixture boils and thickens. Slice the turkey and serve with the vegetables and sauce.

Add the stock to the pan with the wine, brandy, onion, garlic, tomato and herbs.

Tie up the turkey with string, at regular intervals, to help retain its shape during cooking.

Bottom: Turkey pot roast. Top: French-style beef pot roast.

Lion's head meatballs

preparation 20 minutes + overnight refrigeration + 20 minutes soaking
cooking 4 hours 45 minutes
serves 4

chicken stock
1.5 kg (3 lb 5 oz) chicken bones (chicken necks, backs, wings), washed (see Note)
2 slices fresh ginger, cut into 1 cm (½ inch) thick slices
4 spring onions (scallions)

6 dried Chinese mushrooms
100 g (3½ oz) mung bean vermicelli
600 g (1 lb 5 oz) minced (ground) pork
1 egg white
4 garlic cloves, finely chopped
1 tablespoon finely grated fresh ginger
1 tablespoon cornflour (cornstarch)
1½ tablespoons Chinese rice wine
6 spring onions (scallions), thinly sliced
2 tablespoons peanut oil
60 ml (2 fl oz/¼ cup) light soy sauce
1 teaspoon sugar
400 g (14 oz) bok choy (pak choy), halved lengthways, leaves separated

To make the stock, place the bones and 3.5 litres (122 fl oz/ 10 cups) water in a large saucepan and bring to a simmer— do not let it boil. Remove the surface scum over the next 30 minutes. Add ginger and spring onions, and cook, partially covered, at a low simmer for 3 hours. Strain and cool. Cover and refrigerate overnight. Remove the layer of fat from the surface once it has solidified.

Soak the Chinese mushrooms in 250 ml (9 fl oz/1 cup) boiling water for 20 minutes. Drain. Discard the stems and thinly slice the caps. Meanwhile, place the vermicelli in a heatproof bowl, cover with boiling water and soak for 3–4 minutes, or until soft. Drain and rinse. Preheat the oven to 220°C (425°F/Gas 7).

Place the pork, egg white, garlic, ginger, cornflour, rice wine, two-thirds of the spring onion and salt, to taste, in a food processor. Process until smooth. Divide mixture into eight portions and roll into balls with wet hands.

Place 500 ml (17 fl oz/2 cups) of the stock (freeze any remaining stock) in a large saucepan and bring to the boil over high heat. Remove from the heat and keep warm.

Heat the oil in a wok over high heat. Fry the meatballs in batches for 2 minutes each side, or until golden, but not cooked through. Drain.

Place the meatballs, mushrooms, soy sauce and sugar in a 2.5 litre (87 fl oz/10 cup) casserole dish, and cover with the hot stock. Bake, covered, for 45 minutes. Add the bok choy and noodles and bake, covered, for another 10 minutes. Sprinkle with the remaining spring onion, and serve.

Note *To save time, use 500 ml (17 fl oz/ 2 cups) of purchased stock instead of making your own.*

Form the mince mixture into eight large balls using wet hands.

Add the bok choy and noodles to the dish containing the meatballs.

Chicken donburi

preparation 35 minutes
cooking 30 minutes
serves 4

440 g (15½ oz/2 cups) short-grain rice
2 tablespoons oil
250 g (9 oz) boneless, skinless chicken breasts, cut into thin strips
2 onions, thinly sliced
80 ml (2½ fl oz/⅓ cup) shoyu (Japanese soy sauce)
2 tablespoons mirin (sweet rice wine)
1 teaspoon dashi granules
5 eggs, lightly beaten
2 nori sheets
2 spring onions (scallions), sliced

Wash the rice in a colander under cold running water until the water runs clear. Transfer the rice to a heavy-based saucepan, add 600 ml (21 fl oz) water and bring to the boil over high heat. Cover the pan with a tight-fitting lid and reduce the heat to as low as possible (otherwise the rice in the bottom of the pan will burn) and cook for 15 minutes. Turn the heat to very high, for 15–20 seconds, remove the pan from the heat and set aside for 12 minutes, without lifting the lid or the steam will escape.

Heat the oil in a frying pan over high heat. Add the chicken and stir-fry until tender. Remove the chicken from the pan and set aside. Reheat the pan, add the onion and cook, stirring occasionally, for 3 minutes, or until beginning to soften. Add 80 ml (2½ fl oz/⅓ cup) water, the shoyu, mirin and dashi granules. Stir to dissolve the dashi, and bring to the boil. Cook for 3 minutes, or until the onion is tender.

Return the chicken to the pan and pour in the egg, stirring gently to break up. Cover and simmer over very low heat for 2–3 minutes, or until the egg is just set. Remove the pan from the heat. To make the nori crisp, hold it over low heat, moving it back and forward for about 15 seconds, then crumble it into small pieces.

Transfer the rice to a serving dish, carefully spoon over the chicken and egg mixture and sprinkle with the crumbled nori. Garnish with the spring onion.

Cook the onion for about 3 minutes, or until it begins to soften.

Pour the egg into the pan and stir gently to break it up.

Ponzu chicken and noodle hotpot

preparation 15 minutes + overnight refrigeration
cooking 45 minutes
serves 4

ponzu sauce
1 tablespoon lemon juice
1 tablespoon lime juice
1 tablespoon rice vinegar
1 tablespoon tamari
1½ tablespoons mirin (sweet rice wine)
2½ tablespoons Japanese soy sauce
5 cm (2 inch) piece kombu (kelp), wiped with a damp cloth
1 tablespoon bonito flakes

900 g (2 lb) chicken thigh cutlets, cut in half across the bone
10 cm (4 inch) piece kombu (kelp)
200 g (7 oz) dried somen noodles
250 g (9 oz) fresh shiitake mushrooms, halved if large
1 carrot, thinly sliced
300 g (10½ oz) baby English spinach leaves

To make the ponzu sauce, combine all the ingredients in a non-metallic bowl. Cover with plastic wrap and refrigerate overnight, then strain through a fine sieve. Discard any sediment and put the sauce aside.

Place the chicken and kombu in a large saucepan with 875 ml (30 fl oz/3½ cups) water. Bring to a simmer over medium heat. Cook for 20 minutes, or until the chicken is cooked, skimming the scum off the surface. Remove the chicken pieces and strain the broth. Transfer the broth and chicken pieces to a 2.5 litre (87 fl oz/10 cup) flameproof casserole dish or Japanese nabe. Cover and continue to cook over low heat for 15 minutes.

Meanwhile, cook the noodles in a large saucepan of boiling water for 2 minutes, or until tender. Drain and rinse under cold running water.

Add the mushrooms and carrot to the chicken, and cook for 5 minutes. Place the noodles on top of the chicken, then top with the spinach. Cook, covered, for 2 minutes, or until the spinach has just wilted. Stir in 4–6 tablespoons of the ponzu sauce, or to taste. Season with pepper and serve.

Note *Traditionally, this dish would be served in a ceramic nabe dish, for your guests to help themselves.*

Lamb hotpot with rice noodles

preparation 20 minutes + 2 hours marinating
cooking 2 hours
serves 4

2 garlic cloves, crushed
2 teaspoons grated fresh ginger
1 teaspoon Chinese five-spice
¼ teaspoon ground white pepper
2 tablespoons Chinese rice wine
1 teaspoon sugar
1 kg (2 lb 4 oz) boneless lamb shoulder, trimmed and cut into 3 cm (1¼ inch) pieces
30 g (1 oz) whole dried Chinese mushrooms
1 tablespoon peanut oil
1 large onion, cut into wedges
2 cm (¾ inch) piece fresh ginger, cut into matchsticks
1 teaspoon sichuan peppercorns, crushed or ground
2 tablespoons sweet bean paste
1 teaspoon black peppercorns, ground and toasted
500 ml (17 fl oz/2 cups) chicken stock
60 ml (2 fl oz/¼ cup) oyster sauce
2 star anise
60 ml (2 fl oz/¼ cup) Chinese rice wine, extra
80 g (3 oz) tin sliced bamboo shoots, drained
100 g (3½ oz) tin water chestnuts, drained and sliced
400 g (14 oz) fresh rice noodles, cut into 2 cm (¾ inch) wide strips
1 spring onion (scallion), sliced on the diagonal

Combine the garlic, grated ginger, five-spice, white pepper, rice wine, sugar and 1 teaspoon salt in a large bowl. Add the lamb and toss to coat. Cover and marinate for 2 hours.

Meanwhile, soak the mushrooms in boiling water for 20 minutes. Drain. Discard the stems.

Heat a wok over high heat, add the oil and swirl to coat. Stir-fry the onion, ginger and sichuan peppercorns for 2 minutes. Cook the lamb in three batches, stir-frying for 2–3 minutes each batch, or until starting to brown. Return all the lamb to the wok. Stir in the bean paste and black peppercorns, and cook for 3 minutes, or until the lamb is brown.

Add the stock and transfer to a 2 litre (70 fl oz/8 cup) flameproof clay pot or casserole dish. Stir in the oyster sauce, star anise and extra rice wine and simmer, covered, over low heat for 1½ hours, or until the lamb is tender. Stir in the bamboo shoots and water chestnuts, and cook for 20 minutes. Add the mushrooms.

Cover the noodles with boiling water and gently separate. Drain and rinse the noodles, then add to the hotpot, stirring for 1–2 minutes, or until heated through. Serve sprinkled with spring onion.

Stir the bean paste and peppercorns into the lamb and onion mixture.

Stir the bamboo shoots and water chestnuts into the hotpot.

vegetarian

Asian barley pilau

preparation 10 minutes + 15 minutes standing
cooking 35 minutes
serves 4

15 g (½ oz) dried sliced button mushrooms
500 ml (17 fl oz/2 cups) vegetable stock
125 ml (4 fl oz/½ cup) dry sherry
1 tablespoon oil
3 large French shallots (eschalots), thinly sliced
2 large garlic cloves, crushed
1 tablespoon grated fresh ginger
1 teaspoon sichuan peppercorns, crushed (see Note)
330 g (11½ oz/1½ cups) pearl barley
500 g (1 lb 2 oz) choy sum (Chinese flowering cabbage), cut into short lengths
3 teaspoons kecap manis
1 teaspoon sesame oil

Place the mushrooms in a bowl and cover with boiling water, then leave for 15 minutes. Strain carefully, reserving 125 ml (4 fl oz/½ cup) of the liquid.

Bring the stock and sherry to the boil in a saucepan, then reduce the heat, cover and simmer until needed.

Heat the oil in a large saucepan and cook the shallots over medium heat for 2–3 minutes, or until soft. Add the garlic, ginger and peppercorns and cook for 1 minute. Add the barley and mushrooms and mix well. Stir in the stock and mushroom liquid, then reduce the heat and simmer, covered, for 25 minutes, or until the liquid evaporates.

Meanwhile, steam the choy sum until wilted. Add to the barley mixture. Stir in the kecap manis and sesame oil, then serve.

Note *You can buy sichuan peppercorns at Asian food stores.*

Strain the mushrooms, reserving some of the liquid for flavouring the pilau.

Reduce the heat and simmer the pilau until the liquid has evaporated.

Red lentil pilau

preparation 15 minutes
cooking 25 minutes
serves 4–6

garam masala
1 tablespoon coriander seeds
1 tablespoon cardamom pods
1 tablespoon cumin seeds
1 teaspoon whole black peppercorns
1 teaspoon whole cloves
1 small cinnamon stick, crushed

60 ml (2 fl oz/¼ cup) oil
1 onion, chopped
3 garlic cloves, chopped
200 g (7 oz/1 cup) basmati rice
250 g (9 oz/1 cup) red lentils
750 ml (26 fl oz/3 cups) hot vegetable stock
spring onions (scallions), shredded, to serve

To make the garam masala, place all the spices in a dry frying pan and shake over medium heat for 1 minute, or until fragrant. Blend in a spice grinder, blender or mortar and pestle to make a fine powder.

Heat the oil in a large saucepan. Add the onion, garlic and 3 teaspoons of garam masala. Cook over medium heat for 3 minutes, or until soft.

Stir in the rice and lentils and cook for 2 minutes. Add the hot stock and stir well. Slowly bring to the boil, then reduce the heat and simmer, covered, for 15–20 minutes, or until the rice is cooked and all the stock has been absorbed. Gently fluff the rice with a fork. Garnish with spring onion.

Note *If time is short you can use ready-made garam masala instead of making your own.*

Finely blend all the spices in a spice grinder until they make a fine powder.

Potato porcini bake

preparation 30 minutes
cooking 45 minutes
serves 4–6

20 g (1 oz) dried porcini mushrooms
185 ml (6 fl oz/¾ cup) hot milk
125 ml (4 fl oz/½ cup) pouring (whipping) cream
1 kg (2 lb 4 oz) waxy potatoes, unpeeled
30 g (1 oz) butter
1 garlic clove, crushed
60 g (2 oz) spring onions (scallions), sliced
120 g (4 oz/1 cup) grated fontina or gruyère cheese

Lightly brush a large shallow ovenproof dish with oil. Make sure the porcini are free of dirt or grit and put them in a bowl with the hot milk. Cover the bowl and set aside for 15 minutes. Remove the porcini, finely chop them and then return to the milk. Add the cream.

Meanwhile, slice the potatoes fairly thinly and cook in boiling salted water until just tender, then drain well. Melt the butter in a small saucepan and cook the garlic and spring onion until soft.

Preheat the oven to 180°C (350°F/Gas 4). Layer the potato in the dish with the garlic, spring onion and cheese, spooning the porcini mixture over each layer and seasoning with salt and freshly ground black pepper. Bake for 35 minutes, or until golden and tender. Serve hot.

Layer the potato, spring onion and cheese in the dish, spooning the porcini over each layer.

Bottom: Potato porcini bake. Top: Red lentil pilau.

Bean and capsicum stew

preparation 20 minutes + overnight soaking
cooking 1 hour 35 minutes
serves 4–6

200 g (7 oz/1 cup) dried haricot beans (see Note)
2 tablespoons olive oil
2 large garlic cloves, crushed
1 red onion, halved and cut into thin wedges
1 red capsicum (pepper), cut into squares
1 green capsicum (pepper), cut into squares
2 x 400 g (14 oz) tins chopped tomatoes
2 tablespoons tomato paste (concentrated purée)
500 ml (17 fl oz/2 cups) vegetable stock
2 tablespoons chopped basil
125 g (4½ oz/⅔ cup) kalamata olives, pitted
1–2 teaspoons soft brown sugar

Put the beans in a large bowl, cover with cold water and soak overnight. Rinse well, then transfer to a saucepan, cover with cold water and cook for 45 minutes, or until just tender. Drain.

Heat the oil in a large saucepan. Cook the garlic and onion over medium heat for 2–3 minutes, or until the onion is soft. Add the red and green capsicums and cook for a further 5 minutes.

Stir in the tomato, tomato paste, stock and beans. Simmer, covered, for 40 minutes, or until the beans are cooked through. Stir in the basil, olives and sugar. Season with salt and freshly ground black pepper. Serve with crusty bread.

Note 1 cup of dried haricot beans yields about 2½ cups cooked beans. So you can use 2½ cups tinned haricot or borlotti beans instead, if you prefer.

Mediterranean vegetable hotpot

preparation 20 minutes
cooking 40 minutes
serves 4

60 ml (2 fl oz/¼ cup) olive oil
1 onion, chopped
2 garlic cloves, crushed
1 green capsicum (pepper), chopped
1 red capsicum (pepper), chopped
3 zucchini (courgettes), sliced
3 slender eggplants (aubergines), sliced
440 g (15½ oz/2 cups) long-grain rice
250 ml (9 fl oz/1 cup) dry white wine
100 g (3½ oz) button mushrooms, sliced
750 ml (26 fl oz/3 cups) vegetable stock
400 g (14 oz) tin chopped tomatoes
2 tablespoons tomato paste (concentrated purée)
150 g (5½ oz) feta cheese, crumbled

Heat the oil in a large heavy-based saucepan and cook the onion over medium heat for about 10 minutes, or until very soft but not browned. Add the garlic and cook for a further 1 minute.

Add the green and red capsicums and cook, stirring, for 3 minutes, Add the zucchini and eggplant and stir-fry for a further 5 minutes. Add the rice and stir-fry for 2 minutes.

Add the wine, mushrooms, stock, chopped tomatoes and tomato paste. Stir to combine. Bring to the boil, reduce the heat, cover and simmer for 20 minutes. The rice should be tender. Serve immediately, topped with the feta cheese.

Note Like most hotpots and casseroles, this is best made a day in advance to let the flavours develop.

Cook the garlic and onion until the garlic is soft, then add the capsicum.

Add the zucchini and eggplant to the pan and cook for a little longer.

Three-bean chilli

preparation 20 minutes + 2 hours standing
cooking 1 hour 35 minutes
serves 4

220 g (8 oz/1 cup) dried black beans (see Note)
2 tablespoons oil
1 large onion, finely chopped
3 garlic cloves, crushed
2 tablespoons ground cumin
1 tablespoon ground coriander
1 teaspoon ground cinnamon
1 teaspoon chilli powder
400 g (14 oz) tin chopped tomatoes
375 ml (13 fl oz/1½ cups) vegetable stock
400 g (14 oz) tin chickpeas, drained and rinsed
400 g (14 oz) tin red kidney beans, drained and rinsed
2 tablespoons tomato paste (concentrated purée)
1 tablespoon sugar
sour cream and corn chips, to serve

Place the black beans in a large saucepan, cover with water and bring to the boil. Turn off the heat and set aside for 2 hours. Drain he beans, cover with fresh water and boil for 1 hour, until the beans are tender but not mushy. Drain well.

Heat the oil in a large saucepan and cook the onion over low-medium heat for 5 minutes, until golden, stirring frequently. Reduce the heat, add the garlic and spices and stir for 1 minute.

Add the tomatoes, stock, chickpeas, kidney beans and black beans and combine with the onion mixture. Bring to the boil, then simmer for 20 minutes, stirring occasionally.

Add the tomato paste, sugar and season to taste. Simmer for a further 5 minutes. Serve with sour cream and corn chips on the side.

Note *If black beans are unavailable, double the quantity of kidney beans and chickpeas. Do not confuse black beans with Asian black beans, which are fermented soy.*

Tomato and potato stew

preparation 30 minutes
cooking 1 hour 15 minutes
serves 6

60 ml (2 fl oz/¼ cup) olive oil
2 red capsicums (peppers), chopped
2 green capsicums (peppers), chopped
3 onions, thinly sliced
4 garlic cloves, crushed
2 x 400 g (14 oz) tins chopped tomatoes
3–4 sprigs thyme, plus extra, to garnish
2 bay leaves
2 teaspoons caster (superfine) sugar
1.2 kg (2 lb 7 oz) potatoes, cut into chunks
125 g (4½ oz/1 cup) black olives, pitted
parmesan cheese shavings, to serve

Heat the oil in a large, heavy-based saucepan. When the oil is hot, cook the capsicum, onion and garlic over medium heat for 10 minutes, or until softened. Add the chopped tomatoes, 125 ml (4 fl oz/½ cup) water, thyme sprigs, bay leaves and sugar. Season with salt and freshly ground black pepper to taste and leave to simmer gently for 15 minutes.

Add the potato chunks, cover and cook very gently for about an hour, or until tender. Stir in the olives. Garnish with the parmesan shavings and thyme sprigs.

The easiest way to make parmesan shavings is to run a vegetable peeler over the block.

Bottom: Tomato and potato stew. Top: Three-bean chilli.

Spicy vegetable stew with dhal

preparation 25 minutes + 2 hours soaking
cooking 1 hour 35 minutes
serves 4–6

dhal
165 g (6 oz/¾ cup) yellow split peas
5 cm (2 inch) piece of fresh ginger, grated
2–3 garlic cloves, crushed
1 red chilli, seeded and chopped

3 tomatoes
2 tablespoons oil
1 teaspoon yellow mustard seeds
1 teaspoon cumin seeds
1 teaspoon ground cumin
½ teaspoon garam masala
1 red onion, cut into thin wedges
3 slender eggplants (aubergines), thickly sliced
2 carrots, thickly sliced
¼ cauliflower, cut into florets
375 ml (13 fl oz/1½ cups) vegetable stock
2 small zucchini (courgettes), thickly sliced
90 g (3 oz/½ cup) frozen peas
1 large handful coriander (cilantro) leaves

To make the dhal, put the split peas in a bowl, cover with water and soak for 2 hours. Drain. Place in a large saucepan with the ginger, garlic, chilli and 750 ml (26 fl oz/3 cups) water. Bring to the boil, reduce the heat and simmer for 45 minutes, or until soft.

Score a cross in the base of each tomato, soak in boiling water for 30 seconds, then plunge into cold water and peel the skin away from the cross. Cut in half and scoop out the seeds with a teaspoon. Chop the tomato flesh.

Heat the oil in a large saucepan. Cook the spices over medium heat for 30 seconds, or until fragrant. Add the onion and cook for 2 minutes, or until the onion is soft. Stir in the tomato, eggplant, carrot and cauliflower.

Add the dhal and stock, mix together well and simmer, covered, for 45 minutes, or until the vegetables are tender. Stir occasionally. Add the zucchini and peas during the last 10 minutes of cooking. Stir in the coriander leaves and serve.

Simmer the dhal for 45 minutes, or until the split peas are soft.

Add the dhal and stock to the stew and simmer for 45 minutes, or until the vegetables are tender.

Creamy potato casserole

preparation 20 minutes
cooking 40 minutes
serves 4–6

750 g (1 lb 10 oz) all-purpose potatoes (see Notes)
1 onion
125 g (4½ oz/1 cup) grated cheddar cheese
375 ml (13 fl oz/1½ cups) pouring (whipping) cream
2 teaspoons chicken stock (bouillon) powder (see Notes)

Preheat the oven to 180°C (350°F/Gas 4). Peel the potatoes and thinly slice them. Peel the onion and slice it into rings.

Arrange a layer of overlapping potato slices in the base of a large casserole dish. Top the potato slices with a layer of the onion rings. Divide the grated cheese in half and set aside one half to use as a topping. Sprinkle a little of the remaining grated cheese over the onion rings. Continue layering in this order until all the potato and the onion have been used, finishing with a little of the grated cheese.

Pour the cream into a small jug, add the chicken stock powder and whisk gently until the mixture is thoroughly combined. Carefully pour the cream mixture over the layered potato and onion slices, and sprinkle the top with the reserved grated cheese. Bake the casserole, uncovered, for 40 minutes, or until the potato is tender, the cheese has melted and the top is golden brown.

Notes *Waxy or all-purpose potatoes are best to use in this recipe because they hold their shape better when slow-cooked.*

If you have a mandolin, use it to cut the potatoes into very thin slices. If not, make sure you use a very sharp knife.

If you prefer, you can use different types of stock, including vegetable, to vary the flavour.

Tofu, vegetable and noodle hotpot

preparation 10 minutes + 20 minutes soaking
cooking 15 minutes
serves 4

8 dried shiitake mushrooms
500 g (1 lb 2 oz) fresh round rice noodles
3 litres (105 fl oz/12 cups) chicken stock
1 carrot, thinly sliced on the diagonal
100 g (3½ oz) fried tofu puffs, halved
800 g (1 lb 12 oz) bok choy (pak choy), trimmed and quartered
1–1½ tablespoons mushroom soy sauce
6 drops sesame oil
ground white pepper, to season
100 g (3½ oz) enoki mushrooms, ends trimmed

Place the shiitake mushrooms in a heatproof bowl, cover with boiling water and soak for 20 minutes. Drain and remove the stems, squeezing out any excess water.

Meanwhile, place the noodles in a heatproof bowl, cover with boiling water and soak briefly. Refresh with cold water. Gently separate the noodles with your hands and drain.

Place the chicken stock in a large saucepan, cover and slowly bring to a gentle simmer over low heat.

Add the noodles to the simmering stock along with the carrot, tofu puffs, shiitake mushrooms and bok choy. Cook for 1–2 minutes, or until the carrot and noodles are tender and the bok choy has wilted slightly. Stir in the soy sauce and sesame oil, and season with white pepper.

Divide the noodles, vegetables, tofu puffs and enoki mushrooms among four serving bowls, ladle the broth on top and serve immediately.

Sprinkle a little of the grated cheese over each layer of onion rings.

To prepare the enoki mushrooms for the hotpot, trim the ends.

Bottom: Tofu, vegetable and noodle hotpot. Top: Creamy potato casserole.

Lentil bhujia stew

preparation 30 minutes + overnight soaking +
30 minutes refrigeration
cooking 1 hour 10 minutes
serves 4–6

370 g (13 oz/2 cups) green or brown lentils
1 large onion, grated
1 large potato, grated
1 teaspoon ground cumin
1 teaspoon ground coriander
1 teaspoon ground turmeric
90 g (3 oz/¾ cup) plain (all-purpose) flour
oil, for shallow-frying
2 garlic cloves, crushed
1 tablespoon grated fresh ginger
250 g (9 oz/1 cup) tomato paste (concentrated purée)
500 ml (17 fl oz/2 cups) vegetable stock
250 ml (9 fl oz/1 cup) pouring (whipping) cream
200 g (7 oz) green beans, trimmed and cut in half
2 carrots, sliced
2 hard-boiled eggs, chopped
rosemary sprigs, to garnish

Soak the lentils overnight in cold water. Drain well.
Squeeze the excess moisture from the lentils, onion and
potato using a tea towel (dish towel). Place them in a bowl
with the ground spices and flour; mix well and leave for
10 minutes. With floured hands, shape the mixture into
walnut-sized balls and place on a foil-lined tray. Cover and
refrigerate for 30 minutes.

Heat 2 cm (¾ inch) of oil in a heavy-based frying pan. Cook
the balls in batches over high heat until golden brown.
Drain balls by placing on paper towels.

Heat 2 tablespoons of oil in a saucepan and gently fry the
garlic and ginger for 2 minutes. Stir in the tomato paste,
stock and cream. Bring to the boil, then reduce the heat
and simmer for 10 minutes. Add the beans, lentil balls and
carrot. Cook, covered, for 30 minutes, stirring twice. Add
the egg and cook for 10 minutes. Garnish with rosemary.

Variation Split peas can be used in this recipe in place of
the lentils. Soak them in cold water overnight, then drain well
before using.

Ratatouille

preparation 30 minutes
cooking 40 minutes
serves 4–6

100 ml (3½ fl oz) olive oil
500 g (1 lb 2 oz) eggplants (aubergines), cut into
2 cm (¾ inch) cubes
375 g (13 oz) zucchini (courgettes), cut into 2 cm (¾ inch) slices
1 green capsicum (pepper), seeded, cut into
2 cm (¾ inch) cubes
1 red onion, cut into 2 cm (¾ inch) wedges
3 garlic cloves, finely chopped
¼ teaspoon cayenne pepper
2 teaspoons chopped thyme
2 bay leaves
6 vine-ripened tomatoes, peeled and roughly chopped
1 tablespoon red wine vinegar
1 teaspoon caster (superfine) sugar
4 tablespoons shredded basil

Heat 2 tablespoons of the oil in a large saucepan and cook
the eggplant over medium heat for 4–5 minutes, or until
softened but not browned. Remove all the eggplant from
the pan.

Add another 2 tablespoons oil to the pan and cook the
zucchini slices for 3–4 minutes, or until softened. Remove
the zucchini from the pan. Add the capsicum to the pan,
cook for 2 minutes, then remove.

Heat the remaining oil in the pan, add the onion wedges
and cook for 2–3 minutes, or until softened. Add the garlic,
cayenne pepper, thyme and bay leaves, and cook, stirring,
for 1 minute. Return the cooked eggplant, zucchini and
capsicum to the pan, and add the tomato, vinegar and
sugar. Simmer for 20 minutes, stirring occasionally. Stir in
the basil and season with salt and black pepper. Serve the
ratatouille hot or cold.

Note Ratatouille takes quite a long time to prepare and so
is traditionally made in large quantities. It is then eaten over
several days as an hors d'oeuvre, side dish or main meal.

Bottom: Ratatouille. Top: Lentil bhujia stew.

Moroccan tagine with couscous

preparation 20 minutes
cooking 1 hour
serves 4–6

2 tablespoons oil
2 onions, chopped
1 teaspoon ground ginger
2 teaspoons ground paprika
2 teaspoons ground cumin
1 cinnamon stick
pinch of saffron threads
1.5 kg (3 lb 5 oz) vegetables, peeled and cut into large chunks (carrot, eggplant (aubergine),
orange sweet potato, parsnip, potato, pumpkin (winter squash))
½ preserved lemon, rinsed, pith and flesh removed, thinly sliced
400 g (14 oz) tin peeled tomatoes
250 ml (9 fl oz/1 cup) vegetable stock
100 g (3½ oz) dried pears, halved
60 g (2 oz) pitted prunes
2 zucchini (courgettes), cut into large chunks
300 g (10½ oz) instant couscous
1 tablespoon olive oil
3 tablespoons chopped flat-leaf (Italian) parsley
50 g (2 oz/⅓ cup) almonds, toasted

Preheat the oven to 180°C (350°F/Gas 4). Heat the oil in a large saucepan or ovenproof dish, add the onion and cook over medium heat for 5 minutes, or until soft. Add the spices and cook for 3 minutes.

Add the vegetables and cook, stirring, until coated with the spices and the outside begins to soften. Add the preserved lemon, tomato, stock, pear and prune. Cover, transfer to the oven and cook for 30 minutes. Add the zucchini and cook for 15–20 minutes, or until the vegetables are tender.

Cover the couscous with the olive oil and 500 ml (17 fl oz/ 2 cups) boiling water and leave until all the water has been absorbed. Flake with a fork.

Remove the cinnamon stick from the vegetables, then stir in the parsley. Serve on a large platter with the couscous formed into a ring and the vegetable tagine in the centre, sprinkled with the almonds.

Cook the vegetables until they are coated in spices and the outside starts to soften.

Before serving, remove the cinnamon stick with a pair of tongs.

Autumn vegetable stew

preparation 25 minutes
cooking 30 minutes
serves 4–6

185 g (6 oz) frozen broad (fava) beans, thawed (see Notes)
150 g (5½ oz) baby onions (see Notes)
50 g (2 oz) butter
2 teaspoons olive oil
400 g (14 oz) small parsnips
150 g (5½ oz) Jerusalem artichokes
2 tablespoons plain (all-purpose) flour
580 ml (20 fl oz/2⅓ cups) chicken stock
300 ml (10½ fl oz) pouring (whipping) cream
2 teaspoons finely grated lemon zest
1 teaspoon finely grated orange zest
400 g (14 oz) baby carrots, trimmed
500 g (1 lb 2 oz) baby turnips, trimmed

Peel and discard the tough outer skin of the broad beans. Carefully peel the onions, leaving the flat root end attached, then cut a cross through the root end of each onion.

Heat the butter and oil in a large heavy-based saucepan until foamy. Add the onions and cook for 7 minutes over low–medium heat, turning often to colour evenly.

While the onions are browning, peel the parsnips and artichokes, and cut them into bite-sized pieces. Add to the saucepan and toss well. Scatter the flour over the onion, parsnip and artichokes, toss to coat and cook for 2 minutes.

Stir in the chicken stock, cream, lemon zest and orange zest. Bring to the boil, stirring, then reduce the heat and simmer for 7 minutes, or until the vegetables are half-cooked.

Add the carrots and turnips, and toss well. Cover the pan and cook for 4–5 minutes, or until the vegetables are just tender. Season well with salt and freshly ground black pepper, stir in the peeled broad beans to heat through, and serve.

Notes *Fresh broad beans can be used. Add them with the carrots and turnips.*

Baby vegetables have a sweet, delicate flavour. If unavailable, choose the smallest vegetables and cook them for a few minutes longer.

Vegetarian chilli

preparation 15 minutes + 10 minutes soaking
cooking 40 minutes
serves 6–8

130 g (4½ oz/¾ cup) burghul (bulgur)
2 tablespoons olive oil
1 large onion, finely chopped
2 garlic cloves, crushed
1 teaspoon chilli powder
2 teaspoons ground cumin
1 teaspoon cayenne pepper
½ teaspoon ground cinnamon
2 x 400 g (14 oz) tins chopped tomatoes
750 ml (26 fl oz/3 cups) vegetable stock
440 g (15½ oz) tin red kidney beans, drained and rinsed
2 x 300 g (10½ oz) tins chickpeas, drained and rinsed
310 g (11 oz) tin corn kernels, drained
2 tablespoons tomato paste (concentrated purée)
corn chips and sour cream, to serve

Soak the burghul in 250 ml (9 fl oz/1 cup) hot water for 10 minutes. Heat the oil in a large heavy-based saucepan and cook the onion for 10 minutes, stirring often, until soft and golden.

Add the garlic, chilli, cumin, cayenne and cinnamon, and cook, stirring, for 1 minute.

Add the tomato, stock and burghul. Bring to the boil and simmer for 10 minutes. Stir in the beans, chickpeas, corn and tomato paste, and simmer for 20 minutes, stirring often. Serve with corn chips and sour cream.

Stir the garlic and spices into the pan with the onion, and cook for 1 minute.

Bottom: Vegetarian chilli. Top: Autumn vegetable stew.

Potatoes in Mediterranean sauce

preparation 30 minutes
cooking 50 minutes
serves 6

1 kg (2 lb 4 oz) new or baby potatoes, unpeeled and halved
1 tablespoon olive oil
2 onions, finely chopped
3 garlic cloves, crushed
1 teaspoon sweet paprika
400 g (14 oz) tin chopped tomatoes
2 tablespoons lemon juice
½ teaspoon finely grated lemon zest
2 teaspoons soft brown sugar
3 teaspoons tomato paste (concentrated purée)
½ teaspoon dried thyme
12 kalamata olives
1 tablespoon capers, rinsed and roughly chopped
150 g (5½ oz) feta cheese, cubed
1 tablespoon roughly chopped parsley

Boil the potato until just tender. Heat the olive oil in a large saucepan, add the onion and cook until soft and golden. Add the garlic and paprika and cook for another minute.

Stir in the tomato, lemon juice, lemon zest, sugar, tomato paste and thyme. Simmer, covered, for 5 minutes and then add the potato and toss to coat. Simmer, covered, for 20 minutes, or until the potato is cooked through. Stir occasionally to prevent burning.

Remove the pan from the heat and, just before serving, stir through the olives, capers and feta. Season to taste and scatter the parsley over the top before serving.

Stir in the tomato, lemon juice and zest, sugar, tomato paste and thyme.

Cauliflower curry

preparation 20 minutes + 30 minutes marinating
cooking 20 minutes
serves 6

marinade
1 large onion, roughly chopped
1 teaspoon grated fresh ginger
2 garlic cloves, crushed
3 green chillies, chopped
60 g (2 oz/¼ cup) plain yoghurt

1 cauliflower, divided into florets
oil, for deep-frying

curry sauce
2 tablespoons ghee
1 onion, finely chopped
2 tablespoons tomato paste (concentrated purée)
2 tablespoons pouring (whipping) cream
1 teaspoon chilli powder
1½ tablespoons garam masala

To make the marinade, place all the ingredients in a food processor and mix until smooth. Place the marinade in a bowl, add the cauliflower, toss to coat and leave for 30 minutes.

Fill a deep heavy-based saucepan one-third full of oil and heat to 160°C (315°F), or until a cube of bread dropped into the oil browns in 30–35 seconds. Cook the cauliflower in batches for 30 seconds until golden brown all over. Drain on paper towels.

Heat the ghee in a frying pan, add the onion and cook for 4–5 minutes, or until soft. Add the tomato paste, cream, chilli powder, garam masala, 375 ml (13 fl oz/1½ cups) water and salt to taste. Cook, stirring constantly, over medium heat for 3 minutes.

Add the cauliflower and cook for 7 minutes, adding a little water if the sauce becomes dry.

Bottom: Cauliflower curry. Top: Potatoes in Mediterranean sauce.

Potato curry

preparation 20 minutes
cooking 35 minutes
serves 6

curry paste
4 cardamom pods
1 teaspoon grated fresh ginger
2 garlic cloves
6 small red chillies
1 teaspoon cumin seeds
40 g (1½ oz/¼ cup) raw cashew nut pieces
1 tablespoon white poppy seeds (khus) (see Note)
1 cinnamon stick
6 cloves

1 kg (2 lb 4 oz) potatoes, cubed
2 onions, roughly chopped
2 tablespoons oil
½ teaspoon ground turmeric
1 teaspoon besan (chickpea flour)
250 g (9 oz/1 cup) plain yoghurt
coriander (cilantro) leaves, to garnish

To make the curry paste, lightly crush the cardamom pods with the flat side of a heavy knife. Remove the seeds, discarding the pods. Place the seeds and the remaining curry paste ingredients in a food processor, and process to a smooth paste.

Bring a large saucepan of lightly salted water to the boil. Add the potato and cook for 5–6 minutes, or until just tender. Drain well.

Place the onion in a food processor and process in short bursts until it is finely ground but not puréed. Heat the oil in a large saucepan, add the ground onion and cook over low heat for 5 minutes. Add the curry paste and cook, stirring, for a further 5 minutes, or until fragrant. Stir in the potato, turmeric, salt to taste and 250 ml (9 fl oz/1 cup) water.

Reduce the heat and simmer, tightly covered, for 10 minutes, or until the potato is cooked but not breaking up and the sauce has thickened slightly.

Combine the besan with the yoghurt, add to the potato mixture and cook, stirring, over low heat for 5 minutes, or until thickened again. Garnish with the coriander leaves.

Note *White poppy seeds (khus) should not be mistaken for black and do not yield opium. They are off-white, odourless and flavourless until roasted when they have a slight sesame aroma and flavour. If they are not available, replace the poppy seeds with sesame seeds.*

Lightly crush the cardamom pods with the flat side of a heavy knife.

Add the curry paste to the onion and cook until the mixture is fragrant.

vegetarian

Vegetable curry

preparation 20 minutes
cooking 30 minutes
serves 6

250 g (9 oz) potatoes, cut into 2 cm (¾ inch) cubes
250 g (9 oz) pumpkin (winter squash), cut into
2 cm (¾ inch) cubes
200 g (7 oz) cauliflower, broken into florets
150 g (5½ oz) yellow baby (pattypan) squash, quartered
2 tablespoons oil
2 onions, chopped
60 g (2 oz/¼ cup) general purpose Indian curry powder
400 g (14 oz) tin chopped tomatoes
250 ml (9 fl oz/1 cup) vegetable stock
150 g (5½ oz) green beans, trimmed and cut into
4 cm (1½ inch) lengths
90 g (3 oz/⅓ cup) plain yoghurt
40 g (1½ oz/⅓ cup) sultanas (golden raisins)

Cook the potato and pumpkin in a saucepan of boiling water for 6 minutes, then remove. Add the cauliflower and squash, cook for 4 minutes, then remove.

Heat the oil in a large saucepan, add the onion and cook, stirring, over medium heat for 8 minutes, or until starting to brown.

Add the curry powder and stir for 1 minute, or until fragrant. Stir in the tomato and vegetable stock, and combine well.

Add the chopped potato, pumpkin, cauliflower and squash, and cook for 5 minutes, then add the beans and cook for a further 2–3 minutes, or until the vegetables are tender.

Add the yoghurt and sultanas, and stir to combine. Simmer for 3 minutes, or until thickened slightly. Season to taste with salt and black pepper, and serve with chapattis.

Yellow vegetable curry

preparation 20 minutes
cooking 50 minutes
serves 6

60 ml (2 fl oz/¼ cup) oil
1 onion, finely chopped
2 tablespoons Thai yellow curry paste
250 g (9 oz) potato, diced
200 g (7 oz) zucchini (courgettes), diced
150 g (5½ oz) red capsicum (pepper), diced
100 g (3½ oz) green beans, trimmed
50 g (1¾ oz) bamboo shoots, trimmed and sliced
250 ml (9 fl oz/1 cup) vegetable stock
400 ml (14 fl oz) tin coconut cream
Thai basil leaves, to garnish

Heat the oil in a large saucepan, add the onion and cook over medium heat for 4–5 minutes, or until softened. Add the curry paste and cook, stirring, for 2 minutes, or until fragrant.

Add all the vegetables and cook, stirring, over high heat for 2 minutes. Pour in the stock, reduce the heat to medium and cook, covered, for 15–20 minutes, or until the vegetables are tender. Cook, uncovered, over high heat for 5–10 minutes, or until the sauce has reduced slightly.

Stir in the coconut cream, and season with salt. Bring to the boil, stirring frequently, then reduce the heat and simmer for 5 minutes. Garnish with the Thai basil leaves.

Add the beans and cook until all the vegetables are just tender.

Heat the oil in a saucepan, add the onion and cook until turning golden.

Bottom: Yellow vegetable curry. Top: Vegetable curry.

Chu chee tofu

preparation 20 minutes
cooking 15 minutes
serves 6

curry paste
10 small red chillies
50 g (2 oz) red Asian shallots (eschalots), peeled
1 tablespoon finely chopped coriander (cilantro) stem and root
1 lemongrass stem, white part only, chopped
2 tablespoons grated fresh galangal
2 garlic cloves
1 tablespoon ground coriander
1 teaspoon ground cumin
1 teaspoon black peppercorns
½ teaspoon ground turmeric
1 tablespoon lime juice

1 tablespoon oil
1 onion, finely chopped
500 ml (17 fl oz/2 cups) coconut milk
200 g (7 oz) fried tofu puffs, halved on the diagonal
coriander (cilantro) sprigs, to garnish

To make the curry paste, place all the ingredients in a food processor or spice grinder and process until smooth.

Heat the oil in a large saucepan, add the onion and cook over medium heat for 4–5 minutes, or until it starts to brown. Add 3 tablespoons of the curry paste and cook, stirring, for 2 minutes.

Stir in the coconut milk and 125 ml (4 fl oz/½ cup) water, and season with salt. Bring slowly to the boil, stirring constantly. Add the tofu puffs, then reduce the heat and simmer, stirring frequently, for 5 minutes, or until the sauce thickens slightly. Garnish with the coriander sprigs.

Dhal

preparation 15 minutes
cooking 35 minutes
serves 4–6

200 g (7 oz) red lentils
4 cm (1½ inch) piece fresh ginger, cut into slices
½ teaspoon ground turmeric
1 tablespoon ghee or oil
2 garlic cloves, crushed
1 onion, finely chopped
½ teaspoon yellow mustard seeds
pinch asafoetida (optional)
1 teaspoon cumin seeds
1 teaspoon ground coriander
2 green chillies, halved lengthways
2 tablespoons lemon juice
1 tablespoon chopped coriander (cilantro) leaves

Place the lentils and 750 ml (26 fl oz/3 cups) water in a saucepan, and bring to the boil. Reduce the heat, add the ginger and turmeric, and simmer, covered, for 20 minutes, or until the lentils are tender. Stir occasionally to prevent the lentils sticking to the pan. Remove the ginger and stir in ½ teaspoon salt.

Heat the ghee in a frying pan, add the garlic, onion and mustard seeds, and cook over medium heat for 5 minutes, or until the onion is golden. Add the asafoetida, cumin seeds, ground coriander and chillies, and cook for 2 minutes.

Add the onion mixture to the lentils and stir gently to combine. Add 125 ml (4 fl oz/½ cup) water, reduce the heat to low and cook for 5 minutes. Stir in the lemon juice, and season. Sprinkle with the coriander. Serve as a side dish with Indian curries.

Grind all the ingredients for the curry paste in a food processor or spice grinder until smooth.

Add the ginger and turmeric to the lentils and cook until the lentils are tender.

Cheese and pea curry

preparation 30 minutes + 30 minutes draining + 4 hours setting
cooking 40 minutes
serves 6

paneer
2 litres (70 fl oz/8 cups) full-cream (whole) milk
80 ml (2½ fl oz/⅓ cup) lemon juice

curry paste
2 large onions, chopped
3 garlic cloves
1 teaspoon grated fresh ginger
1 teaspoon cumin seeds
3 dried red chillies
1 teaspoon cardamom seeds
4 cloves
1 teaspoon fennel seeds
2 pieces cassia bark

oil, for deep-frying
500 g (1 lb 2 oz) frozen peas
2 tablespoons oil
400 g (14 oz) tomato paste (concentrated purée)
1 tablespoon garam masala
1 teaspoon ground coriander
¼ teaspoon ground turmeric
1 tablespoon pouring (whipping) cream
coriander (cilantro) leaves, to garnish

To make the paneer, place the milk in a large saucepan, bring to the boil, stir in the lemon juice and turn off the heat. Stir the mixture for 1–2 seconds as it curdles. Place in a colander and leave for 30 minutes for the whey to drain off. Place the paneer curds on a clean, flat surface, cover with a plate, weigh down and leave for at least 4 hours.

To make the curry paste, place all the ingredients in a spice grinder or food processor, and grind to a smooth paste.

Cut the solid paneer into 2 cm (¾ inch) cubes. Fill a deep heavy-based saucepan one-third full of oil and heat to 180°C (350°F), or until a cube of bread browns in 15 seconds. Cook the paneer in batches for 2–3 minutes, or until golden. Drain on paper towels.

Cook the peas in a saucepan of boiling water for 3 minutes, or until tender. Drain.

Heat the oil in a large saucepan, add the curry paste and cook over medium heat for 4 minutes, or until fragrant. Add the tomato paste, spices, cream and 125 ml (4 fl oz/½ cup) water. Season with salt, and simmer over medium heat for 5 minutes. Add the paneer and peas, and cook for 3 minutes. Garnish with coriander leaves, and serve hot.

Boil the milk and lemon juice, and stir for a few seconds as the milk curdles.

Cover the paneer curds with a plate, weigh it down and leave it to set.

Indonesian vegetable and coconut curry

preparation 20 minutes
cooking 35 minutes
serves 6

curry paste
5 candlenuts or macadamia nuts
75 g (2½ oz) red Asian shallots (eschalots)
2 garlic cloves
2 teaspoons sambal oelek (Southeast Asian chilli paste)
¼ teaspoon ground turmeric
1 teaspoon grated fresh galangal
1 tablespoon peanut butter

2 tablespoons oil
1 onion, sliced
400 ml (14 fl oz) tin coconut cream
200 g (7 oz) carrots, cut into matchsticks
200 g (7 oz) snake (yard-long) beans, trimmed, cut into
7 cm (2¾ inch) lengths
300 g (10½ oz) Chinese cabbage, roughly shredded
100 g (3½ oz) fresh shiitake mushrooms
¼ teaspoon sugar

To make the curry paste, place the candlenuts, shallots, garlic, sambal oelek, turmeric, galangal and peanut butter in a food processor, and process to a smooth paste.

Heat the oil in a large saucepan over low heat. Cook the curry paste, stirring, for 5 minutes, or until fragrant. Add the onion and cook for 5 minutes. Stir in 60 ml (2 fl oz/¼ cup) coconut cream and cook, stirring constantly, for 2 minutes, or until thickened. Add the carrot and beans, and cook over high heat for 3 minutes. Stir in the cabbage, mushrooms and 250 ml (9 fl oz/1 cup) water. Cook over high heat for 8–10 minutes, or until the vegetables are nearly cooked.

Stir in the remaining coconut cream and the sugar, and season with salt. Bring to the boil, stirring constantly, then reduce the heat and simmer for 8–10 minutes, to allow the flavours to develop. Serve hot.

Process the curry paste ingredients together to a smooth paste.

Add the coconut cream and cook, stirring, until the sauce has thickened.

vegetarian

Curried lentils

preparation 15 minutes
cooking 30 minutes
serves 4

250 g (9 oz/1 cup) red lentils
500 ml (17 fl oz/2 cups) vegetable stock
½ teaspoon ground turmeric
50 g (2 oz) ghee
1 onion, chopped
2 garlic cloves, finely chopped
1 large green chilli, seeded and finely chopped
2 teaspoons ground cumin
2 teaspoons ground coriander
2 tomatoes, chopped
125 ml (4 fl oz/½ cup) coconut milk

Rinse the lentils and drain well. Place the lentils, stock and turmeric in a large heavy-based saucepan. Bring to the boil, reduce the heat and simmer, covered, for 10 minutes, or until just tender. Stir occasionally and check the mixture is not catching on the bottom of the pan.

Meanwhile, heat the ghee in a small frying pan and add the onion. Cook until soft and golden and add the garlic, chilli, cumin and coriander. Cook, stirring, for 2–3 minutes until fragrant. Stir the onions and spices into the lentil mixture and then add the tomato. Simmer over very low heat for 5 minutes, stirring frequently.

Season to taste and add the coconut milk. Stir until heated through. Serve with rice or naan bread.

Dry potato and pea curry

preparation 15 minutes
cooking 20–25 minutes
serves 4

2 teaspoons brown mustard seeds
2 tablespoons ghee or oil
2 onions, sliced
2 garlic cloves, crushed
2 teaspoons grated fresh ginger
1 teaspoon ground turmeric
½ teaspoon chilli powder
1 teaspoon ground cumin
1 teaspoon garam masala
750 g (1 lb 10 oz) potatoes, cubed
100 g (3½ oz/⅔ cup) peas
2 tablespoons chopped mint

Heat the mustard seeds in a dry pan until they start to pop. Add the ghee, onion, garlic and ginger and cook, stirring, until the onion is soft.

Add the turmeric, chilli powder, cumin, garam marsala and potato, and season with salt and freshly ground black pepper. Stir until the potato is coated with the spice mixture. Add 125ml (4 fl oz/½ cup) water and simmer, covered, for about 15–20 minutes, or until the potato is just tender. Stir occasionally to stop the curry sticking to the bottom of the pan.

Add the peas and stir until well combined. Simmer, covered, for 3–5 minutes, or until the potato is cooked and all the liquid is absorbed. Stir in the mint and season well.

Season the lentils and add the coconut milk. Stir until heated through.

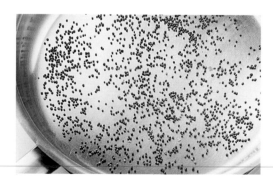

Fry the mustard seeds in a dry frying pan until they begin to pop.

vegetarian

Bottom: Dry potato and pea curry. Top: Curried lentils.

Vegetable curry with spiced noodles

preparation 40 minutes
cooking 35 minutes
serves 4–6

curry paste
5 red chillies, seeded and chopped
1 lemongrass stem, sliced
1 tablespoon chopped fresh galangal
2 garlic cloves, crushed
1 small onion, chopped
1 tablespoon chopped coriander (cilantro)
10 black peppercorns
2 tablespoons lime juice
2 teaspoons oil

2 tablespoons oil
375 ml (13 fl oz/1½ cups) coconut milk
200 g (7 oz) green beans, cut into short lengths
2 small zucchini (courgettes), thickly sliced
1 eggplant (aubergine), cubed
5 makrut (kaffir lime) leaves
2 tablespoons lime juice
1 large handful chopped coriander (cilantro)
1 very large handful chopped basil

spiced noodles
2 tablespoons oil
1 small onion, chopped
1 garlic clove, crushed
½–1 teaspoon dried chilli flakes
½ teaspoon garam masala
200 g (7 oz) thin egg noodles

To make the curry paste, blend all the ingredients in a food processor or blender to make a smooth paste.

Heat the oil in a pan and stir-fry the curry paste for 2 minutes. Add the coconut milk and 125 ml (4 fl oz/½ cup) water and bring to the boil. Reduce the heat and add the vegetables, makrut leaves and lime juice. Cook, covered, until tender. Add the coriander and basil.

To make the spiced noodles, heat the oil in a pan. Cook the onion and garlic over low heat for 5 minutes. Add the chilli flakes and garam masala and cook for 2 minutes. Meanwhile, cook the noodles in boiling water according to packet instructions, or until tender and drain. Add to the onion mixture and toss well. Serve with the vegetable curry.

Lemongrass and galangal are both available from Asian food stores.

Heat the oil in a saucepan and stir-fry the curry paste for 2 minutes.

Chickpea curry

preparation 10 minutes
cooking 40 minutes
serves 4

1 tablespoon ghee or oil
2 onions, sliced
4 garlic cloves, crushed
1 teaspoon chilli powder
1 teaspoon ground turmeric
1 teaspoon paprika
1 tablespoon ground cumin
1 tablespoon ground coriander
880 g (1 lb 15 oz) tin chickpeas, drained and rinsed
400 g (14 oz) tin chopped tomatoes
1 teaspoon garam masala

Heat the ghee or oil in a saucepan. Add the onion and garlic and cook, stirring, until the onion is soft. Add the chilli powder, 1 teaspoon of salt, turmeric, paprika, cumin and coriander. Cook, stirring, for 2–3 minutes.

Stir in the chickpeas and tomato. Simmer, covered, over low heat for 20 minutes, stirring occasionally.

Stir in the garam masala. Simmer, covered, for a further 10 minutes. Serve with naan bread.

Green curry with sweet potato and eggplant

preparation 15 minutes
cooking 25 minutes
serves 4–6

1 tablespoon oil
1 onion, chopped
1–2 tablespoons green curry paste (see Note)
1 eggplant (aubergine), quartered and sliced
375 ml (13 fl oz/1½ cups) coconut milk
250 ml (9 fl oz/1 cup) vegetable stock
6 makrut (kaffir lime) leaves
1 orange sweet potato, cubed
2 teaspoons soft brown sugar
2 tablespoons lime juice
2 teaspoons finely grated lime zest

Heat the oil in a large wok or frying pan. Add the onion and green curry paste and cook, stirring, over medium heat for 3 minutes. Add the eggplant and cook for a further 4–5 minutes, or until softened.

Pour in the coconut milk and vegetable stock, bring to the boil, then reduce the heat and simmer for 5 minutes. Add the makrut leaves and sweet potato and cook for 10 minutes, or until the vegetables are very tender.

Mix in the sugar, lime juice and zest until well combined with the vegetables. Season to taste with salt and serve with steamed rice.

Note *Strict vegetarians should be sure to read the label and choose a green curry paste that doesn't contain shrimp paste. Alternatively, make your own curry pastes.*

Add the chilli powder, salt, turmeric, paprika, cumin and coriander to the pan.

Use a sharp knife to cut the eggplant into quarters, then slice.

Bottom: Green curry with sweet potato and eggplant. Top: Chickpea curry.

Massaman vegetable curry

preparation 25 minutes
cooking 45 minutes
serves 4–6

curry paste
1 tablespoon oil
1 teaspoon coriander seeds
1 teaspoon cumin seeds
8 cloves
½ teaspoon fennel seeds
seeds from 4 cardamom pods
6 red Asian shallots (eschalots), chopped
3 garlic cloves, chopped
1 teaspoon finely chopped lemongrass stems, white part only
1 teaspoon finely chopped fresh galangal
4 large dried red chillies
1 teaspoon ground nutmeg
1 teaspoon white pepper

1 tablespoon oil
250 g (9 oz) baby onions
500 g (1 lb 2 oz) small new potatoes
300 g (10½ oz) carrots, cut into 3 cm (1¼ inch) pieces
225 g (8 oz) tin whole champignons, drained
1 cinnamon stick
1 makrut (kaffir lime) leaf
1 bay leaf
250 ml (9 fl oz/1 cup) coconut cream
1 tablespoon lime juice
3 teaspoons grated palm sugar (jaggery) or soft brown sugar
1 tablespoon shredded Thai basil leaves
1 tablespoon roasted peanuts

To make the curry paste, heat the oil in a frying pan over low heat, add the coriander seeds, cumin seeds, cloves, fennel seeds and cardamom seeds, and cook for 1–2 minutes, or until fragrant. Place in a food processor and add the shallots, garlic, lemongrass, galangal, chillies, nutmeg and white pepper. Process until smooth, adding water as necessary.

Heat the oil in a large saucepan, add the curry paste and cook, stirring, over medium heat for 2 minutes, or until fragrant. Add the vegetables, cinnamon, makrut and bay leaf. Season with salt. Add enough water to cover and bring to the boil. Reduce the heat and simmer, covered, stirring frequently, for 30–35 minutes, or until the vegetables are cooked. Stir in the coconut cream and cook, uncovered, for 4 minutes, stirring frequently, until thickened slightly. Stir in the lime juice, sugar and shredded basil. Add a little water if too dry. Season with pepper and garnish with peanuts.

Process the curry paste ingredients in a food processor until smooth.

Stir in the coconut cream and cook, stirring frequently, until thickened slightly.

Thai red vegetable curry

preparation 10 minutes
cooking 25 minutes
serves 4

1 tablespoon peanut oil
250 g (9 oz) broccoli florets, quartered
250 g (9 oz) cauliflower florets, quartered
500 g (1 lb 2 oz) orange sweet potato, cut into even-size chunks
2 tablespoons Thai red curry paste
500 ml (17 fl oz/2 cups) coconut milk
1 tablespoon lime juice
1 tablespoon fish sauce (optional)
3 tablespoons chopped coriander (cilantro)

Heat a wok over high heat, add the oil and swirl to coat the side. Add the broccoli, cauliflower and sweet potato in batches and stir-fry for 3 minutes. Add 60 ml (2 fl oz/¼ cup) water and cover. Reduce the heat to low for 8–10 minutes to steam the vegetables.

Add the curry paste and cook over medium heat for 30 seconds, or until fragrant. Stir in the coconut milk and simmer for 8 minutes, or until slightly thickened. Add the lime juice, fish sauce and coriander.

Lentil and cauliflower curry stacks

preparation 15 minutes
cooking 50 minutes
serves 6

60 g (2 oz) ghee or butter
2 onions, thinly sliced
2 tablespoons madras curry paste
2 garlic cloves, crushed
180 g (6 oz) button mushrooms, sliced
1 litre (35 fl oz/4 cups) vegetable stock
300 g (10½ oz) brown or green lentils
400 g (14 oz) tin chopped tomatoes
2 cinnamon sticks
300 g (10½ oz) cauliflower, cut into small florets
oil, for deep-frying
18 small (8 cm/3¼ inch) poppadoms
plain yoghurt and coriander (cilantro) sprigs, to serve

Heat the ghee in a large saucepan over medium heat and cook the onion for 2–3 minutes, or until soft. Add the curry paste, garlic and mushrooms and cook for 2 minutes.

Add the stock, lentils, tomato and cinnamon sticks and mix well. Bring to the boil and cook for 40 minutes, or until the lentils are tender. Add the cauliflower in the last 10 minutes and cover. If the curry is too wet, continue to cook, uncovered, until the excess liquid has evaporated. Season to taste with salt and freshly ground black pepper. Remove the cinnamon.

Meanwhile, fill a deep, heavy-based saucepan one-third full of oil and heat until a cube of bread dropped into the oil browns in 15 seconds. Cook the poppadoms in batches for 10 seconds, or until golden brown and puffed all over. Drain on crumpled paper towels and season with salt.

To assemble, place a poppadom on each serving plate and spoon on a little of the curry. Place a second poppadom on top and spoon on some more curry. Cover with the remaining poppadoms and top with a spoonful of yoghurt. Garnish with coriander sprigs and serve immediately.

Add the coconut milk to the wok and simmer until slightly thickened.

Drop the poppadoms into the oil and cook until puffed and golden.

Bottom: Lentil and cauliflower curry stacks. Top: Thai red vegetable curry.

slow cookers

Veal braised with lemon thyme

preparation 15 minutes
cooking 3½ hours
serves 4

2 tablespoons olive oil
1.5 kg (3 lb 5 oz) rack of veal (6 cutlets),
trimmed to a neat shape
2 leeks, white part only, thinly sliced
30 g (1 oz) butter
1 tablespoon plain (all-purpose) flour
1 tablespoon finely grated lemon zest
125 ml (4 fl oz/½ cup) chicken stock
125 ml (4 fl oz/½ cup) dry white wine
2 tablespoons lemon thyme
125 ml (4 fl oz/½ cup) pouring (whipping) cream

Heat the oil in a deep heavy-based frying pan over medium heat and brown the veal well on all sides. Remove the veal from the pan and put in the slow cooker.

Add the leek and butter to the frying pan, reduce the heat and cook, stirring occasionally, for 10 minutes, or until soft. Add the flour to the pan and cook for 2 minutes, stirring continuously. Add the lemon zest and season with freshly ground black pepper. Stir in the stock and wine and bring to the boil, stirring continuously.

Add the leek mixture to the slow cooker. Cook on low for 3 hours, or until the veal is tender and cooked through.

Remove the veal to a plate, cover and set aside. Increase the slow cooker heat to high. Add the lemon thyme and cream and cook, uncovered, for a further 10 minutes. Season to taste. Serve the veal with the sauce and with boiled baby potatoes.

Pork cooked in milk

preparation 15 minutes
cooking 6¼ hours
serves 6

2 kg (4 lb 8 oz) pork loin rack, with 6 chops
6 baby potatoes, peeled and halved
1 large fennel bulb, cut into thick wedges
2 garlic cloves, halved lengthways
2 rosemary sprigs
1 litre (35 fl oz/4 cups) milk
finely grated zest of 2 lemons
juice of 1 lemon

Trim the pork of most of the excess fat. Put the pork, potato, fennel, garlic, rosemary, milk, lemon zest and lemon juice in the slow cooker. Cook on low for 6 hours, or until the pork is tender.

Transfer the pork and vegetables to a serving platter. Cover with foil and set aside to rest for 10 minutes. While the pork is resting, increase the slow cooker heat to high and reduce the liquid left in the bowl. Taste and check for seasoning.

Strain the sauce if you like (you don't need to, but it may look curdled) and serve with the pork and vegetables.

Bottom: Pork cooked in milk. Top: Veal braised with lemon thyme.

Vegetable and cheddar soup

preparation 15 minutes
cooking 3–4 hours
serves 4

2 all-purpose potatoes (about 250 g/9 oz), diced
2 zucchini (courgettes), diced
1 carrot, diced
1 celery stalk, diced
3 spring onions (scallions), finely chopped
1 litre (35 fl oz/4 cups) chicken or vegetable stock
425 g (15 oz) tinned creamed corn
125 g (4½ oz/1 cup) grated cheddar cheese
2 tablespoons finely chopped flat-leaf (Italian) parsley

Put the potato, zucchini, carrot, celery and spring onion in the slow cooker. Add the stock and season well with salt and freshly ground black pepper. Cook on high for 3–4 hours, or until the vegetables are cooked.

Just before serving, stir in the creamed corn, cheese and parsley. Season to taste. Serve when the cheese has just melted and the soup has heated through.

Note *If preferred, you can add some barbecued shredded chicken or chopped ham at the end of cooking, at the same time as the corn and cheddar cheese.*

Onion soup

preparation 20 minutes
cooking 6 hours
serves 4

20 g (¾ oz) butter
1 tablespoon olive oil
1 kg (2 lb 4 oz) brown onions, thinly sliced
250 ml (9 fl oz/1 cup) dry white wine
2 tablespoons brandy (optional)
750 ml (26 fl oz/3 cups) beef stock
4 thyme sprigs
2 tablespoons finely chopped flat-leaf (Italian) parsley

Put the butter, olive oil and onion in the slow cooker. Cook on low for 4 hours, stirring occasionally.

Add the wine, brandy (if using), stock, 250 ml (9 fl oz/1 cup) water and thyme. Cook on high for a further 2 hours. Season to taste with salt and freshly ground black pepper. Sprinkle with the parsley and serve with crusty bread.

Caldo verde

preparation 15 minutes
cooking 4 hours
serves 4

6 all-purpose potatoes, chopped
1 red onion, chopped
2 garlic cloves, crushed
750 ml (26 fl oz/3 cups) vegetable stock
60 ml (2 fl oz/¼ cup) olive oil
1 chorizo sausage (about 180 g/6½ oz), diced
500 g (1 lb 2 oz) silverbeet (Swiss chard) or kale, thinly sliced

Put the potato, onion, garlic, vegetable stock and olive oil in the slow cooker.

Cook on high for 3 hours, or until the potato is cooked.

Using a hand-held stick blender, purée until smooth. Alternatively, transfer to a food processor and blend until smooth. Return to the slow cooker along with the chorizo and silverbeet and cook for a further 1 hour on low. Season to taste with salt and freshly ground black pepper.

Pea and ham soup

preparation 15 minutes
cooking 8 hours
serves 6–8

2 onions, finely chopped
2 carrots, finely chopped
2 celery stalks, finely chopped
1 turnip, finely chopped
440 g (15½ oz/2 cups) split green peas, rinsed and drained
1 smoked ham hock (800 g/1 lb 12 oz) (see Note)
1 litre (35 fl oz/4 cups) chicken stock
2 bay leaves
2 thyme sprigs

Put the onion, carrot, celery, turnip, peas, ham hock, stock, 1 litre (35 fl oz/4 cups) water, bay leaves and thyme in the slow cooker. Cook on low for 8 hours, or until the peas are very soft and the ham is falling off the bone.

Remove the ham bones and meat. When cool enough to handle, cut off any meat still attached to the bone, then cut the meat into small pieces. Return the meat to the soup. Season to taste with salt and freshly ground black pepper.

Note *Ask your butcher to cut the ham hock into smaller pieces.*

Top left: Vegetable and cheddar soup. Top right: Caldo verde. Bottom right: Pea and ham soup. Bottom left: Onion soup.

Cream of mushroom soup

preparation 20 minutes
cooking 2 hours
serves 4

10 g (¼ oz) dried porcini mushrooms
1 leek, white part only, thinly sliced
100 g (3½ oz) pancetta or bacon, chopped
200 g (7 oz) Swiss brown mushrooms, roughly chopped
300 g (10½ oz) large field mushrooms, roughly chopped
125 ml (4 fl oz/½ cup) Madeira (Malmsey) (see Note)
1 litre (35 fl oz/4 cups) chicken or vegetable stock
2 teaspoons chopped marjoram
90 g (3 oz/⅓ cup) light sour cream or crème fraîche
marjoram leaves, extra, to garnish

Soak the porcini in 250 ml (9 fl oz/1 cup) boiling water for 20 minutes. Drain, reserving the soaking water.

Combine the porcini and the soaking water, leek, pancetta or bacon, Swiss brown and field mushrooms, Madeira, stock and half of the chopped marjoram in the slow cooker. Cook on high for 2 hours.

Using a hand-held stick blender, purée the soup in the slow cooker. Alternatively, transfer the soup mixture to a food processor and purée until smooth, then return the soup to the slow cooker.

Stir through the sour cream and cook for a further 5 minutes, then stir through the remaining chopped marjoram. Garnish with marjoram leaves and serve with crusty bread.

Note *Madeira is a fortified wine made in Portugal. Malmsey is the richest and fruitiest of the Madeiras and it can also be drunk as an after-dinner drink. If unavailable, use sherry.*

Cover the porcini mushrooms with boiling water and soak until rehydrated.

Ravioli soup

preparation 20 minutes
cooking 3–4 hours
serves 4

1 small leek, white part only
3 silverbeet (Swiss chard) leaves
1 carrot, diced
1 zucchini (courgette), diced
1 celery stalk, including some leaves, diced
2 whole dried Chinese mushrooms
1.5 litres (52 fl oz/6 cups) chicken stock
1 tablespoon light soy sauce
250 g (9 oz) fresh ravioli pasta, such as chicken and mushroom

Leave the root attached to the leek and slice lengthways a few times. Wash thoroughly under cold water to remove any grit, then drain. Chop the leek into small pieces, discarding the root.

Wash the silverbeet leaves and cut away the thick white stems. Tear the leaves into smaller pieces. Set aside.

Put the leek, carrot, zucchini and celery in the slow cooker. Add the Chinese mushrooms, then pour in the stock and soy sauce. Cook on high for 3–4 hours, or until the vegetables are cooked. About 30 minutes before the end of cooking time, add the silverbeet and ravioli. Cover and continue to cook for a further 20 minutes until the pasta is al dente.

Using kitchen tongs, remove the mushrooms, discard the stems, then thinly slice the mushroom caps and return them to the soup. To serve, ladle the soup and pasta into serving bowls and sprinkle with pepper.

Note *For a vegetarian version, use vegetable stock and a vegetable filled ravioli.*

Bottom: Ravioli soup. Top: Cream of mushroom soup.

Prawn gumbo

preparation 30 minutes
cooking 4¼ hours
serves 4–6

1 onion, finely chopped
1 garlic clove, crushed
1 red capsicum (pepper), seeded and chopped
4 bacon slices, trimmed of fat, diced
1½ teaspoons dried thyme
2 teaspoons dried oregano
1 teaspoon sweet paprika
¼ teaspoon cayenne pepper
60 ml (2 fl oz/¼ cup) dry sherry
1 litre (35 fl oz/4 cups) fish or light chicken stock
100 g (3½ oz/½ cup) par-cooked long-grain rice
2 bay leaves
400 g (14 oz) tin chopped tomatoes
150 g (5½ oz) okra, sliced
1 kg (2 lb 4 oz) raw prawns (shrimp)

Put the onion, garlic, capsicum, bacon, thyme, oregano, paprika, cayenne pepper, sherry, stock, rice, bay leaves, tomatoes and okra in the slow cooker. Cook on low for 4 hours, or until the rice is cooked and the okra is tender.

Meanwhile, prepare the prawns. Peel the prawns, leaving the tails intact, then gently pull out the dark vein from each prawn back, starting at the head end. Refrigerate, covered, until needed.

Stir in the prawns and cook for a further 15–20 minutes, or until the prawns are cooked through. Serve immediately.

Peel the prawns, pulling out the dark intestinal vein.
Remove the heads, keeping the tails intact.

Chicken laksa

preparation 30 minutes
cooking 2½ hours
serves 4

chicken balls
500 g (1 lb 2 oz) minced (ground) chicken
1 small red chilli, finely chopped
2 garlic cloves, finely chopped
½ small red onion, finely chopped
1 lemon grass stem, white part only, finely chopped
2 tablespoons chopped coriander (cilantro) leaves

70 g (2½ oz/¼ cup) laksa paste
750 ml (26 fl oz/3 cups) chicken stock
500 ml (17 fl oz/2 cups) coconut milk
200 g (7 oz) dried rice vermicelli noodles
8 fried tofu puffs, halved diagonally
90 g (3 oz/1 cup) bean sprouts
2 tablespoons shredded Vietnamese mint
3 tablespoons coriander (cilantro) leaves
lime wedges, to serve

To make the chicken balls, put the chicken, chilli, garlic, onion, lemon grass and chopped coriander in a food processor and process until just combined. Roll tablespoons of the mixture into balls with wet hands.

Put the chicken balls, laksa paste, stock and coconut milk in the slow cooker. Cook on high for 2½ hours.

Put the vermicelli in a heatproof bowl, cover with boiling water and soak for 10 minutes. Drain well.

Divide the vermicelli, tofu puffs and bean sprouts among four serving bowls and ladle the soup over the top, dividing the chicken balls evenly. Garnish with the mint and coriander and serve with the lime wedges.

Bottom: Chicken laksa. Top: Prawn gumbo.

Goulash soup with dumplings

preparation 30 minutes
cooking 5¾ hours
serves 6

1 kg (2 lb 4 oz) chuck steak
1 onion, finely chopped
1 garlic clove, crushed
2 tablespoons sweet paprika
pinch cayenne pepper
1 teaspoon caraway seeds
400 g (14 oz) tin chopped tomatoes
750 ml (26 fl oz/3 cups) chicken stock
350 g (12 oz) all-purpose potatoes, cut into 2 cm (¾ inch) dice
1 green capsicum (pepper), halved, seeded and cut into thin strips
2 tablespoons sour cream

dumplings
80 g (3 oz/⅔ cup) self-raising flour
25 g (1 oz/¼ cup) finely grated parmesan cheese
2 teaspoons finely chopped thyme
1 egg, lightly beaten

Trim the steak of any fat and cut into 1 cm (½ inch) cubes. Put the steak, onion, garlic, paprika, cayenne pepper, caraway seeds, tomatoes, stock and potato in the slow cooker. Cook on low for 4½ hours, or until the beef is tender and the potato is cooked through.

Stir in the capsicum, then turn the slow cooker to high and cook for a further 1 hour with the lid off. Season to taste with salt and freshly ground black pepper.

To make the dumplings, put the flour and parmesan in a bowl. Season with salt and stir in the thyme and egg. Transfer the mixture to a floured surface and lightly knead to a soft dough. Using 1 teaspoon of the mixture at a time, roll it into a ball. Drop the dumplings into the slow cooker. Cover and cook on high for 10–15 minutes, or until the dumplings are cooked through.

Gently lift the dumplings out of the slow cooker and divide among serving bowls. Stir the sour cream into the soup and ladle the soup over the dumplings.

Spirali with ham and peas

preparation 20 minutes
cooking 3¼ hours
serves 6

500 g (1 lb 2 oz) spirali pasta
750 ml (26 fl oz/3 cups) chicken stock
250 ml (9 fl oz/1 cup) pouring (whipping) cream
3 small thyme sprigs
1 large strip lemon zest
150 g (5½ oz) smoked ham, diced
2 eggs, lightly beaten
100 g (3½ oz/1 cup) freshly grated parmesan cheese
230 g (8 oz/1½ cups) fresh or frozen peas

Put the spirali in a large heatproof bowl. Pour over boiling water and set aside, stirring occasionally, for 10 minutes.

Drain the pasta and place it in the slow cooker along with the stock, 625 ml (21 fl oz/2½ cups) water, cream, thyme and lemon zest. Cook on low for 3 hours, or until the liquid has almost absorbed and the pasta is tender.

Stir in the ham, eggs, parmesan and peas. Cook, stirring occasionally, for 5–10 minutes, or until the peas are cooked and the sauce has thickened. Season to taste, then serve.

Creamy tomato and chicken stew

preparation 20 minutes
cooking 4 hours
serves 4

1.5 kg (3 lb 5 oz) chicken pieces, trimmed of excess fat
4 bacon slices, fat removed, roughly chopped
2 onions, chopped
1 garlic clove, crushed
400 g (14 oz) tin chopped tomatoes
300 g (10½ oz) small button mushrooms, halved
250 ml (9 fl oz/1 cup) pouring (whipping) cream
2 tablespoons chopped flat-leaf (Italian) parsley
2 tablespoons lemon thyme

Put the chicken, bacon, onion, garlic and tomatoes in the slow cooker. Cook on high for 3 hours, or until the chicken is nearly tender.

Add the mushrooms and cream and cook for 30 minutes, then remove the lid and cook for 30 minutes to thicken the sauce. Stir through the parsley and thyme. Serve with mashed potatoes and green beans.

Apricot chicken

preparation 15 minutes
cooking 4 hours
serves 4

4 x 280 g (10 oz) boneless, skinless chicken breasts
1 garlic clove, crushed
1 tablespoon grated fresh ginger
1 tablespoon ground cumin
1 tablespoon ground coriander
2 tablespoons vegetable oil
30 g (1 oz/¼ cup) plain (all-purpose) flour
400 ml (14 fl oz) tinned apricot nectar
1 tablespoon honey
1 tablespoon lemon juice
60 g (2 oz/½ cup) slivered almonds, toasted
1 handful coriander (cilantro) leaves

Put the chicken, garlic, ginger, cumin, coriander and oil in a flat dish. Toss to thoroughly coat the chicken in the oil and spices. Cover and refrigerate overnight.

Put the flour in a flat dish. Remove the chicken from the marinade and dust with the flour. Place the chicken in the slow cooker with the nectar, honey and lemon juice. Cook on high for 4 hours, or until the chicken is cooked. Season. Top with the almonds and coriander and serve with rice.

Stifatho

preparation 20 minutes
cooking 4¼ hours
serves 4

1 kg (2 lb 4 oz) chuck steak
500 g (1 lb 2 oz) whole baby onions
1 garlic clove, cut in half lengthways
125 ml (4 fl oz/½ cup) red wine
125 ml (4 fl oz/½ cup) beef stock
1 cinnamon stick
4 whole cloves
1 bay leaf
1 tablespoon red wine vinegar
2 tablespoons tomato paste (concentrated purée)
2 tablespoons currants

Trim the beef, then cut into 5 cm (2 inch) cubes. Put the beef, onions, garlic, wine, stock, cinnamon stick, cloves, bay leaf, vinegar, tomato paste and some freshly ground black pepper in the slow cooker. Cook on high for 4 hours.

Stir through the currants and cook for a further 15 minutes. Discard the cinnamon stick and season to taste. Serve with rice, bread or potatoes.

Top left: Spirali with ham and peas. Top right: Apricot chicken. Bottom right: Stifatho. Bottom left: Creamy tomato and chicken stew.

Greek-style stuffed eggplant

preparation 20 minutes
cooking 6 hours
serves 4

2 large eggplants (aubergines)
1 onion, finely chopped
2 garlic cloves, chopped
350 g (12 oz) minced (ground) lamb
60 g (2 oz/¼ cup) tomato paste (concentrated purée)
185 ml (6 fl oz/¾ cup) red wine
400 g (14 oz) tin chopped tomatoes
250 ml (9 fl oz/1 cup) chicken stock
2 bay leaves
1 cinnamon stick
1 tablespoon dried oregano
Greek-style yoghurt, to serve

Halve the eggplants lengthways. Use a sharp knife to cut a deep circle around the flesh, about 1 cm (½ inch) in from the edge. Use a large spoon to scoop out the eggplant flesh, then roughly chop the flesh.

Place the eggplant flesh in a bowl along with the onion, garlic, lamb and tomato paste. Season with salt and freshly ground black pepper and mix well to combine.

Stuff the mixture into the hole in the eggplants, reserving any left-over stuffing, and place the filled eggplants in the slow cooker. Pour over the wine, tomatoes and stock and add the bay leaves, cinnamon stick, oregano and any remaining eggplant stuffing. Cook on low for 6 hours, or until the eggplants are tender.

Remove the eggplants to a serving platter. Season to taste with salt and freshly ground black pepper. Serve topped with a dollop of yoghurt and a Greek salad on the side.

Cabbage rolls

preparation 30 minutes
cooking 2½ hours
serves 4

½ large cabbage
400 g (14 oz) minced (ground) pork
220 g (8 oz/1 cup) par-cooked short-grain rice
50 g (2 oz/½ cup) seasoned stuffing mix or dry breadcrumbs
2 garlic cloves, crushed
1 egg, lightly beaten
1 onion, finely diced
1 tablespoon dijon mustard
1 tablespoon worcestershire sauce
¼ teaspoon white pepper
60 ml (2 fl oz/¼ cup) red wine vinegar
2 bacon slices, thinly sliced
500 g (1 lb 2 oz/2 cups) tomato passata (puréed tomatoes)

Place the cabbage in a large heatproof bowl. Pour over boiling water to cover. Set aside for 5–10 minutes, or until you can separate the cabbage leaves with kitchen tongs. Refresh the leaves in cold water and drain.

Combine the pork, rice, stuffing mix, garlic, egg, onion, mustard, worcestershire sauce, white pepper and 1½ teaspoons salt in a bowl. Add 1 tablespoon of the red wine vinegar.

Use the larger cabbage leaves to roll the parcels, and set the smaller leaves aside for later use. Cut a 'V' shape to remove the large connecting vein in each cabbage leaf. Form some of the pork stuffing mixture into a sausage shape about 2 cm (¾ inch) thick and 4 cm (1½ inches) long and place it in the middle of the cabbage leaf. Roll the cabbage up around the pork, making sure the filling is completely covered. Continue until all of the large leaves have been used.

Thinly shred the reserved small cabbage leaves and place them in the base of the slow cooker. Put the bacon on top, then the cabbage rolls. Top with the tomato passata and remaining vinegar. Cook on high for 2½ hours, or until the pork filling is cooked through

Bottom: Cabbage rolls. Top: Greek-style stuffed eggplant.

Spanish-style pork and vegetable stew

preparation 25 minutes
cooking 4 hours
serves 4–6

1 kg (2 lb 4 oz) boneless pork shoulder
2 hot chorizo sausages, sliced
600 g (1 lb 5 oz) all-purpose potatoes, cubed
1 red onion, diced
2 garlic cloves, chopped
2 red capsicums (peppers), seeded and chopped
400 g (14 oz) tin chopped tomatoes
pinch saffron threads
1 tablespoon sweet paprika
10 large thyme sprigs
1 bay leaf
60 g (2 oz/¼ cup) tomato paste (concentrated purée)
125 ml (4 fl oz/½ cup) white wine
125 ml (4 fl oz/½ cup) chicken stock
2 tablespoons sherry
1 handful flat-leaf (Italian) parsley, chopped

Trim the pork and cut into 4 cm (1½ inch) cubes. Put the pork, chorizo, potato, onion, garlic, capsicum, tomatoes, saffron, paprika, thyme and bay leaf in the slow cooker.

Combine the tomato paste, wine, stock and sherry in a small bowl and pour over the pork and vegetables. Cook on high for 4 hours, or until the pork is tender.

Season to taste with salt and freshly ground black pepper. Stir through the parsley and serve.

Sweet paprika veal goulash

preparation 20 minutes
cooking 4 hours
serves 4

1 kg (2 lb 4 oz) boneless veal shoulder
1 onion, sliced
2 garlic cloves, crushed
1 tablespoon sweet paprika
½ teaspoon caraway seeds
2 bay leaves
625 g (1 lb 6 oz/2½ cups) tomato passata (puréed tomatoes)
125 ml (4 fl oz/½ cup) chicken stock
125 ml (4 fl oz/½ cup) red wine
2 all-purpose potatoes, diced
275 g (10 oz) jar roasted red capsicums (peppers),
drained and rinsed
sour cream, to serve

Cut the veal into 3 cm (1¼ inch) cubes. Put the veal, onion, garlic, paprika, caraway seeds, bay leaves, tomato passata, stock, wine and potatoes in the slow cooker. Cook on high for 4 hours, or until the veal is tender. Stir in the capsicum and cook for a further 5 minutes, or until warmed through.

Taste and season with salt and freshly ground black pepper. Serve with a dollop of sour cream and with cooked fettuccine pasta.

Remove any excess fat, then cut the veal into 2.5 cm (1 inch) pieces.

Bottom: Sweet paprika veal goulash. Top: Spanish-style pork and vegetable stew.

Corned beef with cabbage and potatoes

preparation 20 minutes
cooking 8–10 hours
serves 4–6

1.5 kg (3 lb 5 oz) piece corned beef (silverside)
1 small onion
8 whole cloves
500 g (1 lb 2 oz) small new potatoes (about 12)
1 tablespoon soft brown sugar
1 tablespoon malt vinegar
8 black peppercorns
2 bay leaves
500 g (1 lb 2 oz) savoy cabbage, core attached and
cut into 4–6 wedges

mustard and parsley sauce
1 egg
2 tablespoons caster (superfine) sugar
1 tablespoon plain (all-purpose) flour
1 teaspoon mustard powder
60 ml (2 fl oz/¼ cup) malt vinegar
2 tablespoons finely chopped flat-leaf (Italian) parsley

Rinse the corned beef under running water, pat dry with paper towel and then trim off any excess fat. Peel the onion and stud it with the cloves.

Put the potatoes in the slow cooker in a single layer and top with the corned beef. Barely cover with cold water. Add the onion, the combined brown sugar and malt vinegar, the peppercorns and bay leaves.

Cook on low for 8–10 hours, or until the beef is tender. About 45 minutes before the end of cooking time, arrange the cabbage wedges around the meat, cover and cook until the cabbage is tender. When the beef is cooked, remove to a side plate and cover with foil to keep warm.

To make the mustard and parsley sauce, remove 250 ml (9 fl oz/1 cup) of the cooking liquid from the slow cooker and set aside. Whisk together the egg and sugar in a small bowl, then whisk in the flour and mustard powder. Gradually add the reserved cooking liquid and the vinegar, mixing until smooth. Pour into a small saucepan and stir over medium heat until thickened. Stir through the parsley.

To serve, cut the corned beef into thick slices. Use a slotted spoon to lift the potatoes and cabbage out of the slow cooker to the serving plates. Discard the onion. Serve with the mustard and parsley sauce and with some steamed carrots and green beans if desired.

Note Store leftover corned beef in a bowl with the remaining cooking liquid to cover. Cover with plastic wrap and refrigerate.

Greek lamb with macaroni

preparation 30 minutes
cooking 2¼ hours
serves 4–6

1 kg (2 lb 4 oz) boneless lamb leg
1 large onion, chopped
2 garlic cloves, crushed
400 g (14 oz) tin chopped tomatoes
60 g (2 oz/¼ cup) tomato paste (concentrated purée)
500 ml (17 fl oz/2 cups) beef stock
2 tablespoons red wine vinegar
1 tablespoon soft brown sugar
1 teaspoon dried oregano
200 g (7 oz/2 cups) macaroni pasta
125 g (4½ oz) pecorino cheese, grated

Trim the lamb of any excess fat and cut into 3 cm (1¼ inch) cubes. Put the lamb, onion, garlic, tomatoes, tomato paste, stock, vinegar, sugar and oregano in the slow cooker. Cook on high for 1¾ hours, or until the lamb is tender.

Place the macaroni in a large heatproof bowl and cover with boiling water. Set aside for 10 minutes. Drain and add the macaroni to the slow cooker and stir to combine. Cook for a further 30 minutes, or until the pasta is tender and the liquid has absorbed.

Divide among serving bowls and sprinkle with the cheese.

Lancashire hotpot

preparation 15 minutes
cooking 4 hours
serves 4

4 all-purpose potatoes, sliced
6 baby onions, peeled and left whole
1 tablespoon thyme, chopped
1 kg (2 lb 4 oz) lamb shoulder chops
2 tablespoons worcestershire sauce
125 ml (4 fl oz/½ cup) beef stock
1 handful flat-leaf (Italian) parsley, chopped

In a large bowl, toss together the potato, onions and thyme. Layer the potato and onions in the base of the slow cooker and top with the lamb chops. Pour over the worcestershire sauce and stock. Cook on high for 4 hours, or until the lamb is tender and cooked through.

Season with salt and freshly ground black pepper, and stir through the parsley before serving.

Chutney chops with potatoes and peas

preparation 15 minutes
cooking 4 hours
serves 4

1.2 kg (2 lb 10 oz) lamb forequarter chops
4 all-purpose potatoes, such as desiree, sliced
2 garlic cloves, crushed
240 g (8½ oz) jar tomato fruit chutney
400 g (14 oz) tin chopped tomatoes
125 ml (4 fl oz/½ cup) red wine
125 ml (4 fl oz/½ cup) chicken stock
2 rosemary sprigs
80 g (3 oz/½ cup) fresh or frozen peas

Trim the lamb chops of excess fat. Layer the chops and potato slices in the slow cooker.

Combine the garlic, chutney, tomatoes, wine, stock and rosemary and add to the slow cooker. Cook on high for 4 hours, or until the potato is tender and the meat is falling from the bones.

Stir through the peas and cook for a further 5 minutes. Season to taste before serving.

Chicken agrodolce

preparation 30 minutes
cooking 3½ hours
serves 6

1.2 kg (2 lb 10 oz) chicken pieces, skin removed
1 garlic clove
1 tablespoon dried oregano
2 bay leaves
125 ml (4 fl oz/½ cup) red wine vinegar
125 ml (4 fl oz/½ cup) dry white wine
55 g (2 oz/¼ cup firmly packed) soft brown sugar
220 g (7¾ oz/1 cup) pitted prunes
2 tablespoons capers, rinsed
175 g (6 oz/1 cup) green olives
1 handful flat-leaf (Italian) parsley, chopped

Combine the chicken, garlic, oregano, bay leaves, vinegar, wine and brown sugar in the slow cooker. Cook on low for 3 hours.

Stir in the prunes, capers and olives and cook for a further 30 minutes, or until the chicken is cooked through. Season with salt and freshly ground black pepper and stir through the parsley. Serve with mashed potato.

Top left: Greek lamb with macaroni. Top right: Chutney chops with potatoes and peas. Bottom right: Chicken agrodolce. Bottom left: Lancashire hotpot.

Oxtail with marmalade

preparation 20 minutes
cooking 4¼ hours
serves 4

1.5 kg (3 lb 5 oz) oxtail
160 g (5½ oz/½ cup) marmalade
100 ml (3½ fl oz) sherry
2 tablespoons olive oil
4 all-purpose potatoes, cut into 3 cm (1¼ inch) pieces
2 carrots, sliced
1 onion, thinly sliced
2 bay leaves
1 cinnamon stick
1 orange, peeled and segmented

Cut the oxtail into sections, then combine with the marmalade and sherry in a large bowl. Cover and marinate overnight in the refrigerator.

Heat the olive oil in a large frying pan over high heat and cook the oxtail in batches for about 4 minutes on each side, or until golden brown all over. Set aside.

Put the potato, carrot, onion, bay leaves and cinnamon stick in the slow cooker and sit the oxtail on top. Cook on high for 4 hours, or until the meat is tender. Season with salt and freshly ground black pepper. Top the oxtail with the orange segments and serve with mashed potato.

Remove the peel and pith from the orange, and cut the flesh into segments.

Salmon with horseradish crust and puy lentils

preparation 25 minutes
cooking 4¼ hours
serves 4

400 g (14 oz/2 cups) puy lentils or tiny blue-green lentils
500 ml (17 fl oz/2 cups) vegetable stock
finely grated zest and juice of 1 lemon
1 small green chilli, finely chopped
80 g (3 oz/1 cup) fresh sourdough breadcrumbs
2 tablespoons grated fresh or prepared horseradish
4 tablespoons chopped dill
10 g (¼ oz) butter, melted
4 x 180 g (6½ oz) salmon fillets
50 g (2 oz) English spinach, stalks removed, chopped
1 handful coriander (cilantro) leaves
125 g (4½ oz/½ cup) plain yoghurt, to serve
lemon wedges, to serve

Put the lentils, stock, lemon zest, lemon juice and chilli in the slow cooker. Cook on high for 3 hours.

In a food processor, roughly pulse the breadcrumbs and horseradish until well combined. Stir through the dill and melted butter until the mixture is fairly moist.

Remove any bones from the salmon using your fingers or tweezers, then press the breadcrumb mixture over the top side of the salmon fillets.

In a large non-stick frying pan over medium heat, cook the crumbed side of the salmon for 3 minutes, or until the crumbs are golden. Work in batches if necessary.

Mix the spinach through the lentils in the slow cooker and place the salmon on top. Cook on low for 1 hour, or until the fish is cooked through and flakes when tested with a fork. Remove the salmon to serving plates.

Mix the coriander through the lentils and spoon some lentils onto each plate. Serve the salmon topped with the yoghurt and with lemon wedges on the side.

378

Bottom: Salmon with horseradish crust and puy lentils. Top: Oxtail with marmalade.

Slow-cooked lamb in red wine

preparation 20 minutes + 24–48 hours marinating
cooking 10¼ hours
serves 6

2 kg (4 lb 8 oz) lamb leg
50 g (2 oz) butter, softened
2½ tablespoons plain (all-purpose) flour

marinade
750 ml (26 fl oz/3 cups) red wine, such as burgundy or cabernet sauvignon
60 ml (2 fl oz/¼ cup) brandy
10 garlic cloves, bruised
1 tablespoon chopped rosemary
2 teaspoons chopped thyme
2 fresh bay leaves, torn into small pieces
1 large carrot, diced
1 large celery stalk, diced
1 onion, finely chopped
60 ml (2 fl oz/¼ cup) olive oil

Trim any really thick pieces of fat from the lamb but leave it with a decent covering all over if possible.

Combine the marinade ingredients in a non-metallic baking dish, then add the lamb and turn to coat in the marinade. Cover and refrigerate for 24–48 hours, turning occasionally so the marinade is evenly distributed. Make sure you wrap and rewrap the dish tightly with plastic wrap each time to ensure the strong odours from the marinade do not permeate other foods in the refrigerator.

Put the lamb and marinade in the slow cooker. Cook on low for 10 hours, or until the lamb is tender and cooked.

Carefully remove the lamb to a serving platter using two wide spatulas. Cover the lamb with foil and a tea towel (dish towel) to keep warm while you make the sauce.

Drain off the fat from the liquid in the slow cooker. Transfer the ingredients left in the bowl of the slow cooker to a food processor. Purée, then strain the liquid back into the slow cooker. Turn the slow cooker heat to high. Mix together the softened butter and flour and gradually whisk it into the sauce. Continue cooking for a further 10–15 minutes, or until the sauce has thickened slightly.

Carve the lamb and serve with the sauce. Serve with green vegetables and potato gratin.

Lamb with rice and chickpeas

preparation 25 minutes
cooking 5½ hours
serves 6

500 g (1 lb 2 oz) boneless lamb shoulder steaks
1 onion, chopped
2 garlic cloves, crushed
1½ teaspoons ground cumin
2 teaspoons paprika
½ teaspoon ground cloves
1 bay leaf
750 ml (26 fl oz/3 cups) chicken stock
500 g (1 lb 2 oz/2 cups) tomato passata (puréed tomatoes)
600 g (1 lb 5 oz) tinned chickpeas, drained and rinsed
200 g (7 oz/1 cup) par-cooked long-grain rice
2 large handfuls coriander (cilantro) leaves, chopped

Trim the lamb of excess fat and cut into bite-sized cubes. Combine the lamb, onion, garlic, cumin, paprika, cloves, bay leaf, stock, 500 ml (17 fl oz/ 2 cups) water and the tomato passata in the slow cooker. Cook on low for 5 hours, or until the lamb is tender.

Add the chickpeas and rice and cook for a further 30 minutes, or until the rice is tender. Stir through the coriander and serve.

Turkish meatballs with rice

preparation 30 minutes
cooking 4 hours
serves 4–6

500 g (1 lb 2 oz) minced (ground) beef
½ teaspoon allspice
1 teaspoon ground cinnamon
2 teaspoons ground cumin
1 teaspoon ground coriander
330 g (11½ oz/1½ cups) par-cooked short-grain rice
375 ml (13 fl oz/1½ cups) chicken stock
400 g (14 oz) tin chopped tomatoes
35 g (1 oz/¼ cup) toasted pistachio nuts
2 tablespoons currants
2 tablespoons chopped coriander (cilantro) leaves

Put the beef in a bowl and add the allspice, ½ teaspoon of the cinnamon, 1 teaspoon of the cumin and ½ teaspoon of the coriander. Season with salt and freshly ground black pepper. Using your hands, mix the spices and beef together well. Roll the mixture into small balls.

Put the meatballs in the slow cooker along with the remaining spices, the rice, stock and tomatoes. Cook on high for 4 hours, or until the meatballs and rice are cooked through. Stir through the pistachios, currants and coriander before serving.

Rinse the chickpeas thoroughly under cold running water, then drain.

Bottom: Turkish meatballs with rice. Top: Lamb with rice and chickpeas.

Braised beef short ribs

preparation 15 minutes
cooking 4–5 hours
serves 6

2 kg (4 lb 8 oz) beef short ribs
180 g (6½ oz) bacon slices
2 onions, chopped
1 garlic clove, crushed
1 small red chilli, seeded and thinly sliced
500 ml (17 fl oz/2 cups) beef stock
400 g (14 oz) tin chopped tomatoes
8 bulb spring onions (scallions), trimmed and leaves removed
2 strips lemon zest, white pith removed
1 teaspoon mild paprika
1 teaspoon chopped rosemary
1 bay leaf
1 tablespoon soft brown sugar
1 teaspoon worcestershire sauce
2 tablespoons chopped basil
2 tablespoons chopped flat-leaf (Italian) parsley

Chop the ribs into 4 cm (1½ inch) lengths. Remove the rind and fat from the bacon and cut into 5 mm (¼ inch) dice.

Put the ribs, bacon, onion, garlic, chilli, stock, tomatoes, spring onions, strips of lemon zest, paprika, rosemary, bay leaf, sugar and worcestershire sauce in the slow cooker. Cook on high for 4–5 hours, or until the ribs are tender.

Skim off as much fat as you can from the top. Stir through the basil and parsley. Serve the ribs with mashed potatoes or soft polenta if desired.

Lamb chops in ratatouille

preparation 30 minutes
cooking 7–7½ hours
serves 4–6

1 kg (2 lb 4 oz) lamb forequarter chops
1 eggplant (aubergine), cut into 2 cm (¾ inch) cubes
1 red capsicum (pepper), cut into 2 cm (¾ inch) cubes
1 green capsicum (pepper), cut into 2 cm (¾ inch) cubes
1 red onion, cut into 1 cm (½ inch) cubes
2 tablespoons capers
4 anchovies, chopped
80 g (3 oz/½ cup) pitted kalamata olives, chopped
60 g (2 oz/¼ cup) tomato paste (concentrated purée)
2 garlic cloves, chopped
400 g (14 oz) tin chopped tomatoes
150 g (5½ oz/¾ cup) Israeli couscous (see Note)
1 small handful flat-leaf (Italian) parsley, chopped

Trim the lamb chops of excess fat and cut into pieces. Put the eggplant, capsicums, onion, capers, anchovies, olives, tomato paste, garlic and tomatoes in the slow cooker. Put the lamb chops on top. Cook on low for 6–6½ hours, or until the lamb is tender, stirring occasionally.

Stir in the couscous and continue to cook for another 1 hour, or until the couscous is tender and cooked through.

Season with salt and freshly ground black pepper, and sprinkle with parsley before serving.

Note *Israeli couscous is larger in size than the more familiar Moroccan couscous, and has a chewier texture. It is sold in most gourmet food stores and health food stores.*

Bottom: Lamb chops in ratatouille. Top: Braised beef short ribs.

Chickpea and vegetable curry

preparation 30 minutes
cooking 3–4 hours
serves 4–6

3 garlic cloves, crushed
1 red or green chilli, seeded and chopped
2 tablespoons Indian curry paste
1 teaspoon ground cumin
½ teaspoon ground turmeric
400 g (14 oz) tin chopped tomatoes
250 ml (9 fl oz/1 cup) vegetable stock or water
1 red onion, cut into thin wedges
1 large carrot, sliced diagonally into 3 cm (1¼ inch) chunks
250 g (9 oz) orange sweet potato, sliced diagonally into 3 cm (1¼ inch) chunks
250 g (9 oz) cauliflower, cut into florets
250 g (9 oz) broccoli, cut into florets
2 long, thin eggplants (aubergines), about 100 g (3½ oz) in total, cut into 3 cm (1¼ inch) thick slices
400 g (14 oz) tin chickpeas, drained and rinsed
155 g (5½ oz/1 cup) fresh or frozen peas
165 ml (5½ fl oz) coconut milk
1 small handful coriander (cilantro) leaves, to garnish

Combine the garlic, chilli, curry paste, cumin, turmeric, tomatoes and stock in the slow cooker. Stir in the onion, carrot, sweet potato, cauliflower, broccoli, eggplant and chickpeas. Cook on high for 3–4 hours, or until all the vegetables are cooked.

Add the peas and stir through the coconut milk. Continue to cook for a further 10 minutes, or until the peas are cooked.

To serve, ladle the curry into large bowls and sprinkle with the coriander leaves. Serve with steamed rice.

Note *You can add a little more curry paste if you prefer a stronger curry flavour.*

Yellow curry with vegetables

preparation 30 minutes
cooking 3 hours
serves 4

100 g (3½ oz) cauliflower
1 long, thin eggplant (aubergine)
1 small red capsicum (pepper)
2 small zucchini (courgettes)
150 g (5½ oz) green beans
1–2 tablespoons yellow curry paste
500 ml (17 fl oz/2 cups) coconut cream
125 ml (4 fl oz/½ cup) vegetable stock
150 g (5½ oz) baby corn
1½ tablespoons fish sauce
2 teaspoons grated palm sugar (jaggery) or soft brown sugar
1 small red chilli, seeded and chopped, to garnish
coriander (cilantro) leaves, to garnish

Prepare the vegetables. Cut the cauliflower into florets and cut the eggplant, capsicum and zucchini into 1 cm (½ inch) slices. Cut the beans into 3 cm (1¼ inch) lengths.

Put the cauliflower, eggplant and capsicum in the slow cooker with the curry paste, coconut cream and stock. Cook on low for 2 hours, or until the cauliflower is tender.

Stir in the zucchini, beans, corn, fish sauce and sugar and cook for a further 1 hour, or until the vegetables are tender. Garnish with the chilli and coriander and serve with steamed rice.

Grate the block of palm sugar on the large holes of a metal grater.

Bottom: Yellow curry with vegetables. Top: Chickpea and vegetable curry.

Spicy fish curry

preparation 20 minutes
cooking 2½ hours
serves 4

400 ml (14 fl oz) tinned coconut milk
5 green chillies, seeded and chopped
2 dried red chillies, chopped into pieces
½ cinnamon stick
2 teaspoons grated fresh ginger
2 garlic cloves, finely chopped
4 stalks fresh curry leaves (optional)
1 teaspoon ground turmeric
¼ teaspoon chilli powder
1 teaspoon curry powder
2 tomatoes, finely chopped
250 ml (9 fl oz/1 cup) fish or chicken stock
800 g (1 lb 12 oz) snapper fillets, cubed
2 spring onions (scallions), sliced diagonally
juice of 2 limes, to taste

Put the coconut milk, green and red chilli, cinnamon stick, ginger, garlic, curry leaves (if using), turmeric, chilli powder, curry powder, tomato and stock in the slow cooker. Cook on low for 2 hours, or until the flavours have developed.

Add the fish and cook for a further 30 minutes, or until the fish is cooked through and flakes when tested with a fork. Stir through half of the spring onion and add most of the lime juice, then taste to see if more lime juice is needed. Serve with steamed rice and garnish with the remaining spring onion.

Ma po tofu with pork

preparation 20 minutes
cooking 2½ hours
serves 4–6

2 tablespoons fermented black beans
400 g (14 oz) minced (ground) pork
1 tablespoon finely chopped fresh ginger
3 spring onions (scallions), finely chopped
125 ml (4 fl oz/½ cup) chicken stock
2 tablespoons soy sauce
1 tablespoon chilli bean paste (toban djan)
2 tablespoons Chinese rice wine
450 g (1 lb) firm tofu, cut into 1.5 cm (⅝ inch) cubes
2 garlic cloves, chopped
1 tablespoon cornflour (cornstarch)
2 teaspoons sesame oil
spring onions (scallions), extra, sliced diagonally, to serve

Put the black beans in a bowl of cold water and soak for 5 minutes. Drain and finely chop.

Put the beans, pork, ginger, spring onion, stock, soy sauce, chilli bean paste and rice wine in the slow cooker. Cook on low for 2 hours.

Add the tofu and garlic and stir gently until the tofu is well coated with the sauce. Cook for a further 20–30 minutes, or until the mixture has thickened. Garnish with the extra spring onions and serve with steamed rice.

Finely chop the rinsed and drained fermented black beans with a sharp knife.

389

Sichuan and anise beef stew

preparation 20 minutes
cooking 3 hours
serves 4

1 kg (2 lb 4 oz) chuck steak
1½ tablespoons plain (all-purpose) flour
1 large red onion, thickly sliced
2 garlic cloves, crushed
60 g (2 oz/¼ cup) tomato paste (concentrated purée)
250 ml (9 fl oz/1 cup) red wine
250 ml (9 fl oz/1 cup) beef stock
2 bay leaves, crushed
3 long strips orange zest, about 1.5 cm (⅝ inch) wide
2 star anise
1 teaspoon sichuan peppercorns
1 teaspoon chopped thyme
1 tablespoon chopped rosemary
3 tablespoons chopped coriander (cilantro) leaves

Trim the beef and cut into 3 cm (1¼ inch) cubes. Put all the ingredients except the coriander in the slow cooker. Cook on high for 3 hours, or until the beef is tender.

Season to taste. Stir in most of the coriander and garnish with the remainder. Serve with steamed rice.

Lamb madras

preparation 25 minutes + overnight marinating
cooking 4 hours
serves 4

1 kg (2 lb 4 oz) boneless lamb leg or shoulder
60 g (2 oz/¼ cup) madras curry paste
1 onion, finely chopped
6 cardamom pods
4 cloves
2 bay leaves
1 cinnamon stick
185 g (6½ oz/¾ cup) Greek-style yoghurt
¼ teaspoon garam masala
2 long red chillies, chopped (optional)

Trim the lamb and cut into 3 cm (1¼ inch) cubes. Combine the curry paste and lamb in a large bowl and stir thoroughly to coat. Cover and marinate overnight in the refrigerator.

Put the lamb, onion, cardamom pods, cloves, bay leaves, cinnamon stick and yoghurt in the slow cooker. Cook on high for 4 hours, or until the lamb is tender and cooked through. Season with salt and sprinkle with the garam masala. Garnish with chilli if desired and serve with steamed rice.

Moroccan spiced lamb with pumpkin

preparation 20 minutes
cooking 5 hours
serves 6

1.5 kg (3 lb 5 oz) boneless lamb shoulder
1 large onion, diced
1 teaspoon ground coriander
½ teaspoon ground ginger
½ teaspoon cayenne pepper
¼ teaspoon ground saffron threads
1 cinnamon stick
500 ml (17 fl oz/2 cups) chicken stock
500 g (1 lb 2 oz) pumpkin (winter squash),
cut into 2 cm (¾ inch) dice
100 g (3½ oz) dried apricots
coriander (cilantro) sprigs, to garnish

Trim the lamb of excess fat and cut into 3 cm (1¼ inch) cubes. Put the lamb, onion, ground coriander, ginger, cayenne pepper, saffron, cinnamon stick, stock and pumpkin in the slow cooker. Cook on low for 4 hours. Add the apricots and cook for a further 1 hour.

Season to taste. Transfer to a warm serving dish and garnish with the coriander sprigs. Serve with couscous or steamed rice.

Drunken chicken with rice

preparation 15 minutes
cooking 3 hours
serves 4

1.6 kg (3 lb 8 oz) chicken
2 slices fresh ginger
2 garlic cloves, squashed
2 spring onions (scallions), trimmed
1 star anise
250 g (9 oz/1¼ cups) par-cooked long-grain rice
250 ml (9 fl oz/1 cup) Chinese rice wine
250 ml (9 fl oz/1 cup) chicken stock
light soy sauce, to serve

Trim the excess fat from the cavity of the chicken. Put the ginger, garlic, spring onions and star anise in the cavity.

Put the rice in the base of the slow cooker. Pour over the rice wine and stock and place the chicken on the top. Cook on high for 3 hours, or until the rice is cooked and the chicken juices run clear when the thigh is pierced with a skewer. Serve drizzled with light soy sauce.

Top left: Sichuan and anise beef stew. Top right: Moroccan spiced lamb with pumpkin. Bottom right: Drunken chicken with rice. Bottom left: Lamb madras.

index

the **slow cooking** bible

394

398

Published in 2011 by Bay Books, an imprint of Murdoch Books Pty Limited

Murdoch Books Australia
Pier 8/9, 23 Hickson Road
Millers Point NSW 2000
Phone: +61 (0) 2 8220 2000
Fax: +61 (0) 2 8220 2558
www.murdochbooks.com.au

Murdoch Books UK Limited
Erico House, 6th Floor
93–99 Upper Richmond Road
Putney, London SW15 2TG
Phone: +44 (0) 20 8785 5995
Fax: +44 (0) 20 8785 5985
www.murdochbooks.co.uk

Publisher: Lynn Lewis
Design Concept and Senior Designer: Heather Menzies
Project Manager: Liz Malcolm
Designer: Susanne Geppert
Editor: Zoë Harpham
Production: Renee Melbourne
Index: Jo Rudd

ISBN: 978-0-68134-849-3

Printed by Hang Tai Printing Company Limited, China.
PRINTED IN CHINA. Reprinted 2011.